Lectures on Sculpture

Also from Westphalia Press
westphaliapress.org

Lectures on Sculpture

On the Death of Thomas Banks, Antonio Conova, and John Flaxman

by John Flaxman, R.A.
with an address by
Sir Richard Westmacott, R.A.

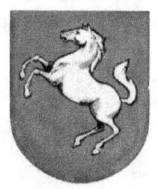

WESTPHALIA PRESS
An Imprint of Policy Studies Organization

Lectures on Sculpture: On the Death of Thomas Banks,
Antonio Conova, and John Flaxman
All Rights Reserved © 2018 by Policy Studies Organization

Westphalia Press
An imprint of Policy Studies Organization
1527 New Hampshire Ave. NW
Washington, D.C. 20036
info@ipsonet.org

ISBN-13: 978-1-63391-722-4
ISBN-10: 1-63391-722-3

Cover design by Jeffrey Barnes:
jbarnesbook.design

Daniel Gutierrez-Sandoval, Executive Director
PSO and Westphalia Press

Updated material and comments on this edition
can be found at the Westphalia Press website:
www.westphaliapress.org

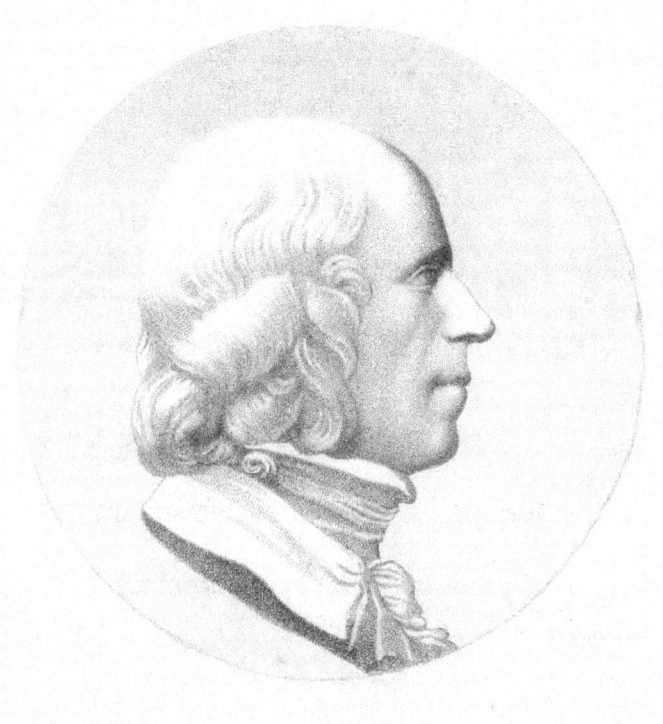

Portrait of Flaxman from a model by himself.

TO

PROFESSOR OWEN, C.B., F.R.S., &c.,

WITH THE WRITER'S GRATITUDE,

FOR WORDS OF TRUE ENCOURAGEMENT,

AND MANY ACTS OF KINDNESS,

This Work

MOST HEARTILY IS DEDICATED.

April, 1875.

LECTURES

ON

SCULPTURE

BY

JOHN FLAXMAN, R.A.

WITH AN INTRODUCTORY LECTURE, AND TWO ADDRESSES TO THE ROYAL ACADEMY
ON THE DEATH OF THOMAS BANKS, IN 1805, AND OF ANTONIO CANOVA,
IN 1822, AND AN ADDRESS ON THE DEATH OF FLAXMAN,
BY SIR RICHARD WESTMACOTT, R.A.

WITH FIFTY-THREE PLATES

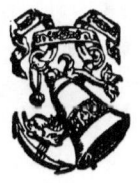

LONDON

GEORGE BELL & SONS

1906

CONTENTS.

———

ADVERTISEMENT.

———◦◦◦———

Mr. Flaxman's Lectures on Sculpture having been
long out of print, and become very scarce, the Publishers have been induced to undertake a New Edition,
in a reduced form, and at a price within the means
of every Student of Art.

In preparing this Edition, a few minor errors have
been corrected, but the Lectures are in every other
respect the same as when first delivered by the
illustrious Author.

In reproducing the illustrations, some pains were
taken to get access to the original drawings used by
Flaxman in his Lectures. Such as could be obtained
were not found available; the Publishers, therefore,
have gone in all cases where it was possible to the
original objects themselves, or to the best copies they
could obtain.

The engravings from Wells Cathedral are taken
from photographs, and may therefore be accepted as
more accurate than the drawings in the First Edition.

EXTRACTS FROM SIR RICHARD WESTMACOTT'S
FIRST LECTURE,

DELIVERED AT THE ROYAL ACADEMY

ON HIS SUCCESSION TO THE CHAIR OF PROFESSOR OF SCULPTURE, AFTER THE DEATH OF FLAXMAN.

"But, gentlemen, I feel that I should be justly accused of want of duty, and of inattention to the Royal Academy, to you, and indeed to our national glory, if I were to suffer this introduction to pass without offering publicly that tribute to the memory of your late lamented Professor which his great talents so eminently call for. His works are before the world; and his excellencies and defects now await that public decree which is to assign him his just place in the Republic of Art.

"If to have procured esteem whilst living, and to have rendered himself useful to his fellow-labourers, both by his practice and the examples he has left us, demand applause, few men have died with stronger claims on posterity.

"The chief qualities which distinguished him as an artist were feeling and purity of style; he was skilled in the intellectual part of his art, and never suffered unnecessary display to weaken the effect of his conceptions: emulous of fame, he sought it on the unerring principles of the best models of antiquity, the only legitimate road by which it could be attained. His whole life was devoted to his pro-

fession; he early habituated himself to the study
of nature, and few applied that study more successfully, or directed his art more happily to those
appeals for which it is more particularly suited;
none excelled him in the learning of his art; and
from his study of the best authors of antiquity, his
mind became stored with their images, and imbued
with their sentiment. During his studies at Rome
he produced those masterly illustrations of Homer,
Hesiod, and Æschylus, which place him as the first
Designer since the revival of Sculpture: these
works evince a thorough knowledge of the principles of his art, and whether considered for composition, and the laws which govern it, for their
acquaintance with the usages and customs of the
ancients, or for their erudition, afford most valuable
examples, and must always be consulted with advantage.

"In a very short period classical sculpture has
been deprived of two of its brightest supports, and
you, gentlemen, have lost a most able instructor;
but neither Italy nor England, in deploring the loss
of Canova or Flaxman, can consider them exclusive
privations. All Europe justly claims the kindred,
and acknowledges the loss.

"To Canova Italy owes her emancipation from
those false perceptions which had, from the influence
of the Bernini school, so long diverted the current
of pure taste. The evil was felt, but the genius
was wanting to establish the true style: the works
which followed the Bernini school were powerless
imitations, without either character or decision, and
from their sameness were equally intolerable with the
fantastic conceits and exaggerations of the former.

"Canova's Dædalus, though a youthful production, showed the value of attention to nature; but his statue of Theseus re-established Sculpture on its true basis, and he was hailed as the restorer of legitimate art.

"To Flaxman the art owes equal obligation. Banks had corrected the grosser impurities, and successfully stemmed the torrent of false taste; but Flaxman not only supported the purity of Sculpture, but carried us within the dominion of Poetry, and taught us its value in art; he boldly passed the barrier which had so long encircled sculpture, and walked freely into the regions of invention. His admiration of simplicity made him regard it in whatever age or examples he discovered it, and gave a general character of originality to his own works, but which it must not be denied sometimes carried him into too close a resemblance of the productions of the earlier revivers of the art.

"But the faults which may be imputed to him are indeed no others than the excess of great and acknowledged beauties; such as a poetical imagination, a devoted admiration of purity, and a warm and enthusiastic genius inspire.

"In comparing and estimating artists who have made the higher department of the profession their study, we ought not to oppose them by forming a judgment of the whole from any particular passages in their works, but to consider their distinguishing characters, and weigh the aggregate of their respective qualities.

"No modern Sculptor has entered so deeply into the recesses of ancient art as Flaxman. His style was founded upon their principles, combined with the simplicity of the Pisani, and others of the fourteenth century; whilst that of Canova was an union of the ideal with Nature. The one attracts us by the originality and sweetness of his invention, the other delights us with a delicacy and beauty peculiar to himself. Execution was with Flaxman subservient to invention, whilst Canova suffered invention to be subordinate, and seduces us by the luxuriance of execution. Each equally felt what belonged to the dignity of Art: simple in their arrangements, sparing in ornament, so that the eye should not be distracted by the pomp of extraneous or unnecessary matter.

" We have two eminently successful examples in Sepulchral Monuments by these Sculptors; the one to a Pope the other to a Judge, in which this principle of feeling is obvious. The class of composition is the same; both are pyramidal, the subject or principal figure occupying the upper region or apex of the triangle, the accessories forming the base: here no more is done than is intended to convey to the spectator the qualities which distinguished the great men whose characters were proposed to be recorded; and if we are arrested by the power and freedom of execution in the principal statue, or by the grace of the accessories in Ganganelli's monument, we are not less charmed with the noble simplicity and classical forms in that of Lord Mansfield.

" The most distinguished proof of Flaxman's powers in Heroical Composition, and the strongest mark of his genius, may be discovered in the colossal group of "St. Michael subduing Satan," now in the gallery of the Earl of Egremont at Petworth, an attempt as successful as daring in colum nar grouping, and which affords an example of the difficulties imposed not only by material, but by the nature of the subject, being overcome without a recourse to adventitious aid, by which the eye or mind might be diverted from the impression proposed, and is strictly within the limits enjoined by Sculpture. I consider it indeed a work not less skilful in the arrangement of its composition than great in its conception. The Archangel is produced in the spirit of the art itself; his countenance denotes a generous indignation tempered by angelic nature; there is an ardour and energy revolving around him which might be supposed to influence him in the execution of his Divine mission; we want no type or wings, but at once admit his presence. The character of the whole is finely marked, and possesses in the choice and structure of form, and in the unity of expression and action, all the ideal qualities appropriate to the exalted subject.

"In the personification of Satan he has been not less succesful. Half-monster and half-man, with all the characterists of mighty stature and Titanic strength, in the malignant subtlety and inflexibility of purpose, in expression, and in the writhing action of the demon, we see him evidently withheld by the presence of a Divine power, in which he is no longer able to sustain himself.

"In alto- or basso-relievo, Flaxman, since the revival of the art, stood pre-eminent. The illustrations from the Lord's Prayer are fine examples of his talents in the simply natural, and in the heroic style in the former; whilst the latter is powerfully displayed in the unrivalled composition of the Shield of Achilles. If examined as compositions by the test of analysis or separation, they will bear the strictest scrutiny; if contemplated for the character each bears to the subject, we would not desire more perfect harmony; if regarded for form, grace, and the taste which pervade the whole, we may pronounce it a work worthy to be ranked with the distinguished discoveries at Dodona."

In a subsequent Lecture delivered by Sir Richard Westmacott, at the Royal Academy, occurs the following passage relating to Flaxman :—

"But the greatest of modern sculptors was our illustrious countryman, John Flaxman, who not only had all the fine feeling of the ancient Greeks (which Canova in a degree possessed), but united to it a readiness of invention, and a simplicity of design, truly astonishing. Though Canova was his superior in the manual part, high finishing, yet in the higher qualities, poetical feeling and invention, Flaxman was as superior to Canova as Shakspeare to the dramatists of his day."

LIST OF PLATES.

The anecdote concerning this monument is this :—M. Ver-schoffel, a Prussian Sculptor, was on a visit to the Rev. M. Langhahn in Switzerland, when Madame Langhahn died on Easter Eve. M. Verschoffel, to console his afflicted friend, immediately carved the lady and her new-born infant, bursting the tomb in the resurrection of the just. It has been introduced on account of the pious and affectionate sentiment it contains.

A BRIEF MEMOIR OF THE AUTHOR.

THE best history of the talents of an artist is to be found by the study of his principal works; for in those are usually displayed the qualities of his mind, the nature of his studies, and the depth of his knowledge; and when the subjects are chosen by himself, they are fair transcripts of his thoughts and affections, and present as true a reflex of his heart and feelings as a clear mirror would the features of his face. Never was this more strongly exemplified than in the present instance. Wherever in the works of Flaxman are found the representations of wisdom, magnanimity, piety, or any of the Christian virtues and charities that exalt human nature, they were the personifications of similar qualities in himself.

This excellent man and admirable artist was born on the 6th of July, 1755, in the city of York, where his father at that time resided, but which he quitted while his son was yet an infant. He very early gave indications of that observation and love

B

for works of art, which distinguished him in maturer
life.   One of the first instances was shewn on the
coronation day of his Majesty George the Third.
His father was going to see the procession, and the
child begged very earnestly that he would bring one
of the medals which were to be thrown to the popu-
lace ; he was not fortunate enough to get one ; but,
on his way home, happening to find a plated button
bearing the stamp of a horse and jockey, rather than
wholly disappoint his little boy, who then was in a
very delicate precarious state of health,* he ventured,
though unwillingly, to deceive him, and gave him
the button.   The young virtuoso took it and was
thankful, but remarked, it was a very odd device
for a coronation medal.   He was then five years
old ; at this age he was fond of examining the
seals of every watch he saw, whether belonging
to friend, or stranger, and kept a bit of soft wax
ready to take an impression of any which pleased
him.   These trivial circumstances are only mentioned to shew how early he began the practice of
seizing every opportunity of improvement in his art,
and of acquiring any knowledge it was right for him
to possess ; indeed, it was a maxim of his, that " we
never are too young or too old to become wiser or
better."

While yet a child he made a great number of
small models, both in plaster-of-Paris, wax, and clay ;

* A very short time previous to this he had been so ill that he
was supposed to be dead, and was laid out under that impression.

some of which are still preserved, and have considerable merit, and were certainly promises of that genius and talent which he faithfully kept in after-years.

When he was about ten years of age, his health had greatly improved ; and, though not strong, he had become a lively active boy, with great enthusiasm of character, which chiefly displayed itself on subjects of generosity, courage, and humanity : this enthusiasm was called forth, in a peculiar and somewhat diverting manner, by reading Don Quixote. He was so much delighted with the amiable, though eccentric hero, and with his account of the duties and honourable perils of knight-errantry, that he thought he could not do better than sally forth, to right wrongs and redress grievances; accordingly, one morning early, unknown to any one, armed with a little French sword (not better than a toy), he set out, without a squire, in quest of adventures which fortunately he did not find.

After wandering about Hyde Park the whole day without meeting enchantor or distressed damsel, not even a castle or drawbridge, he (being rather hungry and more ashamed of his romantic flight) returned home, where his unwonted absence had caused great alarm to his parents, who had sought and inquired fruitlessly for him till evening. He never again emulated the exploits of the knight, though he always retained a great admiration of his character.

He now modelled and drew most assiduously, but

never received more than two lessons from a master, being hurt at having (according to rule) a drawing of eyes only given him to copy, which having done, he shewed them to Mr. Mortimer, a very clever artist, who asked if they were flounders?—this jest not being at all encouraging, his father allowed him to choose his examples, and pursue his studies in his own way, which he did so successfully, that at the age of eleven years and five months he gained his first prize from the Society for the Encouragement of Arts, &c. (which was the silver pallet), for a model. At thirteen he had another ; and the following year was admitted a student at the Royal Academy, then newly established ; and the same year received their silver medal.

About this time he made an acquaintance equally agreeable and serviceable ; it was with a very worthy clergyman, whose wife was one of the most highly-gifted and elegant women of that day ; she was the intimate associate of Mrs. Montague, Mrs. Barbauld, Mrs. Chapone, Mrs. Brooke, &c. At this house, where he was for many years a welcome visitor, he passed frequent evenings in very enlightened and delightful society ; here he was encouraged in studying the dead languages, so necessary to him in his profession : by acquiring these he learned to think with the authors, and to embody the ideas of Homer, Hesiod, and Æschylus, in a manner that no modern artist has exceeded.*

* During his intimacy with this excellent family Mr. Flaxman

Amongst his other engagements in art, he was much employed by Mr. Wedgwood, in modelling for his manufactory; and from the good taste and persevering spirit of the one, and the genius, ability, and industry of the other, was produced that great improvement, in every description of vase, dish, cup, &c., whether for use or ornament, which has been acknowledged throughout the civilised world. A set of chess-men were the most beautiful things of the kind ever produced. A very highly-finished drawing of all the pieces, by Mr. Flaxman, is in the possession of the Wedgwood family.

One of his most admired works, previous to his going to Italy, was a beautiful group of Venus and Cupid, which was executed for Mr. Knight, of Portland-place; another was a monument in Gloucester Cathedral to the memory of Mrs. Morley, who, with her infant, died at sea; the mother and her babe are rising from the waves, and are received by descending angels; it is an exquisite thing, full of that more than mortal beauty so proper to the subject, and at the same time affecting, from the sentiment and expression of the composition.

In 1782 Mr. Flaxman married Miss Ann Denman, an amiable and accomplished woman, who accompanied him to Italy in 1787. Fortunately, his wife possessed that intelligence of mind, and love of art,

---

painted several pictures in oil, one of which was sold at an auction a short time since; the subject was " Œdipus and Antigone," but was ignorantly described in the catalogue as " Belisarius," by Domenichino.

that her society assisted, rather than impeded, the progress of the artist through the studies and difficulties of his profession.

It was not known to any but Mr. Flaxman's nearest connexions, what circumstance determined him to visit Rome. The fact was this: when Sir Joshua Reynolds heard, from himself, that he was married, he exclaimed, "Oh, then you are ruined for an artist!" This observation (which was really unworthy of the man who uttered it) decided what had hitherto been with him a question, whether he should quit England and study for a time in Italy. He was aware of the advantages attending it, and still more convinced that it was considered by the world as essential. He therefore began to contemplate it as a thing to be done, and commenced finishing the works he had in hand, without undertaking others. At length everything was concluded, and knowing that his pecuniary resources would allow him to go without imprudence, he resolved on an absence of two years, a period he thought would be sufficient for his purpose. But when two years had passed away, he found that the business he had undertaken * would not, as yet, permit him to leave Rome; and one engagement succeeded another, until the intended absence of two years became seven.

Throughout this interesting journey, as well as during his residence in Rome, Mr. Flaxman's application was incessant; whether he was drawing from

* The large group for Lord Bristol.

the antique, or making studies from the living groups and figures abounding in the venerable city and its environs, each object, animate and inanimate, was to him beautiful or noble and all-inspiring; no day was lost; and, except his health and strength failed, no hour of the day was suffered to pass without some improvement. Here he executed a group, of colossal size, consisting of four figures, for the late Lord Bristol, Bishop of Derry. The subject was the fury of Athamas, from Ovid's "Metamorphoses." For this great work he received a sum so small that he was a considerable loser by it; indeed, the great loss and vexation this commission brought, made the mention of the subject disagreeable to him. This group, after several removals, first from Rome to Leghorn, and afterwards to Ireland, has at last found its place in Ickworth House, Suffolk, the seat of the present Marquis of Bristol, but, unfortunately, it is but little seen.

He also finished an exquisitely beautiful group, of smaller size, of Cephalus and Aurora, for Mr. Thomas Hope, which remains in that gentleman's collection.

In Rome he made those designs from Homer, Æschylus, and Dante, so much known and admired throughout Europe, more particularly on the Continent. The "Iliad and Odyssey" were for the late Mrs. Hare; the "Tragedies of Æschylus" for the excellent Dowager Countess Spencer; and the "Dante" for Mr. Thomas Hope. These were all admirably engraved in outline by Thomas Piroli, and published in Rome in 1793, and subsequently in London.

In 1794, Mr. Flaxman and his beloved companion returned to their native land,* where his first work was the monument of Earl Mansfield, for Westminster Abbey, the order for which he received previous to his leaving Rome. The figure of the earl is in his judicial robes, sitting, and in the act of giving judgment ; he is supported on each side by Wisdom and Justice, as represented by the ancients; the youth behind the pedestal with the inverted torch is a classical personification of Death.

About the same time he erected a monumental figure of Sir Robert Ladbroke in Spitalfields church. In Westminster Abbey is a noble monument, with a statue of Captain James Montague, crowned by a Victory, which possesses an unusual combination of aërial grace with dignity. The lions on the base are admirable portraits of the magnificent animal from which they were studied, at that time living in the Tower ; the flags behind the statue were added by Mr. Flaxman at his own cost, as he found they

---

* It is not generally known in England that Mr. Flaxman, upon his return from Italy, having paid the duties upon several articles he had brought for his own study, interested himself so warmly for his brother artists, that, through his representations to the proper persons, the duties were taken off all future importations of that kind. This disinterested conduct was acknowledged by the gentlemen then studying in Rome by a letter of thanks bearing all their signatures.

would greatly improve the composition, the excel
lence of the work being always, with him, a prior
consideration to the profit. The removal of this
monument from its original situation in the Abbey,
was considered by Mr. Flaxman as nearly destructive of its effect.

In St. Paul's, the monument of Lord Nelson has a
striking portrait of the hero, wrapped in a pelisse,
and leaning on an anchor; Britannia is pointing out
the glorious example to two young sailors.

In the same cathedral is a monument to Earl
Howe: above is a sitting figure of Britannia holding a trident, the earl stands below her, on her left;
the British lion is watching by him on the other
side; Fame is recording the achievements of the
admiral, while Victory, leaning over her, places a
crown on the lap of Britannia.

To the memory of Captain Millar there is a basso-
relievo of Britannia and Victory raising a medallion
of the Captain to a palm-tree.

There is likewise in St. Paul's a fine statue of Sir
Joshua Reynolds.

Perhaps the most striking family monument ever
executed by Mr. Flaxman, was to the family of Sir
Francis Baring, in Micheldever church, Hants; it
consists of three distinct parts, making an extremely
beautiful whole. In the centre is a sitting figure of
" Resignation," inscribed " Thy will be done;" on
each side is a very fine alto-relievo, also from the
Lord's Prayer; the subject of one,—" Thy kingdom

come;" the other—" Deliver us from evil." **The** tranquil piety of expression in the single figure is finely contrasted with the terrific struggle on the one hand, and the ecstatic joyfulness of the female, who is assisted in rising by angelic beings, on the other.

There are two very interesting monuments in' Oxford to Sir William Jones, one at University College and one in St. Mary's Church, both erected by his lady.

At Christchurch, Hampshire, there is a group, of the late Lady Fitz-Harris and her three children; a most lovely representation of maternal tenderness, which has been much, and deservedly, admired. This was put up in 1817.

A monument to the Yarborough family, at Street Thorpe, near York, is an alto-relievo of two females relieving several poor persons of different ages; it is a singularly fine composition, and remarkable for the natural expression of each individual.

In the same county there is a beautiful monument to the memory of Edward Balme, Esq.—" Instruct the Ignorant." It is a group, in alto-relievo, of an aged man holding a book, in which he reads while a youth and a young female are attentively and affectionately listening.

The memorial in Brighton Church, Northampton-shire, put up by Earl Spencer, to his excellent mother, the late dowager countess, is a proof of how much beauty and real sentiment may be introduced into a simple composition. The monument consists of a tablet, having a figure of Faith at one end, and a group of Charity at the other; this last is one of the most lively conceptions of that virtue ever seen in marble.

A figure of Mrs. Tighe (the authoress of Psyche) merits the same kind of praise, as it possesses the same character of beauty. This went to Ireland.

In Cookham Church, Berks, the monument of Sir Isaac Pocock is a peculiarly affecting representation of the death of that gentleman, which took place suddenly in a boat on the River Thames.

"The good Samaritan," in Layton Church, Essex, to the memory of — Bosanquet, Esq., and a monumental bas-relief to the late Mrs. Bosanquet, are very admirable for feeling and execution. Equally excellent in both is an alto-relievo in St. John's Church, Manchester; and it has the peculiarity of being erected in the life-time of Mr. Clowes, the clergyman of that church, who having been fifty years their exemplary pastor, his parishioners wished in this way to express their love and veneration while he was yet with them ;—he is represented instructing, in their religious duties, Childhood, Maturity, and Age.

In the cathedral at Winchester there is a fine monument for Dr. Wharton.

Salisbury Cathedral has two Gothic monuments, extremely elegant in design and delicately executed.

In Chichester Cathedral there are many of Mr

Flaxman's works: amongst others, a small but very interesting monument to the memory of the poet Collins.

In the city of Glasgow there are two statues larger than life, of Mr. Pitt and Sir John Moore, in bronze; and in Edinburgh the statue of Robert Burns is to be placed in the library of the University.

Many statues and other works he executed for the East Indies. One was a large figure of the Raja of Tanjore; a monument to the missionary Schwartz, in the Raja's territory; two to Lord Cornwallis; and many more for private gentlemen, as well as for the Honourable Company. And it is but justice to mention, what Mr. Flaxman frequently declared, that in all the works he executed for India, he constantly experienced the most liberal treatment, not only in pecuniary concerns, but in the handsome manner his employers expressed their entire approbation of all he did. The last of his works for that country was a statue of the Marquis of Hastings, upon an embellished pedestal, now on its way to Calcutta. This was done by private subscription, and was not quite finished in marble at the time of Mr. Flaxman's decease, but has been completed under the inspection and care of Mr. T. Denman, his pupil and brother-in-law; who has also erected the statue of Mr. Kemble in Westminster Abbey, which was one of the works in hand when the artist was taken from this life.

Mr. Flaxman's grandest work in this country was

the group of the Archangel Michael and Satan, for the Earl of Egremont, and was one of the last productions of the sculptor. This is a work which, in after ages, will be a glory, to the nation, to the memory of the artist, and to the name of the truly noble proprietor; who, besides this group, has a pastoral Apollo, the size of life, the grace and beauty of which are admirable.

The shield of Achilles is a proof of the high classical knowledge, the perfect acquaintance with the human figure, and the truly poetic spirit of him who made the composition. For the variety of its beauties, and its skilful execution, it is unrivalled, and truly worthy of adorning the palace of a sovereign. It reflects infinite credit on the taste and spirit of Messrs. Rundell and Bridge, to have been the means of producing this magnificent work of art.

The friezes on the front of Covent Garden Theatre were designed by Mr. Flaxman; one of them and the figure of Comedy were executed by him.

It is not possible to give a list of all the productions of Mr. Flaxman: those above enumerated were selected as having most interest, though a great number of admirable works must necessarily be omitted.*

* Among the latter works of Mr. Flaxman are two small but beautiful figures of Cupid and Psyche, done for Mr. Rogers; and two others, of equal beauty, though different style, for Sir Thomas Lawrence, of Michael Angelo and Raffaelle: with these should be mentioned two exquisite bas-relievos from Milton, the models for which were finished by Mr. Flaxman; one of them is in a state of considerable forwardness in marble.

It will be right to mention in this place, that the very last work of his hand was making the drawings for all the principal embellishments on the exterior of Buckingham Palace, and had his life been longer spared, he was, at the particular desire of His Majesty, to have executed as many of them as he could undertake, and to have directed the remainder. He took great delight in making the designs, and looked forward with an anxious pleasure to his task—but Infinite Wisdom ordered it otherwise.

————

In 1797 Mr. Flaxman was elected an Associate of the Royal Academy; in 1800 Academician; and in 1810 he was appointed Professor of Sculpture * in the Royal Academy, where he gave his lectures every season, with but few omissions, until the last year of his life, 1826, when his health only permitted him to deliver one. He had, however, written a new one, " On Modern Sculpture," which it has been judged right to publish; it is the tenth and last in the volume.

During the peace of 1802, when Paris was visited by a great number of English, Mr. Flaxman went

* The Professorship of Sculpture was the first in this country, and instituted expressly for Mr. Flaxman, who dedicated most of his evenings to writing the Lectures and making the drawings for them. Few persons can conceive how much time and study he devoted to that purpose. The drawings remain in the possession of his family, as well as a great number of others, studies from nature, and designs from various authors, some of them beautifully finished.

also, for the purpose of seeing again those fine things, he had studied with so much advantage in Italy. Many of his countrymen were at that time introduced to the First Consul; but he refused being one of the number, as he could not submit to pay homage (even for a few minutes) to the man who was the enemy of his country and his king. He also declined, while in that capital, meeting a celebrated French artist, whose talents he admired, but of whose political conduct and principles he had an abhorrence; indeed, it was an invariable rule with him, abroad and at home, to shun, with the greatest care, the society of persons, however brilliant and clever, when he was once convinced that their religious and moral opinions were inimical to the laws of their God and their country. By this conduct he preserved a purity of heart and character rarely to be met with: it was this purity of heart which inspired the delightful cheerfulness and amenity of manner that won the affection of the young and gay, as well as the respect and friendship of those of equal years; the more intimately he was known, the more he was beloved.*

Well might Sir Thomas Lawrence say, in his most eloquent and feeling address to the students, that the death of this exemplary man was "a deep

* In 1820 Mr. Flaxman lost his wife, which was the severest trial he ever experienced, and called for all his pious and humble submission to the will of Providence to support as became his character.

and irreparable loss to Art, to his country, and to Europe."

But still deeper and more irreparable was this loss in the little "circle of affection" in which he lived and died. He was always prepared for the termination of his mortal pilgrimage: this (for him) happy change took place on the 7th of December, 1826, having entered the seventy-second year of his age.

ADDRESS.

Mr. President and Gentlemen,

It is not unknown to you that, by the institution of the Royal Academy, the cultivation and encouragement of painting, sculpture, and architecture, were proposed to be supported from means derived through the public exhibition of original works in those arts. Schools were formed for their practice, and lectures appointed for instruction in their principles; but as the study of sculpture was at that time confined within narrow limits, so the appointment of a professorship in that art was not required, until the increasing taste of the country had given great popularity to the art itself, and native achievements had called on the powers of native sculpture to celebrate British heroes and patriots.

The members of the Royal Academy in this, as in all other public acts, have proved their liberality and patriotism; and it will be no easy task for the person, called to this situation, to prove himself worthy of the confidence he has been honoured with : it remains with him, however, to exert his best endeavours, in a full reliance for support on the same kindness and indulgence which raised him to an exercise of the duty.

INTRODUCTORY LECTURE.

EDUCATION may be distinguished into theoretical and practical. Theory supplies our minds with the principles of science, from which rules are deduced for our future practice; and, indeed, the latter must be considered as immediately succeeding the former by natural connexion and certain consequence, rather than as distinct and independent of theory.

In a general view of human knowledge and exertion, we shall find they have invariably co-operated in whatever has been done most useful and most excellent.

In universities, and the greater public schools, science and literature are taught upon a scale sufficiently extensive to furnish principles and theory for the practice of every useful art and employment; for the same reason in colleges and institutions established for less general purposes, and confined to the cultivation of particular sciences or arts, their systems of education become more valuable and effective as they promote a diligent and successful practice, upon the principles of a sound and rational theory.

The Royal Academy established in this palace, by the munificence of our revered Sovereign, King George III., has continued its exertions, without ceasing, for the improvement of the schools, by supporting its funds, by supplying the best living models, casts from the finest specimens of antiquity, for the student's imitation and practice, and by rewards for the encouragement of distinguished merit.

To these advantages a noble library has been added, containing the most approved works on painting, sculpture, and architecture, which is opened twice a week to the members and students; and to render this system as perfect as possible, and unite the most approved principles, with a diligent practice, professors of eminent merit in painting, architecture, perspective, and anatomy, have been appointed to deliver public instruction: the professorship of sculpture has been added within these few years, which, in relation to the value and beauty of the art it is intended to illustrate, may be justly considered as a valuable addition. It may be anxiously hoped that whoever may be raised to this office, may be capable of honouring his art by the eloquence and precision of his discourses, and the excellence of his practice.

As materials for study constitute one of the chief

means of improvement, sentiments of gratitude will be renewed towards our patron, the Prince Regent, for His Royal Highness's munificent gift of the extensive, magnificent, and invaluable collection of casts from the most sublime works of Greek sculpture.

This collection was executed with great skill and precision from the original marbles, to supply their places on the pedestals of their prototypes, when those originals became the prey of barbarous rapacity.

The pillage was restored by the interference of British justice, and the Regent's magnanimous councils. The Sovereign Pontiff, in acknowledgment, presented the casts to the Regent. His Royal Highness, preferring public advantage to individual gratification, bestowed them on the Schools of Design, to disseminate taste and promote knowledge: thus affording gratification to the artist and connoisseur, and an invaluable subject of contemplation and study to the painter and sculptor.

Permit me to deviate from the direct scope of my subject a few moments, into short but important arguments on the equal injustice and impolicy of removing the works of ancient sculpture from Italy. —We will begin with the injustice, as the more atrocious, although the consequences of such acts will generally prove they were counselled by folly.

The city of Rome, since Constantine removed the seat of empire to Constantinople, has been burnt

seven times, which, in addition to the several cala-
mities of famine, pestilence, sieges, tumults, with the
natural decay produced by time itself, was reduced
to a condition so despoiled and ruinous, that only
six statues were enumerated by a diligent observer.
Poggi, in the beginning of the 15th century, within
the walls; the rest had long been buried under the
mouldering fragments and rubbish of palaces and
temples, once decorations of the Imperial City in
her splendour.   From the latter end of the 15th century, the pontiffs, Italian princes, and nobility have,
with great labour and expense, rescued these wonders of ancient art from the bowels of the earth,
restored their mutilated forms, placed them in galleries and museums, and, with a liberality which the
real love of knowledge alone inspires, have given
the learned traveller and artist, of all conditions and
countries, free access to their treasures.   Let it be
remembered that the ancient Romans, despoilers of
Greece, having long since quitted this stage of life,
—the despoiled Greeks have also long since been
swept away in the lapse of time, so that their successors, in name and territory, of the present day
(a various mixture of barbarous nations), neither
appreciate the possession, nor remember the sufferings of their long past predecessors : the changes
and destruction of succeeding years, have enveloped
the memory of their descendants in such impene-
trable darkness, that we are uncertain whether any
race, or even particular family now living, can fairly

claim the distinction of being their direct repre-
sentatives.

As they cannot now be restored to their original
owners, who can justly and reasonably plead so good
a claim to their possessions, as those whose intelligence, exertions, and benevolence have rescued these
precious remains from their graves, and generously
given them to the public?

These remains were not obtained by the Italian
nobles without considerable expense. The Medici
family appear to have paid 1800 crowns for the
Group of Boxers, when it was first found, one of
the figures being headless, which sum is more than
equal to 2000*l*. value of our money in England at
this day; and Cardinal Borghese built the front
of a church in recompense for the beautiful statue
of Hermaphrodite, lately in the Borghese Villa, on
the Pincian Hill. We may form some opinion of
the sums expended in restoring the works of antiquity from the following instance.

A beautiful and extensive Mosaic pavement, containing two very large circular friezes of figures,—
the subject of one, the Battle of the Lapithæ and
Centaurs, the subject of the other, Tritons and Sea
Monsters,—this was brought to Rome by order of
Pope Pius VI., laid down and restored in the great
hall of the Vatican, at the expense of 60,000 crowns,
about the value of 30,000*l*. of our present money in
England.

Every person desirous to complete a liberal education, receives the rudiments in a school, preparatory to finishing his studies in an university. A like proceeding is requisite to educate a painter or sculptor: he commences his studies in his native academy, and afterwards goes to Italy to make himself acquainted with the originals of those casts and prints he has copied in his own country, there he sees such an accumulation of classical works in the sister arts as cannot fail to decide his choice, form his taste, and lay the certain foundation of a good practice. The claims of Italy to be considered an university for the arts of design are indisputable, for the number and character of her galleries and collections, for the stupendous works of Michael Angelo, Raffaelle, Titian, and the restorers of painting: all of which are painted on walls and cannot be removed, the architectural remains, the relations of those with the classical literature of the country, and of Greece, the warm climate favourable to the study of the human figure, and that general state of tranquillity, and freedom from those dissipations which infect some of the capitals in Europe; all these advantages are peculiarly enjoyed in Rome, Florence, Pisa, and throughout the Pontifical and Tuscan States, and thus possess a union of advantages not possible to be concentrated in any other country in the present state of the world, for completing an education of principles in the arts of design.

Here we will finish the digression and return to

the royal donation, and speak of its extent, character, and value.

The groups, statues, basso-relievos, busts, and fine fragments were sufficiently numerous to have furnished an extensive range of study, supposing there had been no previous collection in the royal schools : the character and value will be best understood by an enumeration of the principal articles, accompanied with such remarks as may imprint on the younger student a strong sense of the excellence which may be transplanted into his own mind from such examples, by diligence and labour.

Let us begin with the Laocoon, which in the time of Pliny was accounted the most consummate work of painting and sculpture ; its sentiment is sublime and pathetic, the forms are noble and expressive, the whole is composed into a continued and varied series of undulations, in agreement with the movements of the serpents which assault Laocoon and his sons, and the writhing agonies their venom has caused. Laborious treatises have been written on this group ; but it is one thing to fill a volume, which captivates by the appearance of enthusiasm and show of learning, and a totally different task to convey sound instruction. Mr. Fuseli in his lectures has given a description of this group equally worthy of a great poet and a painter.

The Apollo Belvidere, so called from the garden of the Vatican, but in reality, the Deliverer from Evil, has been both philosophically and popularly considered as a form animated by such a sentiment as might become a supernatural power revealed to mortal sight. Hints are not wanting in ancient monuments and authors, which lead us to believe that the archetype of this statue was by Phidias.

The Venus of the Capitol, an example of more dignified and less insinuating beauty than the Venus de Medicis,—this statue is certainly a copy from one of the three enumerated by Pliny among the works of Praxiteles.*

The Apollo Sauroctonos, or Lizard Killer, from an antique bronze in the Villa Albani, likewise copied from a work of Praxiteles.*

The Satyr by the same sculptor.*

In the hall are five of these statues, and one group, which may be described in succession.

The colossal statue of Minerva, placed opposite the fire, was discovered twenty-four years since. A duplicate of the same statue has since been found in the neighbourhood of Rome. A bust of the same figure was in the Albani Villa, and another duplicate of the head is in the Marquis of Lansdowne's collection. The frequent repetitions of this statue, the estimation in which it was held by the ancients, may reasonably lead us to believe they are all copies from one by Phidias, mentioned by Pliny, in the enumeration of that sculptor's works : the severe and simple beauty of its character, together with the resemblance to a figure on the reverse of an

* In the Council Room.

Athenian coin, published by Dr. Coombe, in Hunter's collection, gives additional countenance to this opinion.

On the left of this statue sits Menander, and on the right Posidyppus, both comic poets. The learned Visconti has offered arguments, which appear to be unanswerable, for believing them to be the portraits of those authors, which were in the Theatre of Athens.

On the side of the steps next to the window stands a Roman, whose head is covered by his toga, which descends to his feet in majestic abundance. His countenance resembles the Scipio family, and answers in dress to a description of Scipio Nasica, quoted by Ferrarius de re Vestiaria.

The figure of Juno has an air of sublime dignity, the original is in the Capitol.

The Achilles, which faces the Minerva, is an example of heroic strength, in grand and decided form. This statue was in the Borghese Villa; it is now in Paris, with the whole of that collection, which once belonged to the Borghese family.

The group commonly named Papirius and his Mother, but much more likely to be Electra and Orestes, or Penelope and Telemachus, of a pure style and natural sentiment.

The group generally known as Pætus and Arria, but more likely Macareus, son of Œolus, and Canace his wife, or Flamon and Antigone. The sentiment is despair and union; the male figure, whilst he inflicts the mortal wound upon himself, supports with desperate energy his beloved wife, sinking to the ground in death. The lines of this group unite the charms of harmony and force of contrast in the power of expression.

We shall now notice eleven statues in one paragraph, as being one family : they are Mnemosyne the mother and her daughters, the nine Muses, and Apollo their leader. Thalia has the beauty of early youth in modesty ; Melpomene is known by an heroic attitude, similar to Egeus, the father of Theseus or Jason ; Euterpe is distinguished by a regal grace ; Calliope and Clio by Doric simplicity and mental occupation in bodily rest ; Apollo, the leader of the Muses in this series, is known for a celebrated statue among the ancients by some reverses of Nero's coins.

Besides the purposes of study for which these statues are highly valuable in a school of design, their presence has converted the Council Chamber into an Homeric Olympus, where none approach without the mingled sentiment of delight and awe.

In the Plaster Academy is the group of Pylades and Orestes, offering sacrifice ; also the statue of Germanicus delivering an oration.

The Colossal Barberini Faun, remarkable for the terse, elastic forms of muscle and tendon, proper to the mountainous and sylvan habits of the race.

These cursory notices shall be closed with the Diana discharging an arrow, from the original marble in the Gallery of Paris. This beautiful and inte-resting statue has long been the rightful property of the French monarchs: it has been considered by some learned men and professional judges, as nearly resembling the Apollo Belvidere in countenance and general character, to a degree that may warrant opinion that they are both the production of one sculptor. It is also possible the archetypes of these two divinities were introduced in the destruction of Niobe and her family, on the throne of Jupiter, at Elis: the sanction of ancient authors and monu-ments is not wanting to countenance this supposi-tion.

In this enumeration a beautiful modern statue must not be forgotten—it is Paris, by Signor Canova, Marquis of Ischia, and perpetual President, or (in the Italian language) Prince of the Roman Academy: his moral qualities and rank in his art are equally honourable to his country and to himself; gratitude would be wanting not to acknowledge he has mani-fested a passionate desire to serve and respect the Royal Academy of London, and his attention has been prompt and unceasing to the English at Rome.

By such a donation as that we now contemplate, the donor secures to himself satisfaction increasing in proportion to the accumulated advantages result-ing from the use of the gift, the diffusion of know-ledge and taste, the elevation of national character in noble and useful arts; disseminating their advan-tages in a thousand different currents, connected by

the united interests of letters, science, and civilization; the honest wealth of the country promoted;
and by the innocence of such employments, and the
beneficence of their nature, a permanent addition
will be acquired in the general fund of happiness
and contentment.

Long may the Regent enjoy the delights of such
patriotic reflections; and may the rising talents
within these walls satisfy the wishes of their patron,
and fulfil the sanguine expectations, and ardent hope
of this institution and our country.

The object of these lectures has been to lead to
more extensive views in the arts of design, and especially in sculpture.

In the early ages of the world, tents, and the
slightest structures were thought sufficient for the
purposes of habitation; but temples for worship were
raised, or excavated in stone, and adorned by sculpture with the emblems of Theology, and symbols of
Divine Wisdom.

In India the sculptures were mystical attributes
and manifestations. In Assyria they had relation to
the heavenly bodies, and government of the universe.
In Egypt they were hieroglyphical memorials of
divine and human knowledge: this was the earliest
as it will always continue the most important employment of this art, debased indeed according to the
corruptions of systems:—but in that nation which
received the law with signs—wonders to enlighten a
darkened world !—the Almighty directed the figures

of Cherubim to guard the Ark of the Covenant ; but the Ark, the Tabernacle, the first and second Temple, and all their glories have been removed by Divine appointment, and we must look to systems more questionable and less pure for such perfection as we are acquainted with in this art : yet we must not be led to suppose that any art, dependent on intellectual knowledge, can arise to any height of excellence without the assistance of its efficient cause ; and the arts of design in Greece were improved by the Pythagorean and Platonic philosophers, the most enlightened which the heathen world possessed. Less will be said of Grecian art in this place, because it supplies so large a portion of the following discourses, while we turn our thoughts to the more general application and utility of the arts of design, and more especially of sculpture.

LECTURE I.

———◆———

ENGLISH SCULPTURE.

THE arts of design, considered as portions, extend their relations and use through the whole circle of knowledge; they embody ideas, demonstrate the affections and passions; they exhibit the human figure in the highest state of conceivable perfection, and in all of its varieties and gradations. The more common purposes of these arts are to illustrate the several branches of science, from the simplest elements to the most complicated forms and exertions; but their superior concerns appeal to the intellect and the reason, by the representation of superior natures, divine doctrines and history, the perpetuation of noble acts, and assisting in the elevation of our minds towards that excellence for which they were originally intended.

Painting is honoured with precedence, because design, or drawing, is more particularly and extensively employed in illustration of history. Sculpture immediately follows in the enumeration, because the two arts possess the same common principles, expressed by painting, in colour, and by sculpture, in form.

This art, in early ages of most nations, has been chiefly employed in the service of religion, as the symbolical representations of Divine attributes and characteristics abundantly testify, in Egypt, Ethiopia, India, Persia, and ancient Greece; even among the Jews, who were particularly restricted concerning the use of images, on account of their proneness to idolatry, two figures of cherubim were placed by Divine command in the "Holy of Holies," extending their wings over the ark, which contained the covenant between God and man.

If any other testimony were requisite concerning the estimation in which painting and sculpture were held among the ancients, it might be summed up in these observations,—that Plato studied painting, Socrates was a sculptor by profession, and Aristotle may be numbered among the patrons of art, as well as his pupil Alexander, as we learn from the philosopher's will, that he ordered various monumental statues to be made of his friends and relations. This esteem was so general, that not only the best, but the worst characters of antiquity (Nero and Commodus), sought reputation from affecting to encourage, and even to practise them. A further consideration of the state and employment of sculpture among the ancients, particularly the Greeks and Romans, will be necessarily connected with its compendious general history and principles in future discourses, and which may be introduced in the present lecture, by a sketch of its progress in our own country.

Among the ancient Britons, whose dress was a bonnet, hair-cloak, tunic, and long drawers; whose dwellings were huts, and whose cities were woods enclosed by ramparts and ditches, little progress could be expected in the art of sculpture; and indeed no other proofs are come down to us that they had any, excepting some rude coins, apparently imitations of those of Tyre or Carthage, with which countries they had commercial intercourse.

When the Romans had conquered the island, the inhabitants, in imitation of their conquerors, built temples, courts of justice, baths, and all other structures, both public and private, the magnificence of which is not only learned from historians, but proved from immense remains of foundations and mosaic pavements found in various parts of the kingdom, with fragments of statues, groups, sarcophagi, and sepulchral stones, of different ages and workman-ship; on which, however, these remarks may be offered,—that all those works found in Britain, and which we believe were actually performed here, are inferior, both as to principles and execution, to those done by the Romans in their own country at the same period, which is to be accounted for thus; the inhabitants of Britain were instructed in the arts of peace by soldiers, whose knowledge of them was very inferior to their military skill, or by such

artists of little estimation as could be well spared
from Rome or other Italian cities.

Two heads of bronze statues, a Minerva and
Diana,* found in Bath, are examples of sculpture
here during the Roman dominion. The statues, to
which these heads belonged, are believed to have
been the objects of worship in temples dedicated to
those goddesses, formerly existing in that city ; nor
is it impossible that they were British sculpture, as
they are certainly indifferent copies from fine original busts.

The Britons continued to practise the art of casting magnificent works in bronze upwards of 200
years after the departure of the Romans, according
to Speed, who says, "that King Cadwollo being
buried in St. Martin's Church near Ludgate, his
image great and terrible, triumphantly riding on
horseback, artificially cast in brass, was placed on
the western gate of the city, to the further fear and
terror of the Saxons !" We must not, however,
understand, from this bold and poetical description
of Cadwollo's statue, that its expression was the
result of its excellence. If it was terrible as well as
great, that characteristic was the consequence of its
barbarous workmanship : for in the year 677, when
Cadwollo died, the Goths, Franks, Lombards, and
other uncivilized nations, had nearly exterminated
the liberal arts in Europe.

The following general miscellaneous remarks on

* A cast of this head is in Sir John Soane's Museum.

Roman-British Antiquities may be properly offered in this place.

Of the Roman altars and sepulchral tablets, found in Britain, carved in native stone, the workmanship is extremely rude, like that done in Italy under the Gothic and Lombard kings. This observation will include the architectural fragments, as well as human figures in basso-relievo, found at Bath, and belonging to the temples of Minerva and Diana in that city; notwithstanding these temples must have been raised before the time of Constantine the Great, when the Christian religion became the religion of the empire, after which, it is not likely pagan temples of any consequence were erected under the Roman government, if we except the short reign of Julian.

In most of the Roman mosaics found in Britain, the principal object of the design is a Bacchus, or an Orpheus playing on his lyre; those mosaics with the Bacchus are of the best design and workmanship, for which this reason may be given,—that the Bacchus Musagetes was frequently introduced, before the time of Alexander Severus, in sarcophagi and other works, that Divinity being much liked by the Romans, as patron of the drama; consequently, those mosaics are likely to have been done in the course of 170 years, between the reign of Domitian, when the Britons adopted the buildings and decorations of the Romans, and the year 240, when the Orphic philosophy spread its influence in the Roman empire. From this period, to the year 336, the representations of Orpheus may be dated, after which time they were succeeded by Christian characters and symbols.

Fragments of cups and pateras have been found in Cambridge, Colchester, and other places, made of fine red clay, baked and glazed, adorned with basso-relievos, beautifully modelled, of Mercury, Apollo, Venus, and other heathen deities, from large statues still existing, with fine scenic masks, boars, dogs, &c. These were certainly brought from Italy, because great numbers of similar fragments, evidently from the same moulds, are found in Rome and its vicinity.

The Roman coins of Dioclesian, Probus, Licinius, Constantine, his sons, &c., gave examples for diadems, helmets, dress, and the manner of representing busts of their kings, upon the Saxon pennies.

The Roman dress continued in general use in England to the reign of Henry III.: this dress was highly favourable to painting and sculpture, in affording a beautiful variety of folds, and showing the body and limbs advantageously.

The Saxons destroyed the works of Roman grandeur in Britain, burnt the cities from sea to sea, and reduced the country to barbarism again; but when these invaders were settled in their new possessions, they erected poor and clumsy imitations of the Roman buildings themselves had ruined.*

* In the beginning of the sixth century, when the Franks and Germans began to establish themselves in Gaul, they buried

The Saxon painting is rather preferable to **their** sculpture, which, whether intended to represent the human or brutal figure, is frequently both horrible and burlesque. The buildings erected in England, from the settlement of the Saxons to the reign of Henry I., continued nearly the same plain, heavy repetitions of columns and arches. So little was sculpture employed by them, that no sepulchral statue is known in England before the time of William the Conqueror. Previous to this period their names and titles only were engraved on their tombstones. In Winchester Cathedral—"Son of Alfred the Great." In the same church—"Son of William the Conqueror."

Immediately after the Norman Conquest figures of the deceased were carved, in bas-relief, on their gravestones; examples of which may be seen in the cloisters of Westminster Abbey, representing two abbots of that Church, and in Worcester Cathedral those of St. Oswald and Bishop Wulstan, &c.*

their sovereigns in plain stone coffins, without any exterior distinction or inscription, the name of the deceased being written on the inside of the cover. This was done to prevent the tomb being violated for the sake of jewels and other valuables which accompanied the royal corpse,—a common practice in those unsettled barbarous times. Afterwards, in the reign of Charlemagne, who was contemporary with our king Edgar, the French began to decorate the outside of their tombs with statues of the deceased and other ornaments, bearing some resemblance to Roman manner. These are the accounts of the best French Antiquaries, Montfaucon, Buillant, and Felibien; and they may be understood as invariable.

* Plate I.

These are the earliest statues in low relief, introduced about the Conqueror's time, probably by the Normans.

The Crusaders returned from the Holy Wars eager to imitate the arts and magnificence of other countries; they began to decorate the architecture with rich foliage, and to introduce statues against the columns, as we find in the west door of Rochester Cathedral, built in the reign of Henry I.*

Architecture now improved; sculpture also became popular. The custom of carving a figure of the deceased in bas-relief on the tomb seems likely to have been brought from France, where it was continued in imitation of the Romans. Figures placed against columns might also be copied from examples in that country, of which one remarkable instance was a door in the church of St. Germain de Prez in Paris, containing several statues of the ancient kings of France, projecting from columns; a work of the tenth century, of which there are prints in Montfaucon's Antiquities.

Sculpture continued to be practised with such zeal and success, that in the reign of Henry III. efforts were made deserving our respect and attention at this day.

Bishop Joceline rebuilt the Cathedral Church of Wells from the pavement; which having lived to finish and dedicate, he died, in the year of our Lord 1242. The west front of this church equally testi-

* Henry I. and his Queen Matilda.

fies to the piety and comprehension of the bishop's mind; the sculpture presents the noblest, most useful and interesting subjects possible to be chosen. On the south side, above the west door, are alto-relievos of the Creation,* in its different parts, the Deluge, and important acts of the Patriarchs. Companions to these on the north side, are alto-relievos of the principal circumstances in the life of our Saviour. Above these are two rows of statues larger than nature, in niches, of kings, queens, and nobles, patrons of the church, saints, bishops, and other religious, from its first foundation to the reign of Henry III. Near the pediment is our Saviour come to judgment, attended by angels and His twelve apostles. The upper arches on each side, along the west front, and continued in the north and south ends, are occupied by figures rising from their graves, strongly expressing the hope, fear, astonishment, stupefaction, or despair, inspired by the presence of the Lord and Judge of the world in that awful moment.

In speaking of the execution of such a work, due regard must be paid to the circumstances under which it was produced, in comparison with those of our own times. There were neither prints, nor printed books, to assist the artist; the sculptor could

---

* There are many compositions of the Almighty creating Eve, by Giotto, Florence, Buon Amico, Buffalmaco, Pisa, Ghiberti, and Michael Angelo. This is certainly the oldest, and not inferior to any of the others.—Plate II.

not be instructed in anatomy, for there were no anatomists. Some knowledge of optics, and a glimmering of perspective, were reserved for the researches of so sublime a genius as Roger Bacon, some years afterwards. A small knowledge of geometry and mechanics was exclusively confined to two or three learned monks, in the whole country; and the principles of those sciences, as applied to the figure and motion of man and inferior animals, were known to none! Therefore this work is necessarily ill drawn, and deficient in principle, and much of the sculpture is rude and severe: yet, in parts, there is a beautiful simplicity, an irresistible sentiment, and sometimes a grace, excelling more modern productions.*

It is very remarkable that Wells Cathedral was finished in 1242, two years after the birth of Cimabue, the restorer of painting in Italy; and the work was going on at the same time that Nicolo Pisano, the Italian restorer of sculpture, exercised the art in his own country: it was also finished forty-six years before the Cathedral of Amiens, and thirty-six years before the Cathedral of Orvieto was begun; and it seems to be the first specimen of such magnificent and varied sculpture, united in a series of sacred history, that is to be found in Western Europe. It is therefore probable that the general idea of the work might be brought from the east, by some of the Crusaders. But there are two arguments strongly in favour of the execution being English; the family

* Plates II. III. IV.

name of the bishop is English, " Joceline Troteman ;" and the style, both of sculpture and architecture, is wholly different from the tombs of Edward the Confessor * and Henry III.,† which were by Italian artists.

The reign of Edward I. produced a new species of monument.‡ When Eleanor, the beloved wife of that monarch died, who had been his heroic and affectionate companion in the Holy War, he raised stone crosses of magnificent architecture, adorned with statues of his departed queen, wherever her corpse rested on the way to its interment in Westminster Abbey. Three of these crosses still remain, at Northampton, Geddington, and Waltham; the statues have considerable simplicity and delicacy ; they partake of the character and grace particularly cultivated in the school of Pisano, and it is not unlikely, as the sepulchral statue and tomb of Henry III. were executed by Italians, that these statues of Queen Eleanor might be done by some of the numerous travelling scholars from Pisano's school.

The long and prosperous reign of Edward III. was as favourable to literature and liberal arts as to the political and commercial interests of the country. So generally were painting, sculpture, and architecture encouraged and employed, that besides the buildings raised in this reign, few sacred edifices existed which did not receive additions and decorations. The richness, novelty, and beauty of archi-

---

* By Benvenuto.   † Wm. Torrell.   ‡ Plate V.

tecture may be seen in York * and Gloucester Cathedrals, and many of our other churches; besides the extraordinary fancy displayed in various intricate and diversified figures which form the mullions of windows, they were occasionally enriched with a profusion of foliage and historical sculpture, equally surprising for beauty and novelty.

In the chancel of Dorchester Church, near Oxford, are three windows of this kind; one of which, besides rich foliage, is adorned with twenty-eight small statues relating to the genealogy of our Saviour, and the other two with alto-relievos from acts of His life.

It would be endless endeavouring to enumerate the various examples of the passion for sculpture which prevailed in this age. In the Lady Chapel of Norwich Cathedral all the key-stones, twenty or thirty in number, are beautiful alto-relievos from the Virgin Mary's life: three sides of the cloister, belonging to the same church, have key-stones (perhaps one hundred and fifty in number) representing principal passages from the Old Testament as well as the New.

There is a frieze of historical subjects entirely round St. Mary's Church, belonging to Ely Cathedral.

The monuments of Aylmer de Valence Earl of Pembroke, and Edmund Crouchback, in Westminster Abbey, are specimens of the magnificence of such works in the age we are speaking of: the loftiness

* Plates VI. XL. L. and Mr. Carter.

of the work, the number of arches and pinnacles, the lightness of the spires, the richness and profusion of foliage and crockets, the solemn repose of the principal statue, representing the deceased in his last prayer for mercy to the Throne of grace, the delicacy of thought in the group of angels bear· ing the soul, and the tender sentiment of concern variously expressed in the relations, ranged in order round the basement, forcibly arrest the attention, and carry the thoughts not only to other ages, but other states of existence.

It is a gratification to know that the principal sculptors and painters employed by Edward III. in his Collegiate Church (St. Stephen's), now the House of Commons, were Englishmen. In Mr. J. T. Smith's History of Westminster Palace we have many of those artists' names.*

Besides several other works in the reign of Henry VI., three deserve to be particularly mentioned.

First : two statues, King Henry on one side, and Archbishop Chicheley on the other, with a basso-relievo of the Resurrection between them, over the door of All Souls' College, in the High Street, Oxford.

The king's statue has great purity of character, with a peculiar delicacy and grace in the hands, both of which hold the sceptre. The basso-relievo has been carefully defaced, but seems to have possessed merit.

---

* Michael the sculptor ; Master Walter, John of Sonnington. John of Carlisle, Roger of Winchester, &c., painters.

The second of these works is an arch, in Westminster Abbey, which passes from the back of
Henry V.'s tomb over the steps of Henry VII.'s
chapel. This arch is adorned with upwards of fifty
statues : the centre group, on the north face, represents the coronation of Henry V., the lines of
figures on each side, his nobles attending the ceremony. On the south face of the arch, the central
object is the king on horseback, armed *cap-à-pie*,
riding full speed, attended by the companions of his
expedition. The sculpture is bold and characteristic,
the equestrian group is furious and warlike, the
standing figures have a natural sentiment in their
actions, and simple grandeur in their draperies, such
as we admire in the paintings of Raffaelle or Mas-
saccio.

The third of these works is the monument of
Richard Beauchamp, Earl of Warwick, in St. Mary's
Church, Warwick : a gilt bronze figure of the earl,
in the act of prayer, lies on a richly-ornamented
marble pedestal, round which are several beautiful
small gilt bronze statues, standing in niches supporting canopies over them. The figures are so
natural and graceful, the architecture so rich and
delicate, that they are not excelled by any sculpture
in Italy of the same kind at this time, although
Donatello and Ghiberti were living when this tomb
was executed, in the year 1439.*

* Monument in St. Mary's Church, Warwick. The mason,
Thomas Essex ; the sculptor and founder was William Austin

But the building, of all others most intended for a receptacle and display of sculpture, which former ages have left in England for our admiration, is the Lady Chapel of Westminster Abbey, built by Henry VII. to receive his tomb. It has been said the number of statues, within and without this chapel, amounted to three thousand!—perhaps many of these have been destroyed, and in that number every half figure, or animal, may have been reckoned; but certainly, even at this day, the number is very great, and it is another example of the astonishing estimation and employment of sculpture in this kingdom before the Reformation. Many interesting particulars concerning this chapel and tomb, from original documents, are given in Britton's "Architectural Antiquities;" from which, and the "Life of Torrigiano" by Vasari, we may conclude that artist was employed on the tomb only, and had no concern with the building or the statues with which it is embellished. The structure appears to have been finished, or nearly so, before Torrigiano began the tomb; and there is reason to think that he did not stay in this country more than six years, which time would be nearly, if not quite, taken up in the execution of the tomb and some other statues about it, now destroyed, together with the rich pedestal and enclosure. The architecture of the tomb has a

---

of London. Prints, and a description of this monument, in the second volume of Gough's Sepulchral Monuments, and Stothard's Monumental Effigies.

mixture of Roman arches and decoration, very different from the arches of the chapel, which are all pointed ; the figures of the tomb have a better proportion and drawing, in the naked, than those of the chapel ; but the figures of the chapel are very superior in natural simplicity and grandeur of character and drapery.*

From these differences in style, from the indentures with Torrigiano relating to the tomb only, and not to the chapel, and from the names of several English artists, painters, sculptors, founders, and masons, being mentioned in the documents, who were not concerned in Torrigiano's engagement, we may presume the chapel and its sculptures were native productions.

After the observations on this building, we must take a long farewell of such noble and magnificent efforts of art, in raising which the intention of our ancestors was to add a solemnity to religious worship, to impress on the mind those virtues which adorn and exalt humanity.

The greater number of these structures are already gone !—the remaining few are daily crumbling into ruins !—and with what are their places to be supplied ?

The reign of Henry VIII., and those immediately succeeding him, were employed in settling disputes of faith by public executions : as either of the contending religious parties prevailed, this mutual

* Plates VII. and VIII.

and undistinguishing spirit of persecution extended equally to the destruction of man and his ingenious labours.

In the year 1538, Henry VIII. issued an injunction, that all images which had been worshipped, or to which idle pilgrimages had been made, should be taken down and removed from the churches. And in the reign of Edward VI., in the year 1541, his uncle, the Duke of Somerset, the Protector, and Council, ordered all images, without distinction, to be thrown down and destroyed. This was understood, and executed, on pictures, as well as sculpture; and there is good reason to believe that we are indebted to the immense number of these works, which tired the patience of their enemies before their destruction was completed, for what remains of them at this day.

Had the popes of the fifteenth and sixteenth centuries been actuated by the same iconoclastic fury against the remains of Greek and Roman superstition, we should have been unacquainted with the Apollo Belvidere, the Venus of Praxiteles, the Laocoon, the Niobe family, and the other wonders of Grecian art.

Henry VIII., however, in the beginning of his reign, ordered Peter Torrigiano to make for him, and his queen, one of the most magnificent sepulchral monuments ever conceived, and surpassing every thing of the kind in the modern world. Although it was not intended to be so large as that

designed by Michael Angelo for Julius II.,* proposed
to occupy the pavement under the cupola of St.
Peter's in Rome, yet in richness, and the number
of figures, would have much excelled it. The height
was to have been twenty-seven feet, the breadth
twenty, and the depth fifteen. Two steps were to
support the whole work, then a basement of white
marble, ornamented with basso-relievos of the life
of our Saviour, then two pedestals on the basement,
supporting statues of the king and queen as if asleep ;
between them a third pedestal was to rise above
them, supporting the king's statue, completely armed
on horseback ; over this a decorated triumphal arch.
Over the figures of the king and queen, on each
side, a sort of temple, between the columns of which
were to be statues of the fourteen prophets of the
Old Testament, with basso-relievos of their stories,
and angels holding their names, the twelve apostles,
and four doctors of the church, with their angels and
acts ; at the corners of the tomb, the four cardinal
virtues ;†—a chorus of angels, twenty in number, on

* In Della Valle's edition of Vasari.

† A monument to Sir Francis Vere, in the chapel of St. John
the Evangelist, Westminster Abbey, representing four knights
supporting a canopy over the deceased (Pl. LI.).

In the great church of Brede is the monument of Count Engel-
bert and his wife ; he died 1505—the design said to be by Michael
Angelo, the upper part similar to that of Sir Francis Vere. Four
knights bearing armour on a canopy over the Count and Countess,
and at the corners of the base, Cæsar, Regulus, Philip, and
Alexander.

The great Lord Burleigh's monument at Hatfield, Herts, has
the four cardinal virtues bearing the canopy.

the parapet above ; with other statues, one **hundred**
and thirty-three in all, and forty-three basso-relievos
of gilt bronze, with twenty columns in the architecture, of porphyry, oriental alabaster, and serpentine
marble.   The particulars of this magnificent work
are preserved in Speed's "History of England," taken
from the explanation of a drawing the king had
approved.

The commands for destroying sacred painting and
sculpture effectually prevented the artist from suffering his mind to rise in the contemplation or execution
of any sublime effort, as he dreaded a prison or the
stake, and reduced him in future to the miserable
mimicry of monstrous fashions, or drudgery in the
lowest mechanism of his profession !

This unfortunate check to our national ability for
liberal art occurred at a time which offered the most
fortunate and extraordinary assistance to its progress.
The lately-discovered art of printing began to enlighten the European hemisphere with the beams of
knowledge in all directions; copies of the Bible
were generally dispersed ; the philosophies of Plato
and Aristotle were understood and well illustrated ;
mathematics was successfully studied ; so was
anatomy ; linear perspective had been, in a great
measure, perfected by Paul Uccello, the Florentine,
some time before.   These advantages did much
towards the formation of Mantegna, Raphael, Michael
Angelo, Titian, Da Vinci, and Correggio, in common
with the great scientific and literary luminaries of

.he same period, among whom we may boast our
Bacon, Shakespeare, Spenser, and afterwards John
Milton. But the genius of fanaticism and destruction arrested our progress; the iconoclastic spirit
continued, more or less mitigated, till its great explo-
sion during the civil wars, when violence and barbarity became so disgustingly shocking in all respects,
that we shall quit the subject entirely; let it suffice
to say, after the spirit of liberal art had been extinguished among the natives, it was found necessary
to engage celebrated artists from other countries.
Holbein, Rubens, and Vandyke, are the greatest
names among the painters; the sculptors are of less
note. Steevens the Hollander, with De Vere and
others from the Netherlands, Caius Cibber, the
sculptor of the kings at the Royal Exchange, the
bas-relief on the London Monument, and the mad
figures on the piers of Bedlam gates; Sheemacher,
employed on the sculpture of St. Paul's, and Roubiliac,
whose works are justly admired for life and nature,
though their value is diminished by epigrammatic
conceit and frequent meanness of parts.

Yet during the abasement of native art, instances
were not wanting of men who might have risen to
excellence in more favourable times. Christmas
executed a monument to Sir William Pitt and his
lady, at Strathfieldsaye, Hants, which partakes much
of Vandyke's manner. Stone, who was mason to
Charles I., made a monument for Mr. Holles of the
Newcastle family, near Lady Nightingale's in West-

minster Abbey, which has a grandeur of conception by no means common at that time.

Our purpose has been, in this Lecture, to show that ability has not been wanting to excel in sculpture, whenever it has not been prevented by outward circumstances. This has been proved by monuments still in existence, the wrecks only of those prodigious destructions which succeeded each other, without intermission, from the reign of Henry VIII. to that of Charles II. From these wrecks we prove, that from the time Nicolo and John Pisano restored sculpture in Italy, soon after the year 1200, and before the birth of Cimabue the Italian restorer of painting, to the reign of Henry VII., we have works of sculpture in England, in some cases possibly by English artists, in other, and most important instances, certainly by Englishmen, whose names are on record, and whose works may be compared with those of the best Italian artists of the same times. We have likewise seen, since the establishment of the Royal Academy has afforded an advantageous school for study, under the auspices of our gracious sovereign George III., that we have had a sculptor in the late Mr. Banks, whose works have eclipsed the most, if not all, of his continental contemporaries. Further testimony might be added of works by living artists, which have been admired by foreigners, and have raised the British school of sculpture to distinguished eminence in Europe.

We may, therefore, fairly conclude, that whatever attention and encouragement this Institution has bestowed on the art of sculpture, has not only been honourable to the Academy, but advantageous to the **country.**

LECTURE II.

EGYPTIAN SCULPTURE.

In tracing man's early progress and improvement, the most authentic knowledge is obtained from the Bible, not only in religion, but in civilization and arts. In this sacred volume is also a register of patriarchal history, containing accounts of the neighbouring nations long before any other written information that has come down to us. In the Book of Exodus, we are told of Laban's teraphim or images, and the golden calf, made by Aaron and the Israelites, which they worshipped during the absence of Moses on the mount. This violent tendency to idolatry accounts for the strict injunctions, under which they were bound, by divine command, not to worship any image : whilst the same authority commanded statues of cherubim to extend their wings over the Ark of the Covenant, and that the veil of the tabernacle should be adorned with cherubim. This proves the command was not against the images themselves, but the abuse of them for impious and idolatrous purposes, and, on the contrary, is a testimony of approbation of such works, when representing the ministers of God's providence, or the guardians of His holy laws; and indeed it is a most gratifying reflection to a practitioner of the sister arts, that the Almighty condescended to employ them as the handmaids of religion, and that He particularly inspired Ahcliab and Bezaleel to produce the most admirable and lively decorations of angelic forms for His tabernacle. Of these nothing remains but description; all the glories of Solomon's Temple, and that raised after the captivity, with all their beauty and splendour, are swept away by the same appointment which decreed the Jews should no longer be a nation. Were we to search with the most scrutinizing diligence for some specimens of ancient Jewish art, only three could be produced,—the piece of money called a shekel, bearing a cup on one side, and an almond branch on the other; the candlestick with seven branches; and the table of shew-bread, on a bas-relief under the arch of Titus. The porticos of tombs in Palestine, which have been published, bear a strong appearance of Greek restoration.

The magnificent sitting golden Jupiter in the Temple of Jupiter Belus in Babylon, the statue of the Tyrian Hercules, and other divinities of Sidon and the neighbouring cities, are only to be found at present in the ancient writers, and what they were it is impossible for us to judge, unless we may form some conjecture from analogy with Egyptian art,

concerning which information is copious and examples abundant.

Herodotus, an author of the most respectable
integrity and intelligence, informs us " the Egyptians
erected the first altars and temples to the gods, and
carved the figures of animals on stone," and the
great number and variety of Egyptian sculptures
remaining, from the most rude to the most perfect,
give us reason to believe we have specimens from
the earliest to the latest of their productions.

The amazing power of that country,* which, in
the time of their king Amasis, contained 20,000
populous cities; their reputation of being the wisest
nation of antiquity, and on that account visited by
Orpheus, Homer, Thales, Pythagoras, Plato, and
others distinguished for wisdom; the Pyramids, the
Lake Mœris, and other stupendous works and
buildings, of which five immense palaces and thirty-
four temples still remain to astonish posterity;† the
universal and profuse employment of sculpture in
colossal and minute dimensions, for public and
domestic purposes, for the service of the living and
the dead; all induce us to inquire into the principles and quality of their productions. We have
not only the written accounts by ancient authors,
but the demonstrative evidence of remaining works,
that almost the whole of their sculpture was sacred;
that is, representations of divine qualities, attributes,

* Herodotus, Euterpe.   † Citizen Ripand's Report, p. 9.

and personifications; with the exception of the historical series in their tombs and palaces.

Herodotus mentions two statues, one placed before the Temple of Vulcan at Memphis, the other in the city of Sais, by King Amasis, each of which was seventy-five feet long.

The colossal Sphinx,* near the great Pyramid, rises twenty-five feet, although it is nearly buried up to the gullet in sand.

The sitting statues of Memnon, the mother and son of Osmandue, at Thebes, are each fifty-eight feet high. To these we might add a catalogue of similar works, known by remaining fragments, or described by authors. There is a clenched hand in red granite in the British Museum, which belonged to a statue sixty-five feet high.

The Egyptian statues stand equally poised on both legs, having one foot advanced, the arms either hanging straight down on each side, or, if one is raised, it is at a right angle across the body. Some of the statues sit on seats, some on the ground, and some are kneeling; but the position of the hands seldom varies from the above description; their attitudes are of course simple rectilinear, and without lateral movement; the faces are rather flat, the brows, eyelids, and mouths, formed of simple curves, slightly but sharply marked, and with little expression; the general proportions are something more

* Sphinx, in the sacred language of Orpheus, "the soul comprehending all."—Brucker, vol. I., p. 380. —Clemens Alex.

than seven heads high, the form of the body and
limbs rather round and effeminate, with only the
most evident projections and hollows.

Their tunics, or rather draperies, are in many
instances without folds.

Winckelman has remarked, that the Egyptians
executed quadrupeds better than human figures:
for which he gives the two following reasons—first,
that as professions in that country were hereditary,
genius must be wanting to represent the human
form in perfection ; secondly, that superstitious reverence for the works of their ancestors prevented
improvement. This is an amusing but needless
hypothesis; for there are statues in the Capitoline
Museum with as great a breadth, and choice of
grand parts proper to the human form, as ever they
represented in their lions, or other inferior animals.
In addition to these observations on Egyptian statues,
we may remark, the forms of their hands and feet are
gross; they have no anatomical detail of parts, and
are totally deficient in the grace of motion. This
last defect, in all probability, was not the consequence
of a superstitious determination to persist in the
practice of their ancestors, it is accounted for in
another and better way.

Pythagoras, after he had studied several years in
Egypt, sacrificed a hundred oxen in consequence of
having discovered that a square of the longest side
of a right-angled triangle is equal to the two squares
of the lesser side of the same triangle; and thence

it follows, that the knowledge of the Egyptians could not have been very great at that time in geometry. This will naturally account for that want of motion in their statues and relievos, which can only be obtained by a careful observation of nature, assisted by geometry.

The state of Egyptian science in the time of Pythagoras being noticed, leads to another consideration respecting the date of their architecture and sculpture. Most of their great works are mentioned by the ancient writers as being done in the reign of Sesostris, and afterwards. Sesostris lived in the reign of Rehoboam, King of Israel, about the time of the Trojan war, or 1000 years before the Christian era, which shows that the arts of Egypt and of Greece were in a progressive state of improvement at the same time, and from the Greeks residing with them to study theology, philosophy, and science,—from the great intercourse, political and commercial, between the two countries from the heroic times,—from the Greeks being long settled in the city of Naucratis and other parts of Egypt, we may fairly conclude their communication in arts was just as free as in other concerns, which seems the more likely, as there is a considerable resemblance in the features and contour of the early Greek and Egyptian statues.

The Egyptian basso-relievos are generally (but not always) sunk into the ground, which is left level with the highest part of the relief; for which practice two reasons may be assigned—first, that as many of these basso-relievos were cut in very hard stones, basalt or granite, as much time would have been required to clear away the ground about the figure as had been employed in cutting the figure itself; and besides the economy of time, when some hundreds or thousands of these figures were engraven on the sides of a lofty obelisk, or the walls of a temple, the far greater number of them were at a great distance from the eye, fifty, sixty feet or more: in this case the ground being left perpendicular to the figure, the whole circuit of its outline, gave it a greater breadth of shadow and distinctness to the spectator.

These basso-relievos, which we comprehend in the general term of hieroglyphics, or sacred engravings, represent different subjects, according to the place and purpose for which they were employed: in the walls of tombs they represent the profession, actions, and funeral of the deceased; in palaces, wars, negotiations, triumphs, processions, trophies, with the civil, military, and domestic employments of kings.

In temples they were symbolical registers of theology and sacred science; on obelisks, they express hymns to the gods, or praises of their kings. Ammianus Marcellinus has preserved part of a translation by Hesmaneon of the Egyptian hieroglyphics on the obelisk which formerly stood in the centre of the Circus Maximus, and, at present, before the church of St. John de Lateran in Rome. It imports

that the sun, the lord of the universe, gives to
Rameses the kingdom of Egypt and the dominion of
all the earth, in the city of Heliopolis. This translation appears sufficiently justified in the upper lines of
the hieroglyphics, where a divinity is sitting in the
act of bestowing on a man who kneels before him,
stretching out his hands to receive. In the following
line the same man is seen again, taking possession of
an altar, on the side of which is the ox Apis, and on
the top, the mitred hawk, symbol of Osiris. Thus of
the sacred emblems of Egypt.

Our time and purpose will not permit us to dwell
on the stupendous architecture, or laborious wonders,
the labyrinths, tombs, temples, pyramids and palaces
on either side of the Nile, from Upper Egypt till its
discharge through various channels into the Mediter-
ranean ; but we may understand to what extent
sculpture was employed among this people, by a
brief description of the palace of Karnac,* a portion
of Egyptian Thebes. The front of this palace was
420 feet long, its depth nearly three-quarters of a
mile ; it consisted of four great courts of nearly equal
dimensions, comprehended within a long square. The
first court was occupied by four rows of columns,
the second contained 130, the largest eleven feet in
diameter, the smaller seven feet ; the third court was
adorned with six obelisks, ninety feet high, and
colossal statues, and surrounded by various royal
apartments. On each side the entrance of the fourth

* Plate IX.

court was a saloon of granite; the rest of the space
was occupied by porticos, colonnades, and numerous
chambers for officers and attendants. This palace,
with four dependent structures of similar magnificence, but inferior proportions, was approached by
four paved roads, bordered on each side with figures
of animals, fifteen feet long: in one avenue, ninety
lions; in another, sphinxes; in another, rams; and
in the fourth, lions with hawks' heads. From the
ruined state of these avenues, we cannot now have
any computation of the number of animals by which
they were bordered, though it is almost certain they
were not fewer than 300, yet it is possible they
might be many more.

In this place twenty-two colossal statues still
remain, and a great number of granite statues and
fragments the size of nature: besides which, the
walls were nearly covered with basso-relievos and
pictures. The lesser structures in this group of
buildings were adorned in the same manner, and
communicated with the magnificent tomb of Ismandes
or Memnon, before which stood the statue of Memnon,
sixty-five feet high, already mentioned, with the
statues of his mother and son, fifty-eight feet high.
The largest of these was thrown down and destroyed
by Cambyses, the Persian conqueror of Egypt; its
fragments still remain, an ear of which is three feet
three inches long, and a foot four feet across.

The enormous works of Egypt have struck every
foreign visitor with wonder and awe, from Hero-

dotus down to the members of the French Institute. Herodotus says, "one of their buildings is equal to many of the most considerable Greek buildings taken together," and M. Ripand observes, " those works are so prodigious, they make every thing we do look little;" and, indeed, if we consider the execution of a statue sixty-five feet high in so hard a material as granite, the boldest heart would be appalled at the incalculable labour and difficulties of the work!

In the Egyptian sculpture we shall find some excellent first principles of the art.

Their best statues are divided into seven heads and a half; the whole height of the figure is divided into two equal parts at the os pubis; the rest of the proportions are natural and not disagreeable. The principal forms of the body and limbs, as the breasts, belly, shoulders, biceps of the arm, knees, shin-bones, and feet, are expressed with a fleshy roundness, although without anatomical knowledge of detail; and in the female figures these parts often possess considerable elegance and beauty. The forms of the female face have much the same outline and progression towards beauty in the features as we see in some of the early Greek statues, and, like them, without variety of character; for little difference can be traced in the faces of Isis, in her representations of Diana, Venus,* or Terra, or, indeed, in Osiris, although sometimes understood to be Jupiter himself, excepting that in some instances he has a very small

* Plate X.

beard, in form resembling a peg. The hands and feet, like the rest of the figure, have general forms only, without particular detail; the fingers and toes are flat, of equal thickness, little separated, and without distinction of the knuckles; yet, altogether, their simplicity of idea, breadth of parts, and occasional beauty of form, strike the skilful beholder, and have been highly praised by the best judges, ancient and modern.

In their basso-relievos and paintings which require variety of action and situation, are demonstrated their want of anatomical, mechanical and geometrical science relating to the arts of painting and sculpture.

The king or hero * is three times larger than the other figures; whatever is the action, whether a siege, a battle, or taking a town by storm, there is not the smallest idea of perspective in the place, or magnitude of figures or buildings. Figures intended to be in violent action are equally destitute of joints, and other anatomical form, as they are of the balance and spring of motion, the force of a blow, or the just variety of line in the turning figure. In a word, their historical art was informing the beholder in the best manner they could, according to the rude characters they were able to make.

From such a description it is easy to understand how much their attempts at historical representation were inferior to their single statues.

* Plate XII.

What has been hitherto said of Egyptian sculpture describes the ancient native sculpture of that people. After the Ptolemies, successors of Alexander the Great, were kings of Egypt, their sculpture was enlivened by Grecian animation, and refined by the standard of Grecian beauty in proportion, attitude, character, and dress.

Osiris, Isis, and Orus, their three great divinities, put on the Macedonian costume, and new divinities appeared among them in Grecian forms, whose characteristics were compounded from materials of Egyptian, Eastern, and Grecian theology and philosophy.

In the reign of the Roman emperor Hadrian, a number of statues, in imitation of the ancient Egyptian, were made to decorate the canopus in his magnificent villa at Tivoli, several of which have been dug up, and placed in the Capitoline Museum : but Winckelman has remarked of these, that they may be known from the ancient Egyptian sculpture, having no hieroglyphics on them : but besides this distinction, they are entirely unlike the genuine Egyptian, as the drawing and character are Roman, in Egyptian attitudes and dresses.

The ancient authors who give the most satisfactory accounts of Egyptian antiquities are Herodotus, Diodorus Siculus, Josephus, Strabo, Clemens of Alexandria, Iamblicus, and Orus Apollo.

The best modern books on this subject are " Pocock's Voyages," " Savary's Travels in Egypt,"

"Norden's Egypt," and "Denon;" to which may be added the most magnificent work on ancient and modern Egypt publishing in Paris, to be in twelve volumes folio, containing 840 plates, from the observations, researches, accounts, and drawings of the learned men and artists of the French nation who formed the Egyptian Institute.

We must not omit some notice of the sculpture of Persepolis,* palace of the Persian kings, heads of one of the four great monarchies of the ancient world.

This stately ruin, at a small distance from the capital of ancient Persia, was such when visited by Le Bruyn, the Dutch traveller, and our countryman, Sir John Chardin, that no certain plan of it could be ascertained; but from the extent of its site, and the epithet given by the Persian writers, who called it the palace of a thousand columns, it seems to have been a wonder of ancient Asia, as its ruins are of this day. Le Bruyn says, forty columns remained on an extensive basement of masonry, ascended by magnificent flights of steps, approached by gateways and remains of walls, which formerly surrounded the structure, covered with basso-relievos representing the military power, pomp, triumphs and sacrifices of the Persian monarchs. These sculptures have some resemblance to the style of the Egyptian basso-relievos in the palaces of Thebes, allowing for the difference of dress; but as they contain nothing in

* See Plate XII

science, or imitation, particularly favourable to our pursuit of excellence, we shall content ourselves with respecting it as a most venerable monument of ancient history and learning, whilst we follow our course by some observations on Hindu sculpture.

The stupendous excavated temples of Ellora, Ele phantis, and other parts of India, are known in England by representations which do honour to our country.* They are of high antiquity, and adorned throughout with mythological sculpture, the subjects of which are symbols, allegorical personages, and groups of figures expressing various attributes and energies of divine power, providence, and manifestation, according to the Brahmin system, concerning which valuable and extensive information may be obtained from " Moore's Hindu Pantheon," in which there are upwards of 1500 outlines of Hindu painting and sculpture,† faithfully copied from the originals. We may remark on the sculpture, that, although it bears some resemblance to the Egyptian, it is inferior both in science and likeness to nature.‡

After this summary view of sculpture among the early nations of the east, we shall proceed to the

---

* " Journal of a Residence in India," by Maria Graham.

† See Plate XIII.

‡ Matsya Purana Purana, " a direction to the artists in the character, proportions, and attributes of Hindu Divinities." Hayasirus on the same subject, not specified from what Purana taken, in the Imperial Library, Paris.—*Edinburgh Review*, No. 34, Feb. 1811.

principles **and** practice of the art with the Greeks, where, if it was not born, it was advanced to a high degree of perfection : but, as all effects depend on their causes, and ends cannot be produced without adequate means, we shall do well to inquire what branches of science were employed by this distinguished people, to aid them in the representation of form and character ; and here, although we must pause a moment to regret the loss of invaluable treatises by the greatest painters, sculptors, and architects of antiquity, enumerated by Vitruvius and the elder Pliny, yet some short paragraphs those authors have preserved, with the assistance of other ancient writers, and a comparison of these with the numerous and precious remains of ancient works, will compensate for the loss, and give the requisite information.

We find, upon these authorities, that geometry and numbers were employed to ascertain the powers of motion and proportions, optics and perspective (as known to the ancients),—to regulate projections, hollows, keeping, diminution, curvatures, and general effects, in figures, groups, insulated or in relief, with their accompaniments ; and anatomy, to represent the bones, muscles, tendons, and veins, as they appear on the surface of the human body and inferior animals.

In this enlightened age, when the circle of science is so generally and well understood,—when the connection and relation of one branch with another is demonstrated, and their principles applied from necessity and conviction, wherever possibility allows, in the liberal and mechanical arts, as well as all the other concerns of life,—no one can be weak or absurd enough to suppose it is within the ability and province of human genius, without the principles of science previously acquired,—by slight observation only,—to become possessed of the forms, characters, and essences of objects in such a manner as to represent them with truth, force, and pathos at once ! No : we are convinced by reason and experience, that " life is short, and art is long," and the perfection of all human productions depends on the indefatigable accumulation of knowledge and labour through a succession of ages.

The Egyptian arts were in progressive states of improvement, from before the time of Moses to the invasion and subjugation of the country by Cambyses the Persian, a period of about 1000 years, and the arts of Greece, from their rudest beginnings before the time of Dædalus, rose to high perfection in about 900 years, or the reign of Alexander the Great. In the early times of Greece, Pausanias informs us the twelve gods were worshipped in Arcadia, under the forms of rude stones, and before Dædalus the statues had eyes nearly shut, the arms attached to their sides, and the legs close together; but as geometry, mechanics, arithmetic, and anatomy improved, painting and sculpture acquired action, proportion, and detailed parts.

Vitruvius, Book III., lays down some rules used by the most celebrated Grecian artists, taken from their own writings, for the symmetry or proportions of the human figure, and also the geometrical figures which circumscribe its general form and motion.

He says, "if a man lies on his back, his arms and legs may be so extended, that a circle may be drawn round, touching the extremities of his fingers and toes, the centre of which circle shall be his navel;" also, "that a man standing upright, the length of his arms, when fully extended, is equal to his height;" thus, that the circle, and the square, equally contain the general form and motion of the human figure.

He also says "the human figure is eight of its own heads in height, or ten faces, from the chin to the growing of the hair, each face containing three equal parts, &c." From these hints and some others in his work, with some also given by that philosopher and painter, Leonardo da Vinci, in which he has pursued the same profound mathematical train of reasoning, a complete system of proportions and motion may be laid down upon the ancient Greek principles, in a future lecture on that subject.

Concerning the optics and perspective of the ancients he has the following passage : " Agatharcus of Athens made a tragic scene under the direction of Æschylus, and left a commentary upon it; being instructed by that, Democritus and Anaxagoras wrote on the same subject in what manner the extension of rays to the point of sight, by an appointed centre, should answer to the lines by natural reason, so that the certain and uncertain images of buildings should be rendered in appearance by painted scenes, which should be viewed in front on the perspective plain; so that some should seem to retire, and others come forward."

This passage appears to contain as much of perspective as was known to the ancients, and amounts to this—that rays from visible objects meet in the eye as a centre, and that objects should be represented prominent, or retiring, according to their proposed situations. This is certainly all the knowledge of perspective shown in the ancient works of art, however excellent in other respects; and, indeed, from the imperfect description of the eye given by Hippocrates, we have no reason to believe that the nature of vision, or the science of optics, were much understood when Agatharcus, his contemporary, wrote his commentary on perspective.

Pliny says, lib. xxxiv., c. 8, Leontius, the contemporary of Phidias, first expressed tendons and veins—" primus nervos et venas expressit "—which was immediately after the anatomical researches and improvements of Hippocrates, Democritus, and their disciples; and we shall find in the same manner all the improvements in art followed improvements in science.

Diodorus Siculus was informed by the priests, that Dædalus measured the proportions of the Egyptian statues,* and perhaps by this improved the forms of his own works, which he also improved by making his statues walk, that is, setting one foot before the other, and by detaching the arms from the body; yet, notwithstanding, for centuries after, the statues, whether standing or walking, seem equally poised on both feet, having their shoulders, hips, and knees even with each other; and that too in violent actions. In basso-relievos and paintings, when the figure was forcibly exerted, it was generally represented in an awkward and impossible manner, until after the time Pythagoras and Thales had improved geometry, and thus increased the knowledge of circular and triangular powers and relations, which is indispensable to perfectly understanding the curvilinear motion of animal bodies in different directions, and to ascertain its quantity and direction in the limbs.

Pursuing the same observations, we shall find the painters and sculptors did not give the utmost variety and accuracy to their positions and actions, until after Euclid the mathematician had formed his collection of problems.

For want of the same progressive improvement in optics, which would have led to perspective, we find the best ancient pictures and basso-relievos always limited and defective in their fore-shortenings.

The knowledge of anatomy among the early Greeks was so small, that it could have afforded little

* Denon's " Egypt," p. 124. Egyptian statues seven heads and one-third high.

assistance to the artist. Homer, indeed, has described all the wounds mentioned in his poems with anatomical correctness, and on this account has been quoted by Galen, at a time when the science had arisen to considerable eminence. But Pliny observes, "the art of medicine (which among the ancients included anatomy) was in profound darkness from the time of Homer to the age of Hippocrates," and if we examine his treatises on the bones, we shall find their number reckoned, but so rude a sketch of the exterior anatomy, as conveys scarcely any distinct idea of any one part of the body or limbs; yet, from his treatise on the joints, we find that he occasionally dissected parts of the human body. From this imperfect state of the science, even in the time of Phidias and Praxiteles, we must agree in the opinion of your learned professor of anatomy, "that the ancient artists owed much more to the study of living than dead bodies."

Yet different circumstances must sometimes have given anatomical help to artists from early times: the researches of physicians, the observation of bodies left on the field of battle, the preparations of sacrifice or food, and the practice of dissecting quadrupeds among the philosophers:—these several sources will account for all the general and simple anatomical forms we see in Grecian works of art, before the time of Phidias.

What has been adduced is sufficient to show that science must attain a certain perfection before the arts of design can be cultivated with success, and that before the human form can be well represented, some system of proportions must be collected from the measurement of man himself, to regulate the thickness, breadth, and height of the body and limbs, and their parts in the imitation. The powers and extent of motion will be settled by geometry and mechanics ; and anatomy will assist the observation of living nature, by assigning the particular forms which compose masses, and distinguish between the accidents of action and rest.

In considering the assistance afforded by science towards the perfection of art, we observe, that as soon as the painter or sculptor has succeeded in a rude and general resemblance of man, he then attempts the natural differences of sex and age, the civil distinctions of orders, as the soldier and the priest, the king and the slave; he proceeds to the expression of passion and moral qualities, and at last rises to supernatural representation. In this progress he is assisted and directed by the forms of society in which he lives, the principles of philosophy, and the dictates of religion ; these are the natural and regular steps by which art approaches perfection.

The arts of design (particularly sculpture) may be said to be consecrated to religion from the very cradle.

Thus, in the early times, when their figures were ordinary and barbarous, having only the rudest character of imitation, without any of its graces, their gods were distinguished by their symbols only —Jupiter by his thunderbolt, Neptune by his trident, and Mercury by his caduceus : not unfrequently these, and other divinities, were represented with wings, to show they were not mere men.

The symbols, attributes, and personal characteristics, as the arts improved, were derived from the poets,* and influenced by philosophy.

The early figures of Jupiter and Neptune have no beards, but when Homer's verses became the canon of public opinion, the father of gods and men became bearded, and so also did his brother Neptune.

After the first Olympiads, when Mercury was considered a patron of gymnastic exercises, he obtained a youthful figure. It is likely that Hercules was not exhibited with extraordinary muscular strength until the Greek tragedians had settled his character by their impassioned and overpowering descriptions of his acts and labours.

The winged genii on the painted Greek vases were introduced from the Pythagorean philosophy : and female divinities became lovely and gracious in the time of Plato : in fine, the different systems of philosophy, from the beginning of the Ionic sect by Thales to the Alexandrine philosophy, which was prevalent at the coming of Christ, all influenced the arts of design, giving a tone to their excellence, and

* See Plates XIV. and XV.

an indication of their character, which we shall occasionally notice where it is found requisite.

What has here been offered can only be considered as the transient glance of a most extensive prospect, ennobled by monuments of religious institutions, with the symbols and allegories of philosophy; it is enlightened by the wisdom and science of succeeding ages, and delights with an abundant choice of beauty in the higher orders of creation, more particularly expressing mental perfection by bodily form.

For full satisfaction on such a subject, very copious illustration and example are needful: these are to be obtained from the writings of Winckelman, Mengs, Leonardo da Vinci, Reynolds, and Fuseli, with a fuller demonstration from publications of the Pope's museum, the Capitoline museum, Montfaucon, the Herculaneum collection, and various other works on ancient art.

But the admirer of sculpture will receive the most lively satisfaction, and best instruction, from a contemplation of the admirable assemblage in the Townley collection, the invaluable fragments of the Elgin marbles at the British Museum, the casts in the Royal Academy, and elsewhere collected by indi-viduals.

If to these could be added the basso-relievos of Athenians fighting with the Amazons and Centaurs, found at Phigalia in the Argolis, we should indeed possess a most respectable school of sculpture, which, by its assistance in ancient learning, and advancement of the arts, with the consequently profitable improvement in general knowledge (so indispensable to the arts of design), would amply repay any trouble or expense arising in the course of its attainment.*

* In 1815 the frieze of the Temple of Apollo at Phigalia was purchased for £15,000, the expenses of transporting increased the sum to £19,000. There are twenty-three marble tablets; the first eleven numbers represent the combats between the Lapithæ and Centaurs; the remaining, the battles of the Greeks and Amazons. They are the finest works of the kind which have been handed down to us. In the former the ferocity of the brute is contrasted with manly courage; in the latter, female heroism and grace resisting manly strength, awakes our sympathy and calls forth our admiration.

LECTURE III.

————

GRECIAN SCULPTURE.

WHEN we consider the gradual ravages of time, and the more compendious destruction of war, in the eastern portion of Europe, and those countries of Asia from whence the remains of ancient knowledge have been obtained—that the sites of Babylon and Memphis are scarcely known—that Persepolis, Alexandria, Elis, Eleusis, Delphos and Athens are discovered by ruins almost unintelligible, or the remains of their foundations only—that Rome, the eternal city, the mistress of the world, with all her lofty towers, magnificent temples, and imperial palaces, has suffered sevenfold conflagration!!!*— that fourteen thousand exquisite works of Greek and Etruscan sculpture, which decorated this metropolis of the world in her meridian splendour, were so entirely destroyed or overwhelmed by Gothic ignorance, or iconoclastic fury, that in the beginning of the fifteenth century a learned and intelligent observer, Poggio Bracciolini, secretary to Eugenius

* *Vide* Pliny.

the Fourth and Nicholas the Fifth, noticed only six
statues among the other remains of former grandeur
—when we recollect the destruction of the Capitoline and Ulpian libraries, the first and second Alexandrine libraries, one containing 400,000, the other
1,100,000 volumes, together with the general and
undistinguishing Turkish and northern devastations
in every branch of learning and science, throughout
better than one half of the old continent!—from
such a train of reflections, and such a widely-ex-
tended scene of ruin, we might be induced to
suppose that all the nobler monuments of ancient
genius and knowledge were lost for ever.

Upon more accurate inquiry, we shall find the fact
very different from the appearance; and, on the
contrary, whatever was most essential for man's
good, or his information, has by a wonderful providence been preserved! The sacred Scriptures—the
Eastern, the Pythagorean, Platonic, Aristotelian, and
Alexandrine philosophy — copious collections of
geometry, mathematics, astronomy, geography,
medicine, and anatomy—the best poets—the best
historians—catalogues of which have been published
in twenty-three volumes, by the learned J. Christo-
pher Wolff and T. Albert Fabricius, comprehending
an immense body of Eastern, Arabic, Greek, and
Roman literature—if we add to these the stupendous
and admirable architectural remains in Egypt, India,
Persia, Greece, and Italy—the beautiful and nearly
innumerable statues, groups, and basso-relievos

rescued from ancient ruins—the 700 Greek and Roman paintings recovered from the buried cities of Herculaneum and Pompeii, after being lost 1,700 years—exquisite gems and coins discovered, and discovering every day; when we consider that we actually possess such prodigious treasures of ancient science and art, in every branch and species, we must acknowledge we have an overflowing abundance to establish our principles and stimulate our exertions, and that more, although they might gratify our reverence for antiquity, would rather overwhelm than assist the progress of modern genius.

From these sources our present subject will be fully supplied in its progress, its relations to, and assistance from, the circle of science; and, finally, demonstrate that its excellence must depend on the understanding and sentiment which overrules its manual operation. And thus the course of our inquiries will be now directed to the origin of sculpture in Greece.

Some centuries before the Christian era, a sculptor appeared, whose works exacted the praise of poets, the speculations of philosophers, the record of historians, and continued to be preserved with zeal, and spoken of with respect, when sculpture had attained its zenith : this was Dædalus, the countryman and contemporary of Theseus, not inferior perhaps in fame and variety of adventures to that hero, born of a royal race, occasionally the friend or adversary of kings, admired for his works while living, and honoured with a chapel by the Egyptians after death.

To him are attributed many mechanical inventions, fabulous and real: a fine portico to the Temple of Vulcan at Memphis—the Cretan labyrinth, which was a copy of a hundredth part of the Egyptian labyrinth: he made a figure to move like life, by means of quicksilver contained in it. Diodorus Siculus speaks of his works in Sicily; Pausanias mentions those remaining in Greece in his time, nine in number, of which there may be particularly noticed one, a naked Hercules in wood.

"The works of Dædalus are indeed rude, and uncomely in aspect (says Pausanias), but yet they have something as of divinity in their appearance."

Pausanias, besides the high character here given of this statue, mentions it twice in his "Grecian Tour," from which we must understand that it was held in considerable esteem and veneration: this would naturally lead us to hope we are not without some copy of it, in gems, coins, or small bronzes, by which all the most famous works of antiquity were multiplied.

In the British Museum,* as well as in other collections in Europe, are several small bronzes of a naked Hercules, whose right arm, holding a club, is raised to strike, whilst his left is extended, bearing the lion's skin as a shield. From the style of extreme antiquity in these statues—the rude

* See Plate XVI.

attempt at bold action, which was the peculiarity of Dædalus—the general adoption of this action in the early ages—the traits of savage nature in the face and figure, expressed with little knowledge, but strong feeling—by the narrow loins, turgid muscles of the breast, thighs, and calves of the legs—we shall find reason to believe they are copied from the above-mentioned statue.

The same author says the Gnossians had a chorus in white stone, made by Dædalus for Ariadne, which is mentioned in the eighteenth book of the Iliad as youths and damsels dancing hand in hand. The earliest Greek bas-relievos and paintings represent choruses of the Graces and Hours in this manner.

Endæus, the disciple of Dædalus, made a statue of Minerva, which Pausanias saw in the Acropolis of Athens. The learned author of the Introduction to the "Volume of Sculpture," published by the Dilettanti Society, supposes the heads of Minerva, on the early coins of Athens, were copied from this very statue, which seems very reasonable when we compare the style and costume with other works of the highest antiquity; but as our limits neither require, nor allow, of regular history, we shall condense what is most important on this subject into a relation of successive improvements; and here, it should be observed, that in the early times of which we are now treating, their rude efforts were intended to represent divinities and heroes only. Jupiter, Neptune, and several heroic characters have the self same face, figure, and action as the Hercules of Dædalus, described above; the same narrow eyes, thin lips, with the corners of the mouth turned upwards, the pointed chin, narrow loins, turgid muscles, the same advancing position of the lower limbs, the right hand raised beside the head, and the left extended. Their only distinctions were, that Jupiter held the thunderbolt, Neptune the trident, and Hercules a palm-branch or bow—as may be seen in ancient small bronzes, on coins of Athens and Pæstum, and on the most ancient painted vases.

The female divinities were clothed in draperies divided into few and perpendicular folds; their attitudes advancing like those of male figures. The hair of both male and female statues or paintings of this period is arranged with great care, collected in a club behind, sometimes entirely curled, in the same manner as practised by the native Americans, and the inhabitants of the South Sea Islands.

Dædalus and Endæus formed their statues of wood; metal was also used for various purposes of sculpture in the most ancient times, as we learn from Homer, Hesiod, and Plutarch.*

Dipœnus † and Scyllis the Cretan were celebrated for their marble statues, about 776 years before Christ, still retaining much of the ancient manner in the advancing position of the legs, the drawing of

* *Vide* Hesiod, Brazen Age, and Plutarch, Life of Theseus.
† See Plate XVII.

the figure, and the perpendicular folds of drapery disposed in zigzag edges.

Elaborate finishing was soon afterwards carried to excess: undulating locks, and spiral knots of hair-like shells, as well as the drapery, were wrought with the most elaborate care and exactness; whilst the tasteless and barbarous character of the face and limbs remained much the same as in former times. This passion for high finishing of sculpture will reconcile to our reason a passage in Pliny, lib. xxxv., cap. 8, which has frequently been thought to disagree with the general history of ancient painting. He says that "the picture of the battle of the Magnetes, painted by Bularchus, was paid for by its weight in gold, by Candaules, King of Lydia, who was the coeval of Romulus, and lived in the 20th Olympiad, or about 750 years before Christ, thus proving the fame and perfection of the art." According to the same author's account, ancient painting did not arrive at its greatest perfection until after the time of Phidias, or 250 years later; and therefore it is likely that Bularchus's picture was valued chiefly for the same high finishing we see in the earliest marble statues, of which the following are examples :—Colossal busts of Hercules and Apollo in the British Museum, a very ancient statue of Minerva, probably that done by Dipœnus and Scyllis for the Sicyonians; and a priest of Bacchus, lately in the Villa Albani, published by Winckelman in his "Monumenta Inedita" and "Storia

dell' Arte :" to these might be added examples of
extreme finishing in early Greek pateras and other
bronzes.

This observation on Bularchus's picture, and the
sculpture of the same time, will naturally lead to
another of more general comprehension : that the
improvements in sculpture, we have reason to
believe, succeeded those in painting, according to the
dates, as far as we are able to ascertain them, of
remaining works.

Philocles the Egyptian, or Cleanthes the Corinthian, are said to have first introduced outline among
the Greeks, in the practice of which they were
followed by Ardices the Corinthian, and Telephanes
the Sicyonian, who used other lines within the
outline, to express the marking of the body and
limbs ; also, writing the names of those they painted,
which agrees with the earliest paintings on the
Greek vases, as *their* attitudes and peculiarities agree
with early sculpture.* Cimon Cleoneus invented
catagraphy, or the oblique representation of images,
to give different views of the face, looking up,
looking down, and looking backwards. He represented the veins, and the folds and plaits in garments.
This Cimon is mentioned as living before the time
of Phidias, which offers an additional argument
for believing that improvements in painting preceded
those in sculpture, because oblique views of objects,
and the veins of the body and limbs, seem not

* Pliny.

to have been attempted before the time of Phidias, **in** sculpture.

Fortunately for us, the compendious history of painting and sculpture left by Pliny was selected from the writings of the best Grecian artists, and arranged with attention to the several improvements in chronological order, with such perspicuity and comprehension, that whenever, from the brevity of the work, we do not find all we wish for—yet, by attending to the information, prior and subsequent, we shall easily be enabled to supply the defect from other writings, or monuments of antiquity. In this manner we shall satisfy ourselves concerning the progress of sculpture in the 250 years which elapsed between the age of Dipœnus and Scyllis, and that of Phidias.

The better drawing of the figure, with a more careful attention to its parts, more precision and variety of attitude, a less elaborate curling and dressing the hair, the form of the figure better shown through the drapery, are all certain signs of a nearer approach to the age of Phidias.

From the few historical remarks now offered, it is evident that sculpture was 800 years, from Dædalus to the time immediately preceding Phidias, in attaining a tolerable resemblance of the human form, which proves the slow growth of art in the infant state of science; whilst the means of subsistence are precarious, the rights of individuals undefined, and the general attention of society is employed on self-preservation and defence, rather than the increase of comfort or civilization.

Poetry and oratory, the more independent efforts of mind, appear in the earliest states of society, and distinguish man as an intellectual and rational creature, scatter the first seeds of knowledge, lay down theories for the government of future generations, expand the mind, and direct the powers toward whatever is most useful and desirable in the more perfect states of humanity.

The chief occurrences in the early history of Greece are the Argonautic expedition, the war of Thebes, and the taking of Troy; in which particular heroism, or the united achievements of petty states, are interwoven with poetic fiction. Their consequences produced no considerable change in the manners of the people, or the character of the country; but the battles of Marathon and Salamis, which destroyed the Persian army, whose myriads, like locusts, swarmed over the country, struck the first deadly blow to the Persian power, and gave a beginning to the Grecian, or third great monarchy of the world.

An event of so much importance, by changing fortune and transferring power in so large a portion of the civilized part of mankind, raised the character of the Greeks, and particularly the Athenians, the champions of the war; whose heroic ardour, increased by success, sought additional distinction by every great and praiseworthy exertion of body and mind in arts and arms; the accumulated wisdom of ages, and discoveries in science, were taught by their philosophers; their temples and public buildings were raised with a magnificence unknown before, and decorated with all the powers of art.

Æschylus, Euripides, and Sophocles ennobled the minds of the people by their dramatic poetry; the exercises which formed the body to exertion and beauty, and the mind to fortitude and patriotism, were universally practised, cultivated and honoured. In this general spirit of enterprise and improvement, sculpture appeared in the school of Phidias with a beauty and perfection which eclipsed all former efforts.

About 490 years before the Christian era, Phidias flourished, at the same time with the philosophers Socrates, Plato, and Anaxagoras—the statesmen and commanders Pericles, Miltiades, Themistocles, Cimon, and Xenophon—with the tragic poets above mentioned. This period was as favourable in its moral and political circumstances, as in the emulation of rare talents, to produce the display, and encourage the growth of genius.

The city and citadel of Athens had been burnt by the army of Xerxes; but the Greeks, being conquerors, raised more stately edifices in the places of those destroyed. Phidias was engaged by Pericles in the superintendence and decoration of the Temple of Minerva, and other public works. His superior genius, in addition to his knowledge of painting,

which he practised previous to sculpture, gave a
grandeur to his compositions, a grace to his groups,
a softness to flesh, and flow to draperies, unknown
to his predecessors—the character of whose figures
was stiff, rather than dignified; their forms either
meagre or turgid; the folds of drapery parallel, poor,
and resembling geometrical lines, rather than the
simple, but ever-varying, appearances of nature.

The discourses of contemporary philosophers, on
mental and personal perfection, assisted him in
selecting and combining ideas, which stamped his
works with the sublime and beautiful of Homer's
verse.

How this sculptor was esteemed by the ancients
will be understood by such testimonies as the following.* Quintilian says, " His Athenian Minerva
and Olympian Jupiter at Elis possessed beauty
which seemed to have added something to religion,
the majesty of the work was so worthy of the
divinity."

After such positive and magnificent praise as this,
there will be still room for our surprise at the
descriptions, fragments, and other authentic memorials of some works which he conducted and performed.

The Temple of Minerva in the Acropolis of
Athens, erected by Ictinus and Callicrates, was

---

* Pliny says,—"Phidias was most famous throughout all
nations;" and when enumerating the most celebrated sculptors
of antiquity—" but before all, Phidias the Athenian."

under the direction of Phidias, and to him we probably owe the compositions, style and character of
the sculpture, in addition to much assistance in
drawing, modelling, choice of the nude and draperies, as well as occasional execution of parts in
the marble.

The emulators of Phidias were Alcamenes, Critias,
Nestocles, and Hegias; twenty years after, Ageladas,
Callon, Polycletus, Phragmon, Gorgias, Lacon,
Myron, Scopas, Pythagoras, and Perillus.

In this list we certainly have the names of the
sculptors employed on the Temples of Minerva and
Theseus, and as the styles of different hands are
sufficiently evident in the alto and basso-relievos, so
there might perhaps be no great difficulty in tracing
some of the artists by resemblance to others of their
known works.

The two pediments of the Temple of Minerva
were each eighty-eight feet long, filled with compositions of entire groups and statues, from eight to
nine feet high. The subject of the western pediment
related to the birth of Minerva, or rather, perhaps,
her introduction to the gods. The eastern pediment
had the contention of Neptune and Minerva for the
patronage of Athens.

Forty-three metops had combats of the Lapithæ
and Centaurs; and a frieze of 380 feet, round the
wall of the temple under the portico, was decorated
with the procession of the Grecian states in honour
of Minerva, in chariots and on horseback, leading

animals for sacrifice, bearing offerings and presenting the sacred veil, in presence of the gods sitting
upon thrones to witness the solemn ceremony.

The Marquis Nantuel had a drawing made of the
western pediment of this temple, when the statues
were all, excepting one, in their places; and, notwithstanding some mutilation of parts, the whole
was sufficiently entire for the composition to be
perfectly understood.

Specimens of the metops and basso-relievos under
the portico will persuade the beholder, at once, of
their simplicity, grandeur, elegance, and nature;
but, to perfectly judge of their comprehensive excellence, they must be seen and studied.

Within the temple stood the statue of Minerva,*
thirty-nine feet high, made by Phidias of ivory and
gold, holding a Victory, six feet high, in her right
hand, and a spear in her left, her tunic reaching to
her feet. She had her helmet on, and the Medusa's
head on her ægis; her shield was adorned with the
battle of the gods and giants, the pedestal, with the
birth of Pandora. Plato tells us, that the eyes of
this statue were precious stones.†

But the great work of this chief of sculptors, the
astonishment and praise of after ages, was the
Jupiter‡ at Elis, sitting on his throne, his left hand
holding a sceptre, his right extending Victory to the
Olympian conquerors, his head crowned with olive,
and his pallium decorated with birds, beasts, and

* See Plate XIX.   † Greater Hippias.   ‡ See Plate XX.

flowers. The four corners of the throne **were**
dancing Victories, each supported by **a** sphinx,
tearing **a** Theban youth. At the back of the throne,
above his head, were the three Hours or Seasons on
one side, and on the other the three Graces. On the
bar between the legs of the throne, and the panels
or spaces between them, were represented many
stories:—the destruction of Niobe's children, the
labours of Hercules, the delivery of Prometheus, the
garden of the Hesperides, with the different adventures of the heroic ages. On the base, the battle of
Theseus with the Amazons; on the pedestal, an
assembly of the gods, the sun and moon in their cars,
and the birth of Venus. The height of the work
was sixty feet. The statue was ivory, enriched with
the radiance of golden ornaments and precious
stones, and was justly esteemed one of the seven
wonders of the world.

Several other statues of great excellence, in marble
and in bronze, are mentioned among the works of
Phidias, particularly a Venus, placed by the Romans
in the forum of Octavia—two Minervas, one named
Callimorphus, from the beauty of its form; and it **is**
likely that the fine statue of this goddess in Mr.
Hope's gallery is a repetition in marble of Phidias's
bronze, from its resemblance, in attitude, drapery,
and helmet, to the reverse of an Athenian silver
coin. Another statue by him was an Amazon, called
Euknemon, from her beautiful leg: there is **a print**
of this in the Museum Pium Clementinum.

Alcamenes was celebrated for his* Venus Aphrodite, to which Phidias is said to have given the last
touches.

Praxiteles excelled in the highest graces of youth
and beauty. He is said to have excelled not only
other sculptors, but himself, by his marble statues
in the Ceramicus of Athens; but his Venus was
preferable to all others in the world, and many
sailed to Cnidos for the purpose of seeing it. This
sculptor having made two statues of Venus,† one
with drapery, the other without, the Coans preferred
the clothed figure, on account of its severe modesty,
the same price being set upon each. The citizens
of Cnidos took the rejected statue, and afterwards
refused it to King Nicomedes, who would have for-
given them an immense debt in return; but they
were resolved to suffer anything so long as this
statue by Praxiteles ennobled Cnidos. The temple
was entirely open in which it was placed, because
every view was equally admirable. This figure is
known by the descriptions of Liccian and Cedrenus,
and it is represented on a medal of Caracalla and
Plautilla, in the imperial cabinet of France. This
Venus was still in Cnidos during the reign of the
Emperor Arcadius, about 400 years after Christ.
This statue seems to offer the first idea of the Venus
de Medicis, which is likely to be the repetition of
another Venus, also the work of this artist, mentioned
by Pliny.

* See Plate XXI.　　† See Plates XXII. and XXIII.

On the reverse of the Empress Lucilla's medals is a clothed Venus with an apple in her right hand, which, from the grace of its attitude and its resemblance to several antique marble statues, is likely to be the clothed Venus chosen by the Coans.

Among the known works of Praxiteles are his Satyr, Cupid, Apollo the lizard-killer, and Bacchus leaning on a fawn.

Polycletus of Sicyon, the scholar of Agelades, was particularly celebrated on account of his Doryphorus, or lance-bearer,* and Diadumenus,† or youth binding a fillet round his head. The Doryphorus was called the "rule" by artists, from which they studied the forms, outline, or lineaments.

The Discobolus of Myron is ascertained by an antique gem, and the description given by Quintilian, who apologizes for its forced attitude. An ancient example of this figure‡ is in the British Museum.

The Discobolus of Naucydes is universally admired for its form and momentary balance.

The wounded man, in which might be seen how much of life remained, was the famous work of Ctesilaus, and perhaps is the same as the statue commonly called the dying gladiator, but more properly a dying herald or hero, according to Winckelman.

Ctesilaus is known by his wounded Amazon.

* Molliter Juvenem.
† Viriliter Puerum.   This statue was valued at a hundred talents.
‡ See Plate **XXIV.**

The nine Muses by Philiscus of Rhodes are mentioned by Pliny, and the Muses brought by Fulvius Nobilior to Rome; from one of these series must be the greater number of those in the Pope's Museum, of which the comedy is remarkable for grace, and the tragedy for grandeur.*

The Hermaphrodite of Polycles is one of the mo t delicate and graceful productions of antiquity.

The Apollo Philesius (or in love) by Canachus is seen in many fine repetitions in the different galleries of Europe.

The Ganymede borne by the eagle, in the Pope's Museum, is exactly described by Pliny.

The Apollo Belvidere is believed by the learned Visconti to be Apollo 'Αλεξίκακος (the deliverer from evil) of Calamis, mentioned both by Pliny and Pausanias. The history of its removals is given in the "Museum Pium Clementinum."† Only one small antique repetition of this statue has been found.

Admirable and sublime in its beauty as it is, there is a reason which perhaps might render it less popular with the ancients than the moderns. Maximus Tyrius describes a statue by Phidias very similar to this, but more in motion, either discharging an arrow, or preparing to do so. There are traces of this statue in some ancient basso-

* Casts of the Muses in the Royal Academy.

† Museum Capitolinum, and Museum Clementinum, Volume of Statues, p. 21.

relievos, and it is possible the stronger expression of
Phidias's work, together with the authority of his
name, might have diminished the public attention to
Calamis in a comparative production.

The Venus de Medici was so much a favourite of
the Greeks and Romans, that a hundred ancient
repetitions of this statue have been noticed by tra-
vellers. The individual figure is said to have been
found in the forum of Octavia. The style of sculpture seems to have been later than Alexander the
Great, and the idea of this statue appears to have
its origin from the Venus of Cnidos.

We may now notice some statues of great excellence which Pliny has not mentioned, and no wonder
they are omitted, when, of more than 11,000 reckoned
in his history, he professes to give a catalogue of
about five hundred only.

The colossal statues on Monte Cavallo in Rome,
we may fairly presume to be the works of Phidias
and Praxiteles, as inscribed on their pedestals, because the animated character and style of sculpture
seems peculiar to the age in which those artists
lived; and because in the frieze of the Parthenon
there is a young hero* governing a horse, which
bears so strong a resemblance to those groups, that
it would be difficult to believe it was not a first idea
for them by one of those artists.

The heroic statue (by Agasias the Ephesian),
commonly called the fighting gladiator, is shown by

* Bellerophon.

the ingenious and learned Abbate Fea to be Ajax, the son of Oileus, as his figure is so represented on the coins of Locris, his country.

The Hercules Farnese, the style is later than the time of Alexander.

We should now proceed to those precious monuments of art, the ancient groups, in which we see the sentiment, heroism, beauty and sublimity of Greece existing before us ; but these have been described with such pathos and justness of character by your excellent professor of painting,* that nothing more is necessary at present than to show some representations of them.

The group of Laocoon, animated with the hopeless agony of the father and sons, is the work of Apollodorus, Athenodorus, and Agesander of Rhodes. The style of this work, as well as the manner in which Pliny introduces it in his history, gives us reason to believe it was not ancient in his time, as your professor of painting has already observed.

Zethus and Amphion tying Dirce to the bull's horns, an example of filial vengeance for a persecuted mother, is as heroic in conception as vast in execution. The restorations of this group are so bad that they only become tolerable by something like an assimilation of spirit in their union with the ancient and venerable fragment. It is the work of Apollonius, and Tauriscus, of Rhodes.

The group of Hercules and Antæus, in the Palace

* The late Mr. Fuseli.

Pitti at Florence, may be a marble copy from the bronze, on which the copyist inscribed the name of the original artist.

The groups of Atreus bearing a dead son of Thyestes, Orestes and Electra, and Ajax supporting Patroclus, are all examples of fine form, heroic character, and sentiment. There seems to be only one reason for their being omitted by Pliny—that they were, at that time, too recent to have obtained an equal rank in public estimation with the fine works of Phidias, Praxiteles, and their immediate descendants.

The group of Niobe and her youngest daughter, by Scopas, is an example of heroic beauty in maturer age. The sentiment is maternal affection. She exposes her own life to shield her child from the threatened destruction.

The separate statues of the children all partake of the same heroic beauty, mixed with the passions of apprehension, dismay, or death.

To this series belongs that fine example of anatomical study in difficult but harmonious composition, the group of wrestlers.

The beautiful and interesting group of Cupid and Psyche is not mentioned by Pliny, perhaps for the same reason that several other fine works were not—because it was after the times of those great masters, who were looked on as the standards of excellence in his days. It is more likely to have been produced after the reign of Augustus, when the Pythagorean philosophy was revived, from which its subject is taken.

From what has been said, it will appear that sculpture did not arrive at maturity until the age of Phidias, 490 years before the Christian era; and Pliny's chronological catalogue of the most celebrated Greek artists continues 160 years later, or to 330 before Christ: after which time, however, the Laocoon, and several of the finest groups and statues, seem to have been executed. Nor can we believe, from the admirable busts and statues of the imperial families still remaining, that sculpture began to lose its graces until the reign of the Antonines; and, indeed, so strong were the stamina of Grecian genius in the arts of design, that after the time of the Iconoclastes, in the fifth and sixth centuries, when the noblest works were destroyed, even then, and until Constantinople was taken by the Turks in the fifteenth century, the Greeks executed small works of great elegance, as may be seen in the dyptics, or ivory covers to consular records, or to sacred volumes used in the church service.

The works of sculpture here enumerated will show, that nearly all the greatest and most valued productions were of marble, and not bronze, as some have been led to believe; and although several celebrated *statues* mentioned by Pliny were bronze, from which we have marble copies, yet all the *groups*, with two or three exceptions only, are marble, and some of the most admired statues, viz., those of the Venuses and Cupid by Praxiteles, with many others.

Sicyon had long been the workshop of metals in early times. Ægina was also famous for bronze sculpture, and, according to the same author, continued the Egyptian style

Etruscan sculpture must be considered entirely Greek—the work of Greek colonists and their disciples.

The Sicilian sculpture is also Grecian; some of their finest medals in particular are of the Corinthian school.

The principal schools of sculpture were unquestionably Athens and Rhodes: the sculptors of the Laocoon, the Torso Farnese, and the Colossus, were Rhodians; and it is almost incredible that, from this little island, only forty miles long and thirteen broad, the Roman conquerors brought away 3000 statues!

LECTURE IV.

———•———

ON SCIENCE.

In a general view of painting and sculpture, followed by a careful attention to the principles of design requisite to the elevated and extensive practice of those arts, we shall find that they are intimately connected with a considerable portion of the circle of knowledge, whether we regard them as engaged in the representation of the human figure singly, or in the variety of epic and historical composition.

The human figure cannot be represented without an accurate acquaintance with the structure of the bones, muscles, tendons, veins, and nerves, together with a knowledge of the several organs which contribute their functions to the continuation of life, whether the subject is in action or at rest. This information is generally understood to be gained by the science of anatomy; but then, it must be assisted by the geometrical forms of the bones, the mechanical structure and movement of the joints, the laws of extension and contraction in the muscles, with a variety of phenomena relating to the internal economy, and indicated in the exterior of the human form.

The arts of design are connected with all the numerous branches of human knowledge. The doctrines of theology and the ideas of philosophy are manifested to our comprehension by visible figures and symbols. They demonstrate geometrical and mathematical science—illustrate the anatomy and economy of animals—connect the series of natural phenomena and productions, even to the lower strata of the earth, and the depths of the sea. Those arts arrest Time himself in his course, and deliver from his destructive progress the heroes of antiquity, the chorus of Helicon, the synod of Olympus, and theologies of the east; they make intimates of antiquity and posterity; they set before the naturalist the several orders of creation; they exhibit to the geographer men and countries which others have seen for him; and they assist the astronomer in figuring the starry heavens!

Such are the powers and offices of these arts, enlightening an early age with the dawn of knowledge, pouring a fuller blaze upon succeeding times, engaging the affections in worthy contemplations and employment, exalting the intelligence, and assisting its important, its most exalted pursuits.

After our conviction of the utility and excellence of the arts of design, the next inquiry will be, by what course of study shall we be most readily led to a successful practice of them? This question may be answered nearly in the words of Socrates, " by the study of the human form, animated by the human soul ; because the human form is the most perfect of all forms, and contains in it the principles and powers of all inferior forms."

Man was called by the ancients " a little world," because the faculties of his mind determined his claim to intellectual being, whilst his body partook of the common principles of natural existence. Revelation is satisfactory and decided on this subject—

God created man in His own image—

and according to this testimony remaining in the pagan world, they represented divinities, angels, good genii, and heroes, in the most beautiful human forms.

We certainly know that, in those countries where the figure and character of man have been most diligently studied and analyzed, there, consequently, he has breathed in marble, and animated the canvas. The inferior animals and orders of nature have been also most exactly represented. If this assertion required the confirmation of proof, we might appeal to the hall of animals in the Pope's Museum, where, among the specimens of ancient sculpture, are seen entire, and in fragments, quadrupeds, from the most noble to the most inconsiderable,—various orders of birds and reptiles, many remarkable for elegance, and almost every one so natural that they seem nature transformed to stone.

The tetradrachms, or larger silver coins of Macedon, have horses on them of exquisite beauty.

But we possess in England the most precious examples of Grecian power in the sculpture of animals. The horses of the frieze in the Elgin collection appear to live and move, to roll their eyes, to gallop, prance, and curvet; the veins of their faces and legs seem distended with circulation; in them are distinguished the hardness and decision of bony forms, from the elasticity of tendon, and the softness of flesh. The beholder is charmed with the deer-like lightness and elegance of their make, and although the relief is not above an inch from the background, and they are so much smaller than nature, we can scarcely suffer reason to persuade us they are not alive.

In those countries where the arts of design have been more admired for colossal size, and indefatigable labour, than for intelligence and sentiment, the figures of animals were most imperfect in those parts and those expressions least understood in the human figure.

Thus we have positive and negative proof, that the human form, as it is the first in the order and dignity of creation, comprehending the nobler powers, qualities, and forms of inferior creatures, so, by natural consequence, it is the great and principal object of study in the arts of design.

The earliest imitations of the human figure in all nations have been rude, disproportioned, and insipid and these characteristics remain in the more advanced attempts of Mexico, India, and Egypt. The earliest productions of Greece had no superior claim to preference over those of other barbarians. The chief employments in those times were providing food, conducting an attack against their neighbours, or securing themselves from invasion on inaccessible mountains, and within impregnable fortifications. In such a state of society men see objects generally, understand them imperfectly, and represent them rudely.

The human figure—so astonishing in its structure, combining so many principles and powers—so beautiful and engaging in its contour and colours—so varied by sex, age, motion, and sentiment—cannot be represented from cursory and ignorant observation; it must be understood before it can be imitated. Therefore, Greek sculpture did not rise to excellence until anatomy, geometry, and numbers had enabled the artist to determine his drawing, proportions, and motion; then, and not before, a just expression might be infused in the truth and harmony of parts, and the artist endowed his statue with life, action, and sentiment.

The present Lecture will be a compendium of this subject, collected from Hippocrates, Galen, Pliny, Vitruvius, Leonardo da Vinci, and Borelli, considered under the heads of anatomy and outline, proportions and mechanical motion.

The writings of Hippocrates and Galen instruct

us in the science of anatomy among the Greeks, from the time of Phidias to the age of Antoninus Pius, when sculpture had sensibly declined, consequently including those successive periods in which all the nobler works had been produced.

Pliny the elder has preserved a chronological history of artists and their works, from the earliest ages to his own time, extracted from the writings of distinguished painters and sculptors, and containing many of their scientific rules for professional practice.

Vitruvius has preserved from the writings of Greek artists the most approved proportions of the human figure, and the application of diagrams to include and determine the extent of its motion.

Leonardo da Vinci's invaluable memoranda on painting, abound in the most useful observations on the mechanical powers and muscular action of the human frame.

Borelli, a Neapolitan physician, wrote an ingenious treatise on the motion of animals, which was published in the year 1685: to these authors the present Lecture is chiefly indebted, and this general acknowledgment is intended to supersede the necessity of interrupting the course of our subject by particular quotations.

A critical comparison of the noblest examples of ancient sculpture with the contemporary state of science, enables us to determine what they owe to rules, and what to the immediate and particular study of individual nature : this will guard against mistaking faults for beauties, and, above all, establish principles for our own practice.

Our purpose requires that we should leave to the professed antiquary all attention to those times when rude stones were called divinities, as the Ephesian Diana and Samian Juno ; little better than shapeless blocks. We shall, therefore, begin with the earliest attempts at imitation of parts and proportion.

Small bronze statues* exist in different museums of Europe, which stand perpendicularly upright; their legs nearly close together, their arms fixed to their sides, their heads rather large, the hair straight, the eyes full, the nose flattish, the lower part of the face and chin projecting. A little fulness for each breast, and a slight indication of the line formed on each side of the thorax by the terminations of the ribs, are the only parts distinguished in front of the body. The shoulders and arms are meagre, and have little variety in the outline ; the thighs are full, so are the calves of the legs; the joints are scarcely noticed ; their proportions are rather dwarfish, seldom exceeding six heads and a half in height.

The next considerable improvements in the figures are chiefly found on painted vases or basso-relievos of Bacchanalian subjects, or processions of divinities ;† and, as far as we are able to judge from

* See Plate XVI.　　　† Mercury, Venus, Juno, Minerva.

coins,* and the progress of science, we have reason
to believe they were not more than a hundred years
before Phidias. These improvements consisted of
a greater variety and violence of action, a bolder
distinction of the knees, elbows, edge of the pelvis,
the ribs, and the ankles; the muscles turgid and
tendonous, proper to continual and vigorous exertion.

By comparing the monuments of antiquity with
each other, and with contemporary authors, we ascertain their history, unravel their philosophy, and
determine their science. Thus, sculpture executed
in the time of Phidias and his immediate successors,
presents the portrait of the human figure in the
full development of its powers, and perfection of its
beauty, by gymnastic exercises—at the same time
that its anatomical forms are decided with the same
simplicity, elegance, and comprehensive greatness,
which are equally admired in the work of the artist
and the writings of Hippocrates. As a natural and
certain consequence of the sculptor's intelligence
being formed on the physician's instructions, the
system was the simplest and boldest division of parts,
and breadth of masses, that imitation of nature
permits.†

The general forms were, the head rounded, the
face oval, the neck like a portion of a column, the

* Tydeus. Museo Pio Clementino, vol. I. of Statues, No. 7
—Plate A.
† Frieze in the Temple of Theseus.

shoulders one curve from the neck to the bottom of the deltoid muscle, the mass of the body bounded at the bottom by the line of the pelvis (or basin bone), above which the oblique " descensens" muscle projects distinctly. A line divides the front of the body to the gullet of the navel. This is intersected at right angles by curve lines, above the pit of the stomach, from the breast-bone to the arm-pit, produced by the fulness of the breasts. A line nearly semicircular indicates the extremities of the ribs. The abdomen sinks in below the true ribs, and narrows this part of the body across the loins. The arm tapers as it descends to its junction with the hand: it is flattened on the outside below the deltoid, till the rise in the upper part of the lower arm, occasioned by the supinator longus. The inside of the upper arm is also flattened down to the lower internal projection of the humerus.

The lower limb, composed of the thigh, leg, and foot, is rather more than half the whole length of the figure, divided at, and measured from the os pubis. It is longer and stouter than the arm; its general form is tapered down to the ankle; the patella is described by an oval, the inner side of the shin-bone is marked by a curve of thirty degrees, from the upper part of which the calf of the leg projects. The outside of the leg is also curved, and the projection of the inner ankle is rather higher than the projection of the lower ankle.

Such are the general characteristics of outline

and marking in the front view of the human figure, most carefully and rigidly observed in the statues,* basso-relievos, and painted vases, from the age of Pericles and Phidias to the time of Lysippus and Alexander.

The outline of boundary is of necessity the same in the geometrical front and back views of the figure, and they differ only in the interior forms and markings.

The back, from the shoulders to the loins, is comprehended in two generally rounded masses, divided by a narrow channel. The blade-bones, with their muscles, present a rounded flattened form on the greatest projection of each mass. The loins are small, hollowed in, and flat, between the masses above described and the more compressed projection of the nates.

In the side view of the figure, whether in action or at rest, was well observed that wonderful counterpoise of parts, on either side of the centre of gravity, which balances so tall and complicated a structure as the human figure on so small a basement as its feet, the head leaning forward counteracted by the shoulders, these by the abdomen, the abdomen by the nates, and the bending forward of the upper mass as far as the knees, counteracted by the extension of the feet forward, which confirms the support when standing, accelerates progression, and assists a leap with the powers of the lever.

* Apollo Belvidere.

This detail of parts, demonstrated by the ancient works, will convince the younger student that the human figure can only be represented in proportion as it is understood.

Thus the Greeks were enabled to represent the figure with precision, boldness, and character, from their general knowledge of its internal structure and parts, the harmony of its proportions, and the laws of its mechanical motion. These principles of science they derived from the instructions of Hippocrates, and the schools of Pythagoras and Plato.

This mode of proceeding was rational and true, founded on the order of nature, and accounting for effects by their causes, and showing the causes in their effects; it was, consequently, the most successful, and its superiority is proved by the excellence it has produced.

Naked representations of the human figure in Gothic sculpture, from the fifth century to the fourteenth, are destitute of anatomy, proportions and just motion. Those branches of science were neither studied nor understood in those ages, consequently they could not infuse their magic wonders into the labours of painting and sculpture. The ignorant effort was of necessity clumsy, mean, insipid, and unintelligible.

The school of Giovanni di Bologna exhibits defects in the opposite extreme—anatomical pedantry and licentious affectation of graceful movement—the extravagance of which is no less distant from the beautiful simplicity of nature, than the insipid barbarity of Gothic carving and painting.

These comparative observations are introduced as a further confirmation that the excellence of the Grecian theory was the real foundation of excellent practice.

There is reason to believe that those groups and statues which are pre-eminent in the display of anatomical skill were not executed until after the age of Alexander the Great, when Hierophilus and Erasistratus had enlarged the bounds of anatomical science, by numerous dissections in the school of Alexandria. Of this there is abundant evidence, historical and scientific, as well as internal, in the ancient sculpture itself.

After the age of Alexander the Great, anatomical detail became more defined and particular, but without destroying the breadth of masses; for example, the masses in the body and limbs of the young Hercules* in the British Museum are the same, in their general forms, as those of the heroes combating with the centaurs in the Parthenon, or in the frieze of the Temple of Theseus. They are, however, bolder in this statue, in proportion as it is more muscular. The details in front are the mastoidæus, on each side of the neck the clavicle, the pectoral muscle, the edge of the ribs nearly semicircular, the serrati and oblique descendens, the recti of the abdomen, with

* By Lysippus

its horizontal divisions ending at the pubes, which, with the edge of the pelvis, terminates the trunk. The details of the lower limb differ little from the former description, excepting that the knee-pan and the ankle-bones are more strongly marked, the membranous insertion of the biceps is distinct, and the peronæus muscle is seen on the side of the leg.

In the back view of this figure, the trapezius is defined at its insertion in the edge of the scapula, and continued to its pointed termination : above the spine of the scapula it unites in a mass with the supra spinatus, then follows the spine of the scapula, and the whole mass of the scapula is completed by the union of the infra spinatus, the teres minor and the teres major in one form. The acromion is distinctly seen, and the rounded top of the humerus is indicated in the deltoid, which is strongly divided from the muscles of the arm beneath. The protuberance of the triceps is bold ; the biceps is bold, broad, and squared towards the bottom. The bones which form the elbow are carefully distinguished : the head of the ulna in the middle, on the inside of the lower point of the humerus, and on the outside ; the lower condyle or swelling of the same bone at its union with the radius.

In the ages after Phidias, it is true, we observe a greater particularity of anatomical finish and detail ; but, at the same time, we see a choice selection of those simple geometrical forms which in bone, muscle, and tendon are strongest, most efficient and elegant, whether the subject be masculine or **femi-nine**, strong or delicate.

It must not be supposed that those simple geometrical forms of body and limbs, in the divinities and heroes of antiquity, depended upon accidental choice, or blind and ignorant arbitration. They are, on the contrary, a consequence of the strict and extensive examination of nature, of rational inquiry into its most perfect organization and physical well-being, expressed in outward appearance; they are proper to the blossom of youth, and the full flower of maturity; they are the signs of a firm, consistent and harmonious structure, healthful juices and elastic tendon. Such characteristics assist the mind in rising towards the contemplation of real perfection, which is simplicity and unity itself: such forms are directly opposite to those of division, infirmity, and decay.

The group of boxers, and the statue called a fighting gladiator, but in reality the lesser Ajax, exhibit the greatest muscular display in violent action. The forced action of the boxers renders the muscular configuration of their shoulders so different in appearance from moderate action and states of rest, that we may derive a double advantage from the anatomical consideration of their forms: first, we shall learn the cause of each particular form, and, secondly, we shall be convinced how rationally and justly the ancients copied nature.

In the right shoulder of the upper figure, the

acromion of the scapula is distinctly seen ; the backward portion of the deltoid arising from the spine of the scapula; the head of the humerus bone next to the acromion :—the angle and base of the scapula are bordered by a considerable swelling of the teres major, and the trapezius in a continued mass.

The left shoulder of the same figure shews the three divisions of the deltoides distinctly, with the projection of the head of the humerus in the upper part of the middle portion.   The spine of the scapula is marked by a channel under the swelling of the trapezius and supra spinatus, and above the infra spinatus and teres major.

The right arm of the lower figure is forcibly held backwards, which occasions the hindmost portion of the deltoid to fold towards the spine of the scapula. The other muscles of the scapula, and immediately about it, present only a common appearance, because they are not particularly exerted.

The whole left shoulder of this figure is exerted to the utmost in assisting the arm to support the weight of the superincumbent figure.   The whole surface has an opposite appearance to the right arm, which is forced backwards, and therefore the scapula lies in a hollow between the arm and back-bone.   The left shoulder is rounded by its position, and the muscles of the left scapula are swollen by effort into one mass, in which the acromion only makes one very distinct form.

There is the same careful attention to effort, and inaction, in the back of the gladiator throughout its parts, and indeed throughout the figure.

We may now advert to the causes which brought about the anatomical distinction in the forms of the gods.

Hipparchus,* a few years before the birth of Phidias, had formed a public library for the Athenians, in which were placed the works of Homer, which he had collected and arranged; as they were more complete than generally known before, they became more popular. Socrates employed their language in moral discourses, and Plato in images and reasoning to embody and convey the theologies of Orpheus and Pythagoras.

The poets formed tragedies from the "Iliad" and the "Thebais." Homer supplied subjects for the painter and sculptor; his descriptions fixed the persons and attributes of their gods.

Phidias† seems to have been the first in this reformation. Minerva, who had before appeared harsh and elderly, was by him rendered beautiful. His Jupiter was awful as when his nod shook the poles, but benignant as when he smiled on his daughter Venus, according to Homer's description. The anatomical forms selected from powerful nature, presented a massy breast and shoulders, projecting muscles above the hip-bone, the limb strong, without heaviness, and the whole figure mighty.

* Plato's Hipparchus.   † See Plates **XIX.** and **XX.**

The character of the father of gods and men being determined, settled a scale of gradation for his progeny; they were more sublime near him, and less perfect by removal.

Of the sons of Jupiter, Bacchus was the next divinity whose form was sublimated. As Phidias determined the character of the father of the gods, so did the graceful Praxiteles that of Bacchus, who inspires poets, and to whom tragedy was peculiarly dedicated by the Athenians.

Apollo soon became so like his brother Bacchus, that it is not always easy to distinguish one from the other; yet Bacchus has more softness, and Apollo greater energy.

Mercury, as patron of gymnastic exercises, is rather more robust than his brothers.

The masses in the forms of these divinities are little divided; the limbs are simple, flowing in gentle undulation for balance and motion, or quicker curves at the joints.

Hercules, whose labours in difficulty and number were increased by succeeding poets, was more strong and turgid after the time of Alexander the Great, until he became the irresistible hero represented by Glycon in his statue.

Of inferior heroes, Ajax the lesser, and the male figure in the group of Hæmon and Antigone, together with the group of boxers, have the anatomical forms divided with distinctions as numerous as could have been made by any modern.

After the osteology and anatomy of the human figure, we will consider the balance, motion, and mechanical powers according to the ancients.

Pamphilus, the Macedonian painter, under whom pelles studied ten years, was learned in all science, particularly arithmetic and geometry, without which, he declared, art could not be perfected.

How geometry and arithmetic were applied to the study of the human figure, Vitruvius informs us from the writings of the Greek artists, perhaps from those of Pamphilus himself.

A man* (says he) may be so placed with his arms and legs extended, that his navel being made the centre, a circle can be drawn round, touching the extremities of his fingers and toes.

In the like manner, a man* standing upright, with his arms extended, is enclosed in a square, the extreme extent of his arms being equal to his height.

Pliny speaks of improvements in the balance of the figure by some artists, and the neglect of it, and consequent defects, in the works of others.

How well the ancients understood the nature of balance is proved by the two books of Archimedes on that subject; besides, it is impossible to see the numerous figures springing, jumping, dancing, and falling, in the Herculaneum paintings, on the painted vases and the antique basso-relievos, without being assured that the painters and sculptors must have

* Plate XXVI.

employed geometrical figures to determine the degrees of curvature in the body and angular or rectilinear extent of the limbs, and to fix the centre of gravity.

We shall, therefore, proceed in this delightful subject, to some general demonstrations, according to the method of the great Leonardo da Vinci, and the distinguished Borelli, as laid down in his work on the motion of animals.

Extent of motion in the skeleton.*

Front. A, body. B, the head. C, arm. D, thigh and leg.

Side. A, arm. B, leg. C, leg and thigh bent under the figure.

From the top of the head the balance or equi librium of the figure is caused by equality of its parts about the centre of gravity.

When we speak of the centre of gravity, or gravi- tation of the human figure, the principle is referred to by which all bodies upon the earth tend to its centre, as a ray tends to the centre of a circle.

The centre of gravity in the human figure is an imaginary straight line, which falls from the gullet between the ankles to the ground, when it is perfectly upright, equally poised on both feet, with the hands hanging down on each side.†

†Motion is the change of position, caused by inequality of parts about the centre of gravity.

The first motion in the standing figure throws the

* Plates XXVII. XXVIII.   † Plate XXIX.

weight on one leg; in consequence, the centre of gravity, or gravitating line, falls from the gullet on one leg, the shoulder on the same side being lowered, the shoulder on the opposite side raised, the hip and knee sinking below those on the side which supports the weight.

*Preparing to run.**

Preparing to run is throwing the balance beyond the standing foot.

*Striking.**

When the action begins, the figure is thrown back to give force to the blow, and springs forward to the lighter line when the fall of the blow ends the action.

Bearing a Weight.†

The centre of gravity is the centre of the incumbent weight, falling between the feet, if supported by both, or on the supporting foot.

Preparing to Leap.†

To take the spring, the body and thighs are drawn together; the muscles of the leg draw up the heel, so that the figure rests on the ball of the foot; the arms are thrown back—they assist like wings in the impulse. When the figure alights, the arms are raised above the head, and the centre of gravity is near the heels.

* Plate XXX. † Plate XXXI.

Leaning.*

When leaning on more points than one, the **greatest** weight is about that point on which it chiefly rests.

Flying and Falling.*

Flying and falling figures rest on no point, being in motion through the air, but the heaviest portion of the figures rising, denotes flying; as the heaviest portion sinking, determines the falling figure. Without a due attention to these principles, no movement or action can be well expressed, and with their assistance, the finest efforts of ancient and modern art have been produced; the most pathetic, energetic, and graceful attitudes of Raffaelle and Correggio are exemplifications. Excellent lessons on this subject are given by Leonardo da Vinci in his 'Treatise on Painting.'

Every change of position or action in the human figure will present the diligent student with some new application of principles, and some valuable example for his imitation.

It has been observed, that Vitruvius, from the writings of the most eminent Greek painters and sculptors, informs us, that they made their figures eight heads high, or ten faces, and he instances different parts of the figure measured accordingly to that rule, which the great Michael Angelo adopted, as we see by a print from a drawing of his.

* Plate XXXII.

We shall make use of this method in giving the most general proportions of nature and the antique statues.

PROPORTIONS.*

Divisions of the Human Figure in Length.

From the os pubis to the top of the head one half, from the same point to the sole of the foot, the other half.

There are three equal divisions from the acromion of the scapula to the bottom of the inner ankle :—

First, from the acromion to the point in the spine of the ilium, from which the rectus and sartorius muscles begin.

Second, from thence to the top of the patella.

Third, from the top of the patella to the bottom of the inner ankle.

From the bottom of the pubis to the bottom of the patella is the same length as from the bottom of the patella to the sole of the foot, two heads each; but, we must observe, the ancients generally allowed half a nose or more to the length of the lower limbs, exceeding the length of the body and head.

Breadth.

Shoulders	2 heads.
Loins	1 head and 1 nose, or 5 noses.
Across the hips or trochanters.	1 head, 2 noses, or a head and ⅘

* Plate **XXIX.**

Depth.

Chest	1 head, 4 minutes.
Loins	3 noses and ½.
Glutæi	1 head.

Breadth of the Thigh.

Thigh	3 noses.
Calf of the leg	2 noses.
Ankle	1 nose.
Foot	1 head and ½ of a nose long.

Length of the Arm.

From the top of the humerus to the bend of the arm . 1 head and ½.
From the bend of the arm to the first knuckles . 1 head and ½.

Breadth.

Upper arm, front view . . .	1 nose and ½.
Side view of do.	2 noses.
Lower arm, thickest part . .	1 nose and ½.
Wrist	1 nose.

The female figure should not be so tall as the male; the shoulders and loins should be narrower, and the hips broader.

The proportions of the Hercules Farnese, and the Torso Belvidere, are nearly one-fifth more in breadth than other statues; but the ancients varied the proportions according to the character and age of the person. There are examples of the Silenus, and Hercules also when he partook of the same character, exceedingly dwarfish, not exceeding four or five heads in height, and there are examples on some of the Greek vases of figures nine or ten heads high.

PERSPECTIVE.

We have the most satisfactory system of ancient perspective in the principles laid down by Vitruvius: and in Euclid's ' Book of Optics,' which contains no description of the eye, or nature of its vision, but consists of sixty-one propositions, on the manner in which rays pass from objects to the eye, the angles they make, and consequently present them as nearer, or more distant, greater or less, according as they are seen in a parallel or in a diagonal plane; nor does it give rules for the perspective of circles, or the intersections of the visual rays. The modern improvement in perspective which determines depths, enabled Michael Angelo * to give bolder fore-shortenings, and more complicated groups, than the ancients did or could attempt with their imperfect perspective, and which in design, or low relief, has the magical effect of " much in a little."

Such general hints concerning science, employed by the ancients in painting and sculpture, may assis' the young artist in forming principles for the course of his studies, and precede the investigation of the nature and qualities of beauty, which will be offered in the next lecture.

* See Plates XXXIII. and XXXIV.

LECTURE V

BEAUTY.

THAT beauty is not merely an imaginary quality, but a real essence, may be inferred from the harmony of the universe; and the perfection of its wondrous parts we may understand from all surrounding nature; and in this course of observation we find that man has more of beauty bestowed on him as he rises higher in creation.

In the contemplation of our solar system, the splendour of the sun and inferior planets, their magnitude, almost incomprehensible to us, their gravitation, the vastness of their revolutions, bringing the regular succession and return of day and night, with the different seasons, all astonish us in their various circumstances; if we proceed in observation to the starry heavens, crowded with suns, the centres of other systems, we are lost in amazement, and our faculties are overwhelmed.

The objects which surround us on the earth we inhabit are more commensurate to our comprehension and intelligence, and in them we trace wonders,

equally enforcing by their beauty and order, the conviction of power and goodness.

The earth, its history and productions—the sea,
its phenomena and contents — the vegetable and
mineral kingdoms,—have employed, and will continue to employ, the wisest of men in the most
delightful speculations and extraordinary discoveries.

The pursuit of each person must be allotted by his
station, whilst the industry of each contributes to the
circle of knowledge.

Our present object will be, after some general
observations on the animal kingdom, to inquire into
the excellence of man in his real essence, and its
effects on his external appearance—his intelligible
alliance with superior natures, or degeneracy and
abasement in resemblance to the brutes.

Among the many examples in natural philosophy
and history of the gradual and uninterrupted connection of being, from the highest to the lowest, as
far as our perceptions will penetrate, the animal
kingdom offers most striking and stupendous instances.

There is a resemblance in the organization and
bodily form of all animals, which varies by almost
imperceptible gradations, through all the links of
this chain, from man to the worm or vegetable.

The anatomical form and organization of the
ourang-outang bears a near resemblance to the
anatomy of man : this configuration continues in
squirrels, rats, and mice, until the bat, or flying

mouse, unites the race of quadrupeds with birds ; in the same manner, the kangaroo and jei boa, with very short fore legs, and walking on the hind legs only, unite quadrupeds with another class of birds, which do not fly, the penguin, the cassowary, and the ostrich.

The crocodile and alligator unite the race of four-footed beasts with the superior class of reptiles, such as the lizard and the eft, until the frog, being a tadpole in its infant state, belongs to the class ot fishes.

The smaller and more imperfect birds approach to the resemblance of the larger butterflies and moths.

The order of flies at length terminates so exactly in the resemblance of a leaf, that it might be taken for one, did not experiment prove, by the heart, lungs, and anatomical properties, the fly to be perfectly animal ; whilst a totally different organization proves the other to be positively vegetable.

Professor Camper, in the most ingenious and valuable notes to his lectures, shews that the figure and organization of man contain the principles on which the structure of all inferior animals is formed, and from which they are removed by gradual imperfections.

Four-footed animals, although their general forms and anatomy bear strong likeness to the human figure, differ from it in these respects: the brain-pan is less, the nose and jaws have greater projection, their view is downwards, the body is supported in a horizontal line by four legs terminated by paws or hoofs: the interior organization differs in correspondence with the external figure.

The variation of the bird from the beast is, that the nose and jaws of one become a beak in the other, the front legs having lost the paws, are folded up by the sides, and are wings.

In fishes, the head is set immediately on the body; they have no legs, their places are supplied by fins, which guide them through the waters.

All these various orders are wonderfully formed in fitness for the elements they inhabit, and the purposes of their lives. As their history extends through a large and very interesting portion of creation, so the principles of their conformation and powers comprehend a considerable share of natural science.

The forms of the bones and anatomy contain the geometrical forms, as the motions of the body, limbs, and interior, demonstrate the mechanical powers.

The preparation, secretion, and fermentation of the juices are chemical; hydraulics are in the conveyance and motion of the juices; pneumatics in the various modes of breathing; electricity in the effects of heat on the body; and optics in the organs of sight.

Such general observations relate to the bodies of man and other animals; but we must remember that man, even in the structure of his body, is the most perfect of all creatures; and the above remarks are only offered to call the attention to the wonderful extent of creation, and the harmony, order, and beauty of its whole connection and disposition.

But in treating of man in particular, our subject is the most perfect production of Almighty Power in the visible world, the faculties of whose soul place him far above other creatures, and declare the nearer relation he stands in to his divine Creator.

By the wisdom he is endowed with, all creatures are subjected to his dominion; by his affections he is enabled to perform all the charities of life—to prefer the interests of others to his own—to distinguish personal beauty as the indication of good disposition and health—to trace his Creator in his works, and offer the homage of his worship: in all which he is superior to the brute animals, whose exertions are the consequence of instinct for the preservation of themselves and progeny, and whose reasoning has never been discovered to go beyond these purposes, or some particular attachment.

As the affections of man stimulate and engage him in every act, so his understanding directs the means, and looks to the end in every employment through life. These modify the exterior of the face and figure, according to constant habit or momentary impulse.

The passionate are known by quick fiery glances, swollen brows, dilated nostrils, the mouth a little open, the movements of the whole figure sudden, the muscles of the body being disposed to rigidity and contraction.

The melancholy have a general dejection of look, the exterior corners of the eyes and eyebrows tending downwards, a universal slowness of motion and disregard of outward objects.

Every passion, sentiment, virtue, or vice, have their corresponding signs in the face, body, and limbs, which are understood by the skilful physician and physiognomist, when not confused by the working of contrary affections or hidden by dissimulation.

In the formation and appearance of the body, we shall always find that its beauty depends on its health, strength, and agility, most convenient motion and harmony of parts in the male and female human figure, according to the purposes for which they were intended; the man for greater power and exertion, the woman for tenderness and grace. If these characteristics of form are animated by a soul in which benevolence, temperance, fortitude, and the other moral virtues preside, unclouded by vice, we shall recognize in such a one perfect beauty, and remember that "God created man in His own image."

We know that sickness destroys the complexion and consumes the form, until that which was once admired for grace and attractive loveliness becomes a ghastly spectre; and is it not equally evident that brutal ferocity, revenge, hypocrisy, or any other of the malignant passions, still more effectually destroy the very traces of beauty by reducing man to a savage beast in his most degraded state?

The most perfect human beauty is that most free from deformity either of body or mind, and may be therefore defined—

The most perfect soul, in the most perfect body.

Doubts can scarcely be entertained that there are principles of beauty, because various opinions prevail in different countries on the subject.

Men are in different states of mental and bodily improvement, from the most savage to the most civilized countries, and we know that many successive ages must pass in the confirmation of moral habits, the right direction of reason and elevation of intellect, before man can judge, with any tolerable ability, of mental or natural beauty, their causes, relations, and effects: and that in all states of society there must be allowance for prejudice and climate. But we shall certainly find that the wisest and the best men in all ages and countries have held nearly the same doctrine on this subject.

The excellence of intellect and moral beauty was asserted by Menu, the Indian legislator, Confucius, the Chinese philosopher, Zoroaster, the Persian sage, and by the Egyptian priests.

Pythagoras, who had studied their wisdom, understood the dispositions of the mind by its influence expressed in the exteriors of the body; and accordingly, Iamblichus, his biographer, tells us he would observe the countenance, figure, looks, movements, manner of speaking, and tone of voice, until he was accurately acquainted with any one's character.

Our present purpose particularly requires we should consider the sentiments of the most celebrated Greeks on beauty, the connection of mental and bodily beauty, and their expression in the human form.

Homer constantly endows his gods with personal beauty, accommodated to their mental perfection and immortal power, and his heroes with the attributes of gods : thus, as he gives to Jupiter the epithets of "Counsellor" and "Provident," he describes his hair as "divine," "ambrosial," and his nod as making the world tremble : Juno, he calls the "ox-eyed," and the "white-armed;" Minerva, "the blue-eyed virgin." Achilles, the hero of the "Iliad," is the handsomest man that went to Troy ; his epithets are, "divine," "god-like," "swift-footed;" Agamemnon is called "the king of men;" Nestor and Ulysses are said to be "in council like the gods;"—all expressing the union of mental and bodily excellence.

That the same sentiments continued in aftertimes, we have the coeval testimonies of the most illustrious philosophers, tragedians, orators, and artists.

In Plato's Dialogue of Phædrus, concerning the beautiful, he shews the power and influence of mental beauty on corporeal, and in his dialogue, entitled "the Greater Hippias," Socrates observes in argument, "that as a beautiful vase is inferior to a beautiful horse, and as a beautiful horse is not to be compared to a beautiful virgin, in the same manner, a beautiful virgin is inferior in beauty to the immortal gods ;" " for," says he, " there is a beauty* incorruptible, ever the same." It is remarkable that immediately after, he says, " Phidias is skilful in beauty."

Aristotle, the scholar of Plato, begins his ' Treatise on Morals' thus—" Every art, every method and institution, every action and council, seems to seek some good; therefore, the ancients pronounced the beautiful to be the good."

Much, indeed, might be collected from this philosopher's treatises on morals, poetics, and physiognomy, of the greatest importance to our subject; but for the present we shall produce only two quotations from Xenophon's 'Memorabilia,' which contain the immediate application of these principles to the arts of design.

In the dialogue between Socrates and the sculptor Clito, Socrates concludes that " Statuary must represent the emotions of the soul by form ;" and in the former part of the same dialogue, Parrhasius and Socrates agree that " the good and evil qualities of the soul may be represented in the figure of man by painting."

In the applications from this dialogue to our subject, we must remember philosophy demonstrates

---

* The word in Greek is καλὸς—used in the same sense by Plato and Aristotle.

that rationality or intelligence, although connected with animal nature, rises above it, and properly exists in a more exalted state.

From such contemplations and maxims, the ancient artists sublimated the sentiments of their works expressed in the choicest forms of nature; thus they produced their divinities, heroes, patriots, and philosophers, adhering to the principle of Plato, that "nothing is beautiful which is not good;" it was this which, in ages of polytheism and idolatry, still continued to enforce a popular impression of divine attributes and perfection.

In the highest order of divinities, they represented, as far as possible, the energy of intellect above the material accidents of passion or decay.

Jupiter * was most placid as most mighty, either extending victory as the reward of fortitude and patriotic emulation, or holding the thunder and sceptre, emblems of his sovereignty in the government of the universe; excepting when destroying the Titans,—he is then in heroic action.†

Observations on the Bust of Jupiter.

A fine remark is made by Winckelman (perhaps suggested by Mengs), that the brow and hair of this head have some resemblance to those of the lion; the beard and hair are full, the expression is benevolence and wisdom, the age, maturity of power.

* See Plate XX.   † See the Gem of this subject.

Neptune resembles Jupiter in countenance and person; his hair is more disturbed by the winds, or wetted by the element he governs; he is nearly or entirely unclothed.

Pluto continues the likeness of the Saturnian family, observable in Jupiter and Neptune : he sits in solemn state, the ruler of the lower world—he is covered with drapery—his eyes have a sceptre-like stare—and the hair, falling over his forehead, adds gloom to his countenance.

Apollo, Bacchus, and Mercury, distinguished by their youth and beauty, preserve the resemblance of their father Jupiter.

The energetic Apollo Alexicacos, or the driver-away of evil, commonly called Belvidere, is " severe in youthful beauty;" he supplies Homer's description to the sight—his golden locks are agitated—his countenance is indignant—the quiver is hanging on his shoulder—and he steps forward in the discharge of his arrow.

Apollo in love, or companion of the Muses, is majestic yet graceful, strongly resembling Bacchus, who, in the height of youthful beauty, is frequently leaning on a faun, or a muse, or reclining on Ariadne ; his grace and softness approaches to, and sometimes really becomes, female delicacy.

Mercury is a mediate character between Apollo and the youthful Hercules ; he unites the sublime beauty of divinity with corporeal, heroic strength, as patron of gymnastic exercises, and as messenger of the gods from heaven to earth, from earth to heaven.

The characteristics of elevated beauty are continued in the youthful Cupid, Hercules, when a child, strangling the serpents, and the young Ganymede. Heroes, whether considered by the ancients as the immediate progeny of a divinity and a mortal, or as having traced their descent from divinity more remotely, are of muscular forms, in which strength, activity, and beauty blend, but in such a manner that by bodily exertion and agility they have been successful combatants and conquerors. Mental power characterizes the divinity, bodily exertion the hero. Such is Oileus Ajax, the Hæmon, Zethus, and Amphion.

Achilles is the example of masculine beauty among the heroes, as Hercules is of unconquerable force.

In the faces of the dying Achilles and Laocoon, pain and death produce nothing like distortion, the elevation of noble minds is seen in their sufferings.

The train and ministry of Bacchus afford more variety than that of any other divinity—the sacred instructors—the bearers and dispensers of wine and grapes—fauns and satyrs of different ages—dancing and mad Bacchanals.

The sacred instructors are bearded : men of noble characters entirely clothed. Silenus, bearded, with a pleasant countenance, between good fellowship and philosophy—a rather spare and elegant figure with a faun's tail, entirely naked. Such a one nurses the infant Bacchus in Perrier's statues.

Two genii, the frequent attendants of Bacchus, on either of which he often leans, are Ampelus and Acrates. Ampelus is a faun, nervous and sprightly; Acrates dwarfish, round-bellied, and sometimes hairy.

The fauns are youthful, sprightly, and tendinous; their faces round, expressive of merriment, not without an occasional mixture of mischief.

Satyrs, the lowest order in the train of Bacchus, are strong resemblances to different quadrupeds, their faces and figures partake of the ape, the ram, or the goat, they have sometimes goats' legs, and always either goats' or horses' tails.

The giants are towers of human strength to the waist; but instead of legs, their figures terminate in the huge folds of serpents' tails; their heads resemble the Saturnian family, but lowering with brutal ferocity; two small serpents are on their heads, perhaps to indicate the torments in the lower regions, according to Hesiod.

Ocean, and great rivers, as the Nile, Euphrates, Tigris, and Tiber, resemble the Saturnian family in countenance, hair, and beard; their figures Herculean and full of flesh.

The Tritons, and inferior sea-divinities, are robust men to the middle, ending with fishes' tails; their faces are like either the giants' or fauns'; finny hair covers their heads, and gills are on their jaws.

Juno is the first of the goddesses, as sister and wife

of Jupiter: she possesses the highest degree of beauty: her character is lofty and imperial.

Minerva is sometimes seen as the patroness of peaceful arts, in attitude highly dignified, yet simple, clothed in full drapery, and holding an olive branch; but she is most frequently seen armed, in her four-crested helmet and ægis bearing the terrors of Medusa's head, holding her spear and shield, as the virgin-goddess of war. In both characters she is the representative of wisdom.

Venus,* the example and patroness of beauty, appears more frequently in poetic numbers, and rapturous description, than any other heathen divinity. She was the delighting and frequent theme of Homer, Hesiod, Apollonius Rhodius, Virgil, and indeed most of the ancient poets. Plato distinguishes the celestial from the earthly Venus, and Pliny mentions a statue by Phidias of Venus Urania, or the heavenly. The Venus of Alcamenes and the Venus de Medicis are certainly of Plato's latter class; they perfectly agree with Hesiod's description—

The lovely modest Goddess rising from the sea, accompanied by Love, and followed by Desire.

The Graces are seen in ancient sculpture as three lovely, youthful sisters, embracing each other. They were always clothed till after the time of Socrates. In the earlier ages they formed a chorus hand in hand, as described by Pindar.

* See Plates XXI. XXII. and XXIII.

The Greek and Latin names of these goddesses, *Charites* and *Gratiæ*, which signify the exercise of kind affections, or the charities of life, are well personified by the tender union of sisters.

The character and action of these goddesses have given the epithet *graceful* to easy, undulating motion.

The sea-nymphs are graceful in the extreme: their beautiful movements are as various as the waves on which they are borne; each appears a foam-produced Venus.

The whole universe was peopled by congenial beings, substantiated by philosophers, described by poets, represented with the glow of life by painters and sculptors.

In heaven were good demons, or angelic spirits, winged victories, winds, and hours.

On earth, the genii of mountains, trees, rivers and fountains, fauns and satyrs.

In the infernal regions, furies and chimæras.

In an assemblage comprehending such an extent of gradation, with its different races of variety, whatever could be chosen from nature, or deduced from reasoning, evident or abstracted, was employed, from the most beautiful, through various removals and descents, to the most gross and terrific.*

It would be endless to enumerate the foreign divinities of Syria, Egypt, Arabia, Persia, Africa, Spain, Gaul, Germany, and Britain, which during the Roman power received Greek and Roman forms

* Terrific—Pan, Medusa.

and personifications; and, if this were done, **we** could learn nothing novel from it, in relation to our present subject. We should, however, be more certainly led to this conclusion—that whatever traces of grandeur or beauty were found, they would be discovered as pillage and transfer, from ancient Greece.

This much being said more particularly in respect to the countenances and heads of statues, which have been the chief subjects of former Lectures, we will offer a few general remarks on hands and feet.

The proportion of the hand, (it is well known,) from its junction with the wrist to the end of the middle finger, is the length of a face; the breadth across the four lower knuckles does not exceed half the length, or a nose and a half. With these proportions, the beauty of the female hand consists in a fulness and roundness of form, gently dimpled over the first knuckles; the fingers long, round, tapering towards the end, with scarcely any indication of joints.

The male hand, with nearly the same proportions, has more squareness of form and joints, and has little indication of bone or tendon in the youthful figure.

The foot is about a head and a half-nose in length; the breadth, in a straight line across the upper joint of the little toe, being one-third, or a nose and a half.

The beauty of the female foot consists in a rounded

form, dimpled over the first joints of the toes, which are very delicate, with exceedingly gentle indications of the joints, and turned by an almost imperceptible diagonal from the great toe.

The foot of the male figure of youth shews no more of its anatomical structure than the female, but has a greater squareness of form. In more advanced age, or more muscular character, the male foot shows more of tendon and bone ; but in form square and broad, the part of the tibia forming the inner ankle is neatly defined, as is also the lower part of the fibula, forming the outer ankle with the tendon of the peroneus muscle; the knuckles of the toes are more strongly marked.

In both male and female the great toe is large in comparison with the others, and separated from them by a distinct space.

The boundaries of personal beauty are the Apollo and Hercules ; a more slender form than the Apollo is *maigre*, and one more covered with flesh than the Hercules must be clumsy; as one in which the parts are more forcibly marked than in the Laocoon would be a dissected figure.

Such are the regulations and forms of beauty in the human face and figure, which allow of infinite modification and variety, but not transgression.

By these general remarks on the principles of beauty, the student will be excited to a spirit of research, which every one must exert for himself in the various galleries and museums already published, to be found in the library of the Royal Academy, and other public and private repositories, and ancient monuments; but this must be in addition to the most diligent and continual study of choice nature.

LECTURE VI.

----•----

COMPOSITION.

HAVING introduced the Lectures on Sculpture by an inquiry concerning its relations and connection with the circle of general knowledge—stated some important facts in its ancient history—considered the application of science, the observation of nature, and the speculation of mental qualities more particularly evident in the nobler works of Grecian sculpture— we may now proceed to that great effort in which the artist sums up all his knowledge, embodies all his science, and exerts his utmost powers, under the standard of passion, or sentiment, in composition.

To avoid repeating that which it is scarcely possible to think or say better on the present subject, I shall refer the student to the excellent principles and doctrines in the Lecture on Composition by the professor of painting *—to consider with attention what he has delivered on invention and design, on dignity of conception, and pathos of sentiment—to imprint on his memory, with peculiar care, the

* Mr. Fuseli.

gradual elevation to a climax in the example of Rembrandt's " Ecce Homo "—and the degradation of subject to the disgusting in " the Blinding of Samson," by the same painter.

The maxims to be collected from these paragraphs of that admirable discourse have equal force in both arts; and as they have been laid down for the regulation of painting, it is equally important they should be implicitly followed in sculpture; for as the theories of painting and sculpture, so far as the study of colours makes no distinction, are nearly the same, the lectures on painting impart a share of instruction to the sculptor, little less than that which is received by the painter.

Composition, in the arts of design, is the grouping of figures in succession or action, and immediately follows the intelligible imitation of the human figure.

The early compositions of Greece in poetry, painting, and sculpture, celebrate heroic deeds and sacred mysteries; as the combat of Theseus and the Minotaur, of Eteocles and Polynices, of Hercules and the Centaurs, Dejanira carried off by Nessus, processions of divinities, and the initiations of Bacchus and Ceres on painted vases, coins, votive basso-relievos, and ancient wells. Their barbarous violence of angular action, or simple formality of movement, is expressed in a gross execution.

These were among the first bold attempts of painting and sculpture:—to emerge from the servility of hieroglyphical writing and symbolical figure;

speaking to the feelings, instead of to the memory; proclaiming to the spectator's transient view the delivery of a people, the fall of a city, or the Divine superintendence.

When the power of Asia was transferred to Greece, the sciences, the graces, and the muses, bestowed on the arts truth, beauty, and inspiration. Painting and sculpture became more dignified. Colossal statues of prodigious size arose in the cities, like guardian genii overlooking their states. Their attributes and pedestals were adorned with compositions from poetry and theology. The porticos were animated with the heroes of other times. In the friezes of the temples, the Athenians and Amazons, the Lapithæ and Centaurs, the Greeks and Persians fought again, whilst assemblies of gods and demigods rose to the sky in their pediments. Such was the state and magnificence of sculpture in Greece, which is so far important to us, as it makes us acquainted with the celebrated compositions of Grecian artists.

Phidias did not only ennoble Athens and Elis with colossal statues of Minerva and Jupiter of ivory and gold, but he adorned their insignia and pedestals with compositions from the grandest subjects in the poems of Homer and Hesiod. On the outside of Minerva's shield was the battle of the Athenians and the Amazons; on the inside the contest of the gods and giants; on the pedestal was the birth of Pandora.

On the throne of Jupiter were the destruction of Niobe's children, the labours of Hercules, the delivery of Prometheus, the garden of the Hesperides, with other incidents of the heroic ages.

On the base, the battle of Theseus and the Amazons; on the pedestal an assembly of the gods. the Sun and Moon in their cars, and the birth of Venus.

These compositions excelled whatever had appeared before in beauty, grace, and compass, in the same proportions as Phidias excelled his predecessors; and their numerous repetitions testify the esteem of the ancients, and give us possession of the spirit and character of the works themselves, in friezes, basso-relievos, and painted vases.

Minerva received in the assembly of the gods, on the pediment of her temple at Athens, we know from the drawing of it preserved by the Marquis Nanteul.

Of the marriage of Pelops and Hippodamia, on the temple of Jupiter at Elis, we may perhaps form some conception from a magnificent painted vase in the British Museum, on which are two quadrigas, and various human figures.

The battles of the Athenians with the Amazons and the Persians, beheld by assemblies of the gods, in the temples of Minerva and Theseus, and the Propylæum of Athens, together with the frieze lately discovered at Phigalia, are admirable examples of simplicity and energy.

When the states of Greece ceased to be free, they could no longer raise noble temples from the spoils of their enemies, and blazon their own struggles for freedom, or proclaim their divinities on friezes and pediments;—but, with the same love of their country, they employed their genius on inferior memorials of their heroic or deified ancestors, for porticos, libraries, halls, or tombs. The wars of Troy * and Thebes, the stories of their ancient families and kings, expanded by the tragic poets from the episodes of Homer, have bestowed on us those invaluable compositions—the discovery of Achilles, his contest with Agamemnon, the death of Ægisthus and Clytemnestra, Orestes and the Furies, Orpheus and Eurydice, Medea and Jason, Œdipus Coloneus, and the death of Meleager.

The principal compositions of Roman sculpture, the best of which, there is reason to believe, were executed by Greek artists, are those of the arches raised to Titus, Trajan, Marcus Aurelius, Severus, and Constantine—the Trajan, Antonine, and Theodosian columns. They breathe the spirit of the people they commemorate—war, conquest, and universal dominion !

In the Greek compositions, the countenances and figures are of exalted beauty ; the actions display the limbs and body with the greatest variety, energy, and grace ; the subjects are heroic or divine. They have a kindred sublimity with Homer, of patriotism

* The destruction of Priam's family — Neoptolemus killing Priam ; Ajax seizing Cassandra at the shrine of Minerva ; Æneas bearing Anchises. A Vase in Mr. Thomas Hope's possession, and A. L. Millin's Antique Vases, vol i. p. 25, 26.

with Tyrtæus, the noble flights of Pindar, the terrors of Æschylus, and the tenderness of Sophocles!

The Roman compositions owe no inspiration to the Muses, urge no claim to the epic or dramatic. They are the mere paragraphs of military gazettes—vulgar in conception, ferocious in sentiment. On the columns and arches above mentioned, the principal objects are mobs of Romans, cased in armour, bearing down unarmed, scattered Germans, Dacians, or Sarmatians —soldiers felling timber, driving piles, building walls or bridges, carrying rubbish, shouldering battering-rams, killing without mercy, or dragging and binding captives. The forms of their bodies and limbs are interrupted by mail or plate armour, and most of the heads so brutal and savage as to excite compassion for the barbarians who have fallen into their hands.

From this abasement of sculpture in Italy we shall willingly turn again to the compositions of the Greeks, and observe that this people, who had embodied the false divinities of Olympus, and widely spread their fame by the perfection of their representations, the same people were the first to declare the sacred oracles of truth, under the Christian dispensation, by the mute eloquence of painting and sculpture.

Different subjects of Holy Writ are mentioned by the writers of those times, which no longer exist.

Some mosaics, ivory carvings, and illuminations, which have escaped the destruction of Moslem fanaticism, abundantly indicate the beauty of those more considerable works we have lost.

Seven or eight Greek Christian compositions were mentioned in a former lecture, as having been standards to the Italian painters, from which they scarcely ventured to deviate for ages, viz., The creation of Adam and of Eve, the Nativity,* the Transfiguration, the Crucifixion, the Resurrection, the Glorification, the Last Judgment,† with some others; those amply prove that the sacred flame remained in Greece which kindled light and life in the modern arts of Western Europe.

Grecian composition may be traced in the biblical basso-relievos of Orvieto by Nicolas and John Pisani; in the noble bronzes of the life of Christ on the pulpits of St. Lorenzo in Florence, by Donatello; on the bronze gates of St. John's Baptistery, in the same city, by Lorenzo Ghiberti, and in the paintings of Raffaelle and Michael Angelo.

The Greek poets conducted their works on a plan of composition which equally governs painting and sculpture.

Homer's Iliad is a whole, united in its parts by connection, and varied by gradation.

The sentiment throughout is wrath, beginning with the dissension of the kings, continued by the vengeance of the Trojans, and ended by the destruction of Troy's hope and bulwark in the death

* See Plates II. XXXV. XXXVI.   † Plate XXXIX.

of Hector. The characters have a varied individuality.

Achilles is the hero who, like the sun, enlightens and heats all by the blaze of his presence; his absence is darkness and dismay.

There is the same unity in connection and gradation of characters and circumstances to be found in the Prometheus of Æschylus.

Vulcan, Force and Strength, Mercury, Ocean, and the Nymphs are but contingents to the adamantine spirit of Prometheus, whom the threats of Jupiter could not move, nor convulsions of the universe terrify: the interest is in him, to which the ministering violence, admonition, consolation or tenderness of the inferior characters, give subordinate relation.

The principles of composition require that the story should be a perfect whole, and that one character should be supreme, to which all the inferior ones should have some relation by connection or separation. The individual variety of character is equally in the order of nature.

Aristotle and Horace, in their " Art of Poetry," (besides the above mentioned,) propose various rules, which equally govern the poet, painter, and sculptor; and that no doubt may be entertained concerning the practice of the ancient artists, Horace tells us that " the poet and painter are regulated by the same principles."

For the sake of clearness, the rules of composition shall be given under distinct heads :—

First, a poet speaks by words.

The painter and sculptor by action.

Action singly, or in series:—the subject of composition being comprised in the arts of design, thus the story of Laocoon is told by the agony of the father and sons, inextricably wound about in the folds of serpents.

The anger of Achilles is shewn by drawing his sword on Agamemnon in the council of the kings. And every action is more perfect as it comprehends an indication of the past, with a certainty of the end, in the moment chosen.

Ananias, falling in the contractions of death at the feet of St. Peter, proves a divine authority in the apostle's rebuke, whilst Sapphira, counting the silver, leads to the nature of his offence. See Raffaelle's Cartoon.

In the group of Hæmon and Antigone, he supports the expiring woman, whilst he kills himself with the same sword which slew her, shewing his death to be a consequence of hers.

Expression distinguishes the species of action in the whole and in all the parts; in the faces, figures, limbs, and extremities. Whether the story be heroic grave, or tender, it is the very soul of composition—it animates its characters and gradations, as the human soul doth the body and limbs—it engages the attention, and excites an interest which compensates for a multitude of defects—whilst the most admirable execution, without a just and lively expression, will be disregarded as laborious inanity, or contemned as an illusory endeavour to impose on the feelings and the understanding.

The general forms of masses in composition have been enumerated and ably described by the professor of painting; but as these particularly concern the sculptor, whose whole study is form, a repetition will not be useless.

The forms are the pyramid erect, inverted, or lateral, the circle and the oval; they may be radiated, and the whole will have a flame-like undulation in effect, from the ever-varying succession of curves in the outline and action of the human figure.

The parts will be more simple and rectilinear in repose, more angular in violent action,* and partaking of gentle curves when the subject is tender, and the person elegant: when the limbs are entwined as struggling, or in any sympathetic act either of force or tenderness, the joints, the general curves and views of the limbs, should never be exactly and mechanically the same, but partake of the wonderful variety of nature, in which all faces, all bodies, and all efforts are different. This gives life and motion.

What has been said above is equally applicable to the group or basso-relievo, but the application must be accommodated to the subject.

The entire group is independent of back-ground, and that additional contrast or effect produced by

* Athenian and Amazon.

the adjunction of secondary figures and objects it is one whole, whose idea is perfect, and action satisfactory in itself; it is to be seen in every view, and each view must exhibit a different group, preserving a succession of beautiful forms and distinct lines, without impairing the energy of sentiment.

The basso-relievo may be considered in effect as a picture without colouring, whose back-ground is light, a little subdued, the figures thereon being chiefly of the middle tint, with touches of strong dark in the depths, and bright lights on the higher projections. This species of sculpture is not intended to be seen in many views like the entire group; but it has this advantage, that more groups than one may be on the same back-ground, and sometimes a succession of events in the same story; a greater force is given to harmony, or contrast of lines, by the number of groups and figures, as well as the projection of their shadows.

The ancients, who considered simplicity as a characteristic of perfection, represented stories by a single row of figures in the bas-relief, by which the whole outline of the figure or group, the energy of action, the concatenation of limbs, the flight or flow of drapery were seen with little interruption; but there are instances of the best times in low relievo, where many horsemen are advancing before each other, the nearer horse hiding the hinder parts of the preceding, and sometimes part of the rider, without causing the least confusion of effect, as in the frieze from the Temple of Minerva in Lord Elgin's collection.

There are noble examples, also, of groups and figures rushing in the same reiterated line through the composition; but even in basso-relievo, it must be remembered, the work is sculpture, which allows no picturesque addition or effect of back-ground; the story must be told, and the field occupied by the figure and acts of man.

All art, as the imitation of nature, must be allied by the same relations, and submit to the same laws which govern nature itself: thus, a certain view of the human figure is most fit to express its spring and motion in running or striking, and consequently the quantity of the figure seen in that view; another quantity will more properly belong to a different exertion or repose.

The story may require that the upper part of one figure should be principal, whilst, perhaps, the lower parts are concealed by an intervening object; some figures may be running in different directions, more crowded, or separate. To regulate these spaces and quantities harmoniously, concerns the sculptor in his composition, equally with the poet or musician in theirs. This is to be done by the same means, according to different modes of manifestation; and the 3rds, 5ths, and 8ths, with their subdivisions taken by gross calculation in the arts of design, not exact measurement, will produce the same agreeable effect in lines, light and shadow, space and the arrangements of colours, as is produced by similar quantities in music.

One simple instance only shall be given of opposition, and another of harmony, in lines and quantities :* two equal curves, set with either their convex or concave faces to each other, produce opposition; but unite two curves of different size and segment, they will produce that harmonious line, termed graceful, in the human figure.

Concerning the quantity of light and shadow in a group, if the light be one-third, and shadow two-thirds, the effect will be bold. If the light be one part, and the shade four, it will be still bolder, and accord with a tragic or terrific action; but the more general effect of sculpture is two-thirds of light on the middle of the group, with a small proportion of very dark shadow in the deeper hollows.

An attention to the materials of sculpture will naturally lead us to the description of its legitimate subjects. The grey solemn tints of stone, the beautiful semi-transparent purity of marble, the golden splendour, or corroding darkened green of bronze, reject as incongruous all subjects and characters which have not some dignity or elevation.

The awful simplicity of those forms whose eyes have neither colour nor brilliancy, and whose limbs have not the glow of circulation, strikes the first

* Opposition and harmony of lines.
    Opposition) (( )
    Harmony ∫. ½.

view of the beholder as beings of a different order
from himself.

Angels, spiritual ministers, embodied virtues,
departed worthies, the patriot or general benefactor,
shining in the splendour of his deeds, or gloomy and
consuming memorials of the great in former ages —
such subjects distinguish temples, churches, palaces,
courts of justice, and the open squares of cities. At
the same time that they symbolize their several
purposes, they may be comprehended in the three
classes of sublime, heroic, and tender.

The sublime represents all supernatural acts and
appearances, such as assemblies of the gods, or falls
of the giants, &c. In the higher class of Christian
subjects are the different acts of Creation, the
Angels appearing to the Shepherds, the Transfiguration, the Ascension, and the Judgment.

In this class can be nothing common in idea,
person, or action; the idea, whether simple or com-
plex, must be such as cannot be seen in nature; the
beauty and dignity of the persons should be more
than human, and the action, whether forcible or
pathetic, should be action in its essence.

Of the heroic class of compositions, we may account
the battles of the Athenians and Amazons, and of
the Athenians and Persians, in the Temples of Minerva and Theseus in Athens, and the Temple of
Apollo at Phigalia, with such subjects as the story
of Orestes, and the death of Ægisthus, in the ancient
basso-relievos.

Of the tender, or pathetic, are the Death of
Meleager, Antiope comforted by Zethus and Amphion ; to which may be added, such Christian
subjects as Michael Angelo's Holy Family and
Charity : for although these last two are paintings,
their compositions are so perfectly sculptural, that
they may, without impropriety, be admitted into the
present arrangement.

Another class of subjects may be observed among
the ancient basso-relievos, which may be termed the
graceful, from the prevalence of elegant female
figures in the pageants of marine divinities, or in the
festive choruses.

The characteristics of Grecian composition, in the
best ages, are simplicity and distinctness, in all the
examples of painting and sculpture which have come
down to us.* Where the story does not require
much action, it is told by gentle movements, and the
figures, whether grouped or single, have a sufficient
portion of plain back-ground left about them to
shew the general lines with the forms of the limbs
and draperies perfectly intelligible.

Where complication and force of action may be
required, it is done with a grace of concatenation
which adds continuity to the act, without causing
it to be less distinct. And in such as are all agitation
and violence, the force of striking, the rush of flight,
the agony of dying, and the prostration of the dead,
in which union of action is enforced by repetition,

* Hesperides

and difference of situation by contrast,—still the
same distinctness is preserved.*

In the great compositions of modern times, the
Last Judgment of Michael Angelo, and the Fall of
the Angels, by Rubens, there are multitudes and
legions in comparison with the separate figures and
single groups in the most considerable of the ancient
works. The beholder is thunderstruck by angels
falling in groups and forked masses, amalgamating
in the vivid flashes, and darkening in the sulphurous
smoke, in the various dismay, horror, terror, and
torpor of deadened intellect in their lost condition.
In this picture the undulation of groups, the play of
lines, the entwining of limbs, and the breadth and
quantities of light and shade, may be studied by the
painter and sculptor with equal advantage.

The Last Judgment, by Michael Angelo, is, however, a more consummate work, and the parent from
which Rubens's Fall of the Angels has derived its
being.

If the Judgment is inferior to the Falling Angels
in general effect—in the breadth of light and shade
—the strength of approaching parts—the gradual
distance of those which retreat, by diffusion of
middle tint and the vivid variegations of reflex, it is
superior in the sublimity and extent of character
and action — in the gradations of sentiment and
passion, from exalted beatitude to the abyss of hopeless destruction—in the kinds and species of these

* Phigalia, in the Royal Academy.

degrees—in relations to the theological and cardinal
virtues, opposed to the seven deadly sins—in force
of conception—in uncommon, original, distinct, and
fit appropriation in the groups or separate figures.
The sentiment of particular figures and groups is in
the whole, and all the parts penetrating, sympathetic, and true.

Despair plunges headlong downwards; the fall of
the contentious is aided by strife and blows; the
malignant, drawn downwards by the fiends, is tor-
mented in his way by the biting serpent; for some
there is a terrific contest between angels and in-
fernals.*

Among the happy, brotherly love is evident in
three figures which shoot upwards together, whose
faces, seen a little beyond each other, appear to be
reflections of the same self; several rise to the
heavenly region by the attractions of purity, piety,
and charity.

In this stupendous work, in addition to the genius
of the mighty master, the mechanical powers and
movements of the figure, its anatomical energy and
forms, are shewn by such perspective of the most
difficult positions, as surpass any examples left by
the ancients on a flat surface or low relief, and are
only to be equalled in kind, but not in the proportion of application, in the front and diagonal views
of the Laocoon, and all the views of the Boxers,
which are both entire groups.

* See Plate XXXVII.

By such observations on these works, so far as composition and design are common to the sister arts, the sculptor perceives the scope and power of his own art.

It is true, that sublime and extensive works are seldom required in the slow and difficult process of sculpture; but he who loves the honourable exercise of his art, and the intellectual delight of worthy exertion, will endeavour to prepare himself for all difficulties: besides, the combinations and particular groups will be more or less concerned in the studies of every day; and as the electric fluid pervades all matter, so the same spirit and principles which inform these works, penetrate the whole study of the human figure.

The lines of Grecian composition enchant the beholder by their harmony and perfection; and this portion of study seems to have been highly improved by Pamphilus, the learned Macedonian painter, who denied that any one could succeed in the study of painting without arithmetic and geometry. The application of these two sciences is very evident in the arts of design: by arithmetic, the proportions of the human figure and other animals are reckoned, and the quantities of bodies, superficies, or light and shade ascertained; geometry gives lines and diagrams for the motion, outline, and drapery of the figure, regulated by the harmony of agreeable proportions, or the opposition of contrast. The effect is evident in the groups of Laocoon and the Boxers, the bas-relief of the Niobe family, and that of the rape of Proserpine ; but this magic bond of arrangement was utterly lost when the other perfections of Grecian genius were overwhelmed in barbarism, nor in any degree recovered until late in the resurrection of the arts, and then they were reproduced by the same means which had discovered them.

The study of geometry became more general, and had been applied with more success to the improvement of science and art, after the learned Greeks, who fled from Constantinople, settled in Italy.

Leonardo da Vinci and Michael Angelo were greedy partakers in this abundant harvest of knowledge. Michael Angelo* shewed his sensibility to the play of lines in his picture of the Holy Family, in which the Virgin, sitting on the ground, receives the infant Jesus, whom Joseph, stooping behind, presents over her right shoulder.

Leonardo da Vinci, who had devoted much time to mechanical and geometrical studies, composed the Contest for the Standard, intended to be painted in the great hall of the old palace of Florence. This was indeed a prodigy in modern advancement, and the first great example of complicated grouping since the arts flourished in ancient Greece.

Michael Angelo's mind seems at this time to have been employed on the powers, forms, and views of the human figure singly ; and perhaps the admirable groups in the ceiling, and the Last Judgment, of the

* See Plate XXXVIII

Sistine Chapel, were the consequence of Leonardo da Vinci's example. We are sure the several hunts of the lions, hippopotamus, and crocodile, were painted by Rubens in emulation, if not imitation, of Leonardo's Battle of the Standard; and such is their merit, that in them you see the men strike, the horses kick, the wild animals roaring, turn and rend their hunters, with a grandeur of lines equal to the vivacity of action and passion. In comparing these with similar subjects in ancient basso-relievos, particularly with those on the arch of Constantine, in which Trajan hunts the lion and boar, modern genius shines with uncommon brilliancy, and Trajan with his followers, and the animals they attack, are tame, insipid, and unnatural.

In comparing ancient and modern compositions, we shall find the excellence of each was derived from the systems and moral habits of the times and countries. The Greeks admired, encouraged, and cultivated personal beauty by gymnastic exercises and public rewards in the Olympian meeting of the states; consequently, what they admired they represented. The most choice selection of countenance and form, the most elegant display in the folds of drapery, were seen in their councils of divinities; in combats and heroic adventures, grace, elasticity of action, and personal courage were conspicuous.

The modern arts have been more zealously employed to commemorate the acts and events of that dispensation which governs their conduct, and determines their future condition ; and even in their celebrations and memorials of political occurrences, or private characters, they are always combinations of the moral virtues, or the influences of providential direction. What has been done, and what may be done from such subjects, is proved by Michael Angelo's Old Testament,* and Judgment, in the Sistine Chapel—the Calling of S. Paul, and the Martyrdom of S. Peter, in the Pauline Chapel—the Plagues in the last days of the Church, by Signorelli, in the Cathedral of Orvieto—the cartoons of Raphael—the scriptural basso-relievos by John and Nicholas Pisani,† Donatello,‡ and Lorenzo Ghiberti.§ These subjects are more than sufficient to employ the greatest human powers, comprehending whatever is most sublime or beautiful in energy or repose— most tender, most affectionate, most forcible, or most terrific.

An additional distinction between the subjects of ancient and modern composition is occasioned by parental affection, and domestic charities, being cherished in the Christian dispensation much more powerfully than in the Grecian codes : to these graces of benevolence we owe those lovely groups— the Holy Families of Raffaelle and Correggio, and the Charity ‖ of Michael Angelo, unequalled by any ancient composition of a mother and children, and one of the finest groups in existence.

---

* See Plate XXIII. † Adam and Eve. ‡ Entombing.
§ Bronze gates, Giving the Law. ‖ See Plate XXXIV.

In a discourse on the composition of sculpture, some observations may be expected on sepulchral monuments and equestrian statues; but little need be said concerning them at present, because the sculptor capable of producing a fine group, or alto relievo of three or more figures, need only limit the compass of his powers, or submit them to architectural arrangements, and he will execute either one or the other without difficulty. Two or three examples will be sufficient. A monument to Sir Francis Vere, Westminster Abbey*—the Tomb of Madame Langhahn*—and Michael Angelo's design for Julius II.'s monument—a description of it is given in the lecture on English sculpture (page 27). But let him always remember, that the entire group, and the alto- or basso-relievo, are the only legitimate sculpture.

All those monuments of the later Italian school, in which entire figures are mingled with those of low relief on pyramidal back-grounds, are mean attempts to unite the effects and perspective of painting with the force and severity of sculpture, as ineffectual as injudicious, and as they partake in the qualities of both arts, cannot properly be ranked in either.

The sculptor must not forget that his art is limited in comparison with painting; colours and their effects are beyond his bound; whether the act he represents was performed in the bright mid-day sunshine or the darkness of midnight concerns him not,

* See Plates LI. LII.

his forms must be equally perfect, and his expression equally decided. Even basso-relief, a tree or two, some rude stone, a flat column, or a wall, slightly marked in the back-ground, must indicate a forest, a mountain, or a palace, without detailing a portrait of their component parts.

Such are the limits which circumscribe the sculptor; but it is a limitation by which he is in a measure delivered from the restraints of time and space, which strengthen his powers by concentration, and by which he is privileged to disregard inferior objects for the human figure, the most perfect of all forms, with all the gradations of intelligence, affection, sentiment, action, or passion, capable of being expressed in it, individually or in numbers, and in the different orders of being, from the exalted supernatural agent to the lower gradations which terminate in brutal nature.

What has been delivered comprises some of the rules for composing, and observations on composition, the most obvious, and perhaps not the least useful. They have been collected from the best works and the best writings, examined and compared with their principles in nature. Such a comprehensive view may be useful to the younger student, in pointing his way, preventing error, and shewing the needful materials; but, after all, he must perform the work himself. All rules, all critical discourses, can but awaken the intelligence, and stimulate the will, with advice and directions for a beginning of that which is to be done. They may be compared to the scaffolding for raising a magnificent palace; it is neither the building nor the decoration, but it is the workman's indispensable help in erecting the walls which enclose the apartments, and which may afterwards be enriched with the most splendid ornaments.

Every painter and sculptor feels the conviction that a considerable portion of science is requisite to the productions of liberal art; but he will be equally convinced that whatever is produced from principles and rules only, added to the most exquisite manual labour, is no more than a mechanical work. Sentiment is the life and soul of fine art; without it, it is all a dead letter. Sentiment gives a sterling value, an irresistible charm, to the rudest imagery or most unpractised scrawl. By this quality a firm alliance is formed with the affections in all works of art. With an earnest watchfulness for their preservation, we are made to perceive and feel the most sublime and terrific subjects, following the course of sentiment through the current and mazes of intelligence and passion to the most delicate and tender ties and sympathies of affection;—the benign exertions of spiritual natures; the tremendous fall of rebel Angels or Titans; the immoveable fortitude or contending energy of patriotism; the sincerity of friendship, and the irresistible harmony of connubial, maternal, fraternal, and filial love.

Such effects are produced by the communication of

the artist's own choicest feelings and faculties, embodied and enforced by the uninterrupted and constant observation and imitation of whatever is strikingly excellent in nature.

In these discourses on subjects extensive and various in their relations will be found many defects, both of matter and example, and some of these the author is not ashamed to acknowledge may exist beyond the limits of his intelligence to perceive, or his power to correct; yet he cherishes a hope of removing some of the errors, and adding such improvements as his abilities permit, with a desire that the lectures on sculpture may in time become a portion not unworthy of the noble theory and plan of education for the sister arts, as pursued in the Royal Academy.

LECTURE VII.

———

STYLE.

THE introduction to a theory, whether of science or art, practical or abstracted, should contain such a compendious view of the subject as will connect all the branches or members with the principle on which they depend for their essential quality and peculiar characteristic distinction; so that our view of the whole should comprehend the parts of which it is composed, and our inquiries concerning the parts should be guided and regulated by that common prin ciple in which they are all united.

This universal and indispensable maxim, applied to a course of lectures on sculpture, will naturally lead us to some well-known quality which originates in the birth of the art itself—increases in its growth —strengthens in its vigour—attains the full measure of beauty in the perfection of its parent cause—and, in its decay, withers and expires. Such a quality will define the stages of its progress, and will mark the degrees of its debasement;—it will point out how, and when, proportions were obtained by measure and calculation—when geometrical figures, more simple or complicated, decided form·· ·how the harmony of lines in composition produce energy by contrast, and sympathy by assimilation. Such a quality immediately determines to our eyes and understanding the barbarous attempt of the ignorant savage—the humble labour of the mere workman—the highest examples of art conducted by science, ennobled by philosophy, and perfected by the zealous and extensive study of nature.

This distinguishing quality is understood by the term style, in the arts of design. This term, at first, was applied to poetry, and the style of Homer and Pindar must have been familiar long before Phidias or Zeuxis were known ; but, in process of time, as the poet wrote with his style or pen, and the designer sketched with his style or pencil, the name of the instrument was familiarly used to express the genius and productions of the writer and the artist ; and this symbolical mode of speaking has continued from the earliest times through the classical ages, the revival of arts and letters, down to the present moment, equally intelligible, and is now strengthened by the uninterrupted use and authority of the ancients and the moderns.

And here we may remark, that as by the term style we designate the several stages of progression, improvement, or decline of the art, so by the same term, and at the same time, we more indirectly refer to the progress of the human mind, and states of society; for such as the habits of the mind are, such will be the works, and such objects as the understanding and the affections dwell most upon, will be most readily executed by the hands. Thus the savage depends on clubs, spears, and axes for safety and defence against his enemies, and on his oars or paddles for the guidance of his canoe through the waters: these, therefore, engage a suitable portion of his attention, and, with incredible labour, he makes them the most convenient possible for his purpose; and, as a certain consequence, because usefulness is a property of beauty, he frequently produces such an elegance of form as to astonish the more civilized and cultivated of his species.* He will even superadd to the elegance of form an additional decoration in relief on the surface of the instrument, a wave-line, a zig-zag, or the tie of a band, imitating such simple objects as his wants and occupations render familiar to his observation—such as the first twilight of science in his mind enables him to comprehend. Thus far his endeavours are crowned with a certain portion of success; but if he extend his attempts to the human form, or the attributes of divinity, his rude conceptions and untaught mind produce only images of lifeless deformity, or of horror and disgust.

When we consider these weak and inefficient attempts for a moment, with what astonishment shall we turn to the almost breathing statue, whose mimic

* New Zealand canoe.

flesh seems yielding to the touch! whose balance
alarms with the expectation of movement! whose
countenance beams with the sweetest charities of
humanity! or, like the Jove of Phidias (if it were
possible), adds to the interest of religion. In these
opposite descriptions we contemplate the productions
of man just emerging from gross and savage nature,
and civilized man, formed to moral habits, intellectual enjoyments, and delighting to trace the Creator
in his works.

Such is the difference between the beginning and
the perfection of art. To mark this progress and its
gradations is the object of our present inquiry : nor
will our time be unprofitably employed; for if, by
the characteristics of style, we can secure landmarks
on the road to excellence, we may avoid the danger
of deviating into the paths of error.

The characters of style may be properly arranged
under two heads—the natural and the ideal.

The natural style may be defined thus : a representation of the human form, according to the distinctions of sex and age, in action or repose, expressing
the affections of the soul.

The same words may be used to define the ideal
style, but they must be followed by this addition—
" selected from such perfect examples as may excite
in our minds a conception of the supernatural."

By these definitions will be understood, that the
natural style is peculiar to humanity, and the ideal
to spirituality and divinity.

In our pursuit of this subject we are aware of the propensity to imitation common in all, by which our knowledge of surrounding objects is increased, and our intellectual faculties are elevated; and we consequently find in most countries attempts to copy the human figure, in early times, equally barbarous, whether they were the production of India, Babylon, Germany, Mexico, or Otaheite. They equally partake in the common deformities of great heads, monstrous faces, diminutive and mis-shapen bodies and limbs. We shall, however, say no more of these abortions, as they really have no nearer connection with style than the child's first attempts to write the alphabet, can claim with the poet's inspiration or the argument and description of the orator.

We shall now proceed to mark the character, and trace the progress of style, not from the earliest dawn, but rather from the sunrise of human intelligence, when the imitative faculty is assisted by rule, and corrected by reflection—when the representation partakes, in some degree, of man's dignity in countenance and figure. In this state we find painting and sculpture among the Egyptians, whose application to geometry, and inquiries concerning the animal structure, enabled them to give a general, though imperfect, proportion and outline to their figures, whose forms, however, were more determined by simple geometrical lines, than a scrupulous attention to nature.

Professions in Egypt (as before observed) being

hereditary, the son was obliged to follow his father's occupation, and as the same particular talent could not be expected through a series of generations, the painting or sculpture would have little concern with genius or study; their productions would be determined by the family recipe, and the works must be mechanical labour, not liberal art.

The proportions of Egyptian figures are about seven heads in height—in slighter works of painting and relievo frequently more, the breadth of the figure agreeing with the height. The face is generally youthful, even when a beard, in the form of a peg, is added to the chin—we may suppose intended to signify advancement in years. The nose, eyes, eyebrows, mouth, and extended line of the cheeks, are formed of simpler curves than are usually seen in nature. The countenances greatly resemble each other, and the expression is placid, with a mixture of cunning. The shoulders are high and forward; the body marked only by the projection of the breast and abdomen, being narrow above the hips. The arms are rounded, gradually tapering from the shoulder downwards to the elbow; bend of the arm and wrists without any resemblance to form of bone and tendon in those joints. The thighs and legs formed by a general rounded resemblance to nature, but equally deficient with the arms as to ignorance of and incorrectness in the joints. The calf of the leg, and the form of the tibia in the front view, as well as the hands and feet, are careless and un decided. The fingers and toes are rounded, parallel to each other, straight, and without distinction of joints.

The attitudes of Egyptian statues have little variety; if standing, one leg is a little advanced, the arms hang down close to the sides; sometimes one arm is laid across the breast. Figures sitting on seats have the legs and thighs forming right angles in the side view, and in front the legs are parallel to each other. Sometimes the figure sits on the ground, with the legs drawn near the body in parallel lines; sometimes the figure is kneeling.

In the historical or allegorical bas-relievos of the Egyptians, their subjects are composed in the most evident and common manner, certainly without artifice or system, on the one hand, as, on the other, they are devoid of elegance or choice.

The drapery of the Egyptian statues is close, and seldom interrupted by folds.

The Egyptian animals are superior works of art to their human statues; and a reason for this is, that inferior animals are more easily represented.

The style of Egyptian sculpture is simplicity in the extreme, and the magnitude of their colossal works is awful; but the simplicity is so excessive, that one face, and one set of forms, have extended an universal monotony of resemblance, as far as possible, through the differences of age and sex. The surface of the body and limbs betrays great ignorance in the knowledge of the bones, muscles, and tendons, which produce the forms in the surface; and although this people have been celebrated for their skill in geometry, their basso-relievos and painted compositions demonstrate that they had not advanced sufficiently to determine the balance and motion of the human figure by the rules of that science.

The Egyptian sculptors astonish us by their indefatigable labour, but, considered as artists, they are but beginners; their works little more than bodies without souls, the dead letter of the art, whose purpose was, symbolically, to deliver an historical fact, a philosophical precept, or a divine mystery; but never to charm by life, sentiment, heroic power, or spiritual beauty.

The Hindu sculpture has been thought to resemble the Egyptian; but the latter nation has given greater beauty to the countenance, with a better proportion to the figure, although some smaller Hindu works of bronze and ivory have the detail of parts finished with great delicacy; and the events of Hindu mythology have furnished various extraordinary and poetical compositions,* more singular and elegant than have been hitherto seen in the published antiquities of Egypt.

The arts of design in China have been also supposed to bear some resemblance to those of Egypt; but the architecture is wholly different in character and principle. The sculpture of the two nations seems

* Vishnu's Elephant, Horse, and Goose. From Moore's Hindu Pantheon.

to have little in common; and whatever painting they practised in ancient times might be native, or foreign, received from India or Greece, but, for centuries past, we know too much of their intercourse with Europe not to be sure that their best works have been matured by foreign instruction.

Having incidentally mentioned the arts of these two countries in relation to those of Egypt, we will proceed in our inquiries concerning style, by an examination of early works in Greece.

Fortunately for us, we have a mass of undoubted evidence existing, so extensive in its nature, and yet so perfect in coincidence, as will excite surprise when we consider the succeeding tides of destruction it has escaped, and the long series of ages it has endured.

Homer and Hesiod have introduced us to so accurate a knowledge of the military, rural, and domestic habits of the heroic ages, and have distinguished the persons with such peculiar character and life, that we seem to ourselves acquainted and intimate with the kings, warriors, judges, elders, husbandmen, and shepherds; we are present in their councils, their encounters for fame and victory; we partake in the culture of their fields, and the abundance of their harvests, and the still, clear evening: with them we watch the sky, the Hyades, the Pleiades, Orion's strength, the Bear, and all the glittering stars which crown the heavens!

We are now familiar with the plans and military

architecture of Mycenæ,* Argos, and Tiryns, Cyclo-
pean works, the dominion and residence of Agamemnon
and his ancestors, as published by Sir William Gell,
but previously discovered and drawn by M. Fauvel,
the French consul in Athens.

Another source of information concerning Greek
style and design will be found in the painted vases,
and early coins of the country :† the numerous collections of vases published by Sir William Hamilton,
Tischbein, Millin, Millingen, &c. form an endless
treasure to the artist and the antiquary, supplying
every species of example and illustration.

Coincident and satisfactory information concerning
early Greece expands in proportion with the progress
of that people towards the high rank they occupied
among the nations of antiquity. Their theologians,
philosophers, poets, statesmen, mathematicians, anatomists, and artists, have left unerring guides in their
writings and monuments, for us to trace the steps by
which they reached excellence, and by that means to
determine the different styles and characters of their
works.

We may in this place repeat a popular observation,
that the institutions and climate of Greece were
equally favourable to personal beauty, and consequently to the study of painting and sculpture; for
as the genial sunshine and mild breezes rendered
only light clothing requisite, and in some cases
rejected the incumbrance wholly, the body and limbs

* See Plate XIV. † Macedonia or Thrace.

being commonly seen, naturally led to the contemplation of form in the human figure, and comparison of beauty in the parts between one subject and another.

The Pentathlon, or five Olympic games, of wrestling, boxing, throwing the quoit, running, and riding one or more horses at full speed, engaged all the noble youth of Greece in the honourable contest, and improved the powers of the body and limbs by the force of exertion, and added grace to beauty by facility of motion. Of what importance this power and beauty of person, accompanied by such dexterity and agility, was to the possessor we are informed by the consequences : a conqueror in one of the games was honoured as if he returned from the conquest of foreign enemies—crowned with olive—drawn to the city in a chariot by four horses—and a breach was made in the wall for his entrance; his statue was erected in the sacred wood, and the most celebrated poet sang his praises. He that obtained the prize three times, was complimented with a statue, the portrait of his face, and the particular lineaments of his figure. Among the celebrations of this kind were verses which hail the conqueror by name, with the epithet of Καλὸς, the Beautiful; and, indeed, the sublimest of their philosophers do not fail in their discourses, with a pious reverence, to refer this beauty to a correspondent spiritual beauty in the divine source of all perfection. So much was the beauty of the human form esteemed in Greece, and such the motives from which it was cultivated !

We may observe in this place, that Grecian art began where Egyptian art ended.

The Egyptian statuaries were hereditary laborious mechanics; their works were lifeless forms, menial vehicles of an idea, or the fixed slaves of uniformity in a temple or a palace.

In Greece, painting and sculpture were liberal arts: they were studied by the noblest and best-educated persons; they were improved by the accumulation of science; they were employed to excite and celebrate virtue and excellence; and, finally, to exalt the mind of the beholder to the contemplation of divine qualities and attributes.

Neither our present limits, nor the intention of this Academy, permit us to extend our inquiries beyond a rational theory to regulate the study of design; but strictly within these limits we may observe that in whatever instances the institutions of Greece cultivated and rendered more powerful the virtuous exertions of mind and body, the arts of design also were animated by their beneficial effects, to a degree which surpassed the other nations of antiquity, and have laid a foundation of principles and practice for all succeeding ages.

We shall now endeavour to trace the characters of style which marked the distinct periods of Grecian art.

*The early statues strongly resemble the Egyptian

* Plates XVI. XVII.

in attitude, in form, in want of outline and anatomical distinction ; they have also nearly the same expres-sion of countenance.

The compositions on painted vases immediately succeeding this period offer little variety of subject : —Acts of the heroic ages, the encounter of Theseus and the Minotaur, the duel of Eteocles and Poly-nices,* Hercules strangling the Lion ; to these may be added Bacchanalian dances.

The drawing of the figure, as well as the choice of subjects, indicate the state of society ; the compressed abdomen and spare limbs prove habits of activity in war and in the race ; the Bacchanalian dances shew the introduction of mysteries and pageants in an increasing polytheism, and both seem perfectly con-sistent with the manners of the early inhabitants of fortified cities.

The early arts of Greece were interrupted in their progress by a succession of political commotions and destructive wars, and we scarcely perceive any im-provement in them until the time of the Seven Sages, of Pythagoras and Esop, who were all contemporaries, about 130 years before Phidias. They increased the intellectual light of their country by foreign travel and laborious study, they reformed the laws and morals, improved science and the useful arts of astro-nomy, geometry, numbers, harmony, and medicine, including the animal structure and economy. Their

* Mercury leading Juno, Venus, and Minerva.

philosophy taught a purer system of divinity and providence, and the works of the poets were made known in public libraries.

The benign influence of such advantages was felt in the arts of design, and prepared them for that beauty and perfection with which they were subsequently graced in the times of Pericles, Alexander, and his successors.

The works of the age we are now speaking of embraced a greater variety of subjects, in composition more copious; the Bacchanalian dances were in greater number,—the labours of Hercules, Nessus and Dejanira, processions of the gods, and acts in the Theban war. Pausanias describes the chest of Cypselus, Tyrant of Corinth, covered with a great number of heroic stories in relief.

Although the Grecian sculpture was considerably advanced after the age of the Seven Wise Men, some of the old barbarism still remained. Much of the ancient face and figure continued. In painting and bas-relief the faces were profiles, whatever might be the position of the figure.* The limbs were distorted, because the artist was unacquainted with the structure of the joint, and the lines of its perspective. The breasts, general curves of the ribs on each side of the thorax, the bend of the arms, and a small projection for the knee-pan, were the chief, and almost the only, indications of bone and muscle. That infinite variety of compounded lines, requisite

* Hercules seizing the Tripod from Apollo.

to draw or carve the features of the face, in any even the most common views, were beyond the skill of these times. They, therefore, substituted the easier method of making the eyes, nose, and mouth of nearly simple curves, whose extremities turned upwards in the same direction. Simple geometrical forms were equally employed in the folds of drapery —parallel curves across the body or limbs—perpendicular parallels in falling drapery, and zig-zags, like reversed steps, for the edges of the drapery. Thus in the early efforts of design, geometrical formality supplied the place of the ever-varying forms in nature.

In compositions which required an increased number of figures, two were seldom grouped; and when this was done, the group was frequently awkward, and sometimes impracticable. In the course of this period, however, the figure was better drawn, the parts were more defined; and on a nearer approach to the age of Phidias there were some attempts to distinguish between divinity and mortality.

The early arts above described represented the persons and habits of a race chiefly occupied in the exercises of war and hunting, agriculture and the care of flocks and herds, living in the open air, and defending themselves from their enemies by impregnable fortifications on rocks; their arts consisting in the fabrication of instruments for agriculture and war, the architectural construction of walls and citadels, to which may be added potter's vessels for

domestic use and sacred offices, on which they in
dulged the more intellectual powers, by tracing heroic
traditions and religious processions.

The Doric simplicity in this style of art is imposing from its determined expression, and awful
by an uncommon and barbarous character. The processions consist of uniform repetitions: their actions
are violent, stiff, and angular oppositions; but these
being faithfully transcribed from the grosser appearances of human character, expression, and action,
laid a sure though rude foundation of principles for
the superstructure of excellence afterwards raised on
them by succeeding improvements.

From the age of Pericles to the death of Alexander the Great, Greece was the focus of admiration
to the world. Greece destroyed the Persian power,
the terror of all nations. Nor was the mental
progress of this people less admirable than their
military achievements—their science was extended
and enlarged by the succession of their wise men—
their philosophers taught more distinctly and publicly the doctrine of a Deity, and the subordinate
agencies of His providence throughout the visible
and invisible universe. Their poets harmonized
their minds by numbers, and enriched their imaginations by presenting the range of whatever is sublime
and beautiful in visible nature or mental abstraction.

Such was the spirit of patriotism, that the richest
citizens did not endeavour to exceed others in the

magnificence of their houses or tables, but employed their wealth for the security and defence of their country, and in raising noble public buildings and works for the service of religion, and in honour of public and private virtue.

We shall not be surprised that in a period of such combinations, two works of sculpture were produced, which are numbered among the seven wonders of the world,* the Olympian Jupiter, by Phidias, and the Colossus of Rhodes. These were equal in size to the most enormous Egyptian statues, but they resembled them only in bulk and prodigious height.

The Olympian Jupiter and the Colossus of the Sun, appeared to be animated and intelligent—not with the life and intelligence of man, but of supernatural existence, whose finished beauty and wondrous majesty seemed immortal.

The magnificence of this period † furnished two other works likewise enumerated among the seven wonders,‡ to which the great sculptors added the most admired decorations; but as these works were architectural, we shall return to our subject—the style of sculpture.

Quintilian's "Twelfth Book of Institutions" presents a compendious view of the progressive improvements of style in painting and sculpture in the following passage :—

---

* See Plate **XX.**
† The great Pyramid and the Sphinx of Memphis, &c.
‡ Mausolus.

" The first of those whose works attracted notice, not for the sake of antiquity only, were Polygnotus and Aglaophon, called famous painters, so studious of the simple colour, that they could be considered only as rude beginners, and the first that made essays towards the production of future art, especially compared with Zeuxis and Parrhasius, who followed soon after. The first of these discovered the rules for light and shadow, and the latter is said to have been more accurate in the examination of his lines. For Zeuxis enlarged the body and limbs, following Homer, who was pleased with powerful forms, even in women; but Parrhasius so circumscribed all, that he was called the Legislator, because the figures of the gods and heroes, as delivered by him, were followed by others as if from necessity.

" Painting flourished particularly from the time of Philip to the successors of Alexander, but in divers qualities—by the care of Protogenes—by the rules of Pamphilus and Melanthius—by the facility of Antiphilus—by the imagination of Theon the Samian ; and from the genius and grace with which he was endowed, Apelles was the most excellent.

" Euphranor caused himself to be admired, being among the most distinguished for the best studies, and at the same time a wonderful painter and sculptor.

" There was a like difference in the statues : the more hard, approaching the Tuscan style, were by Callon and Egesius ; the less rigid by Calamis ; the more soft than those already mentioned (that is to say, more resembling flesh) were by Miron. Polycletus excelled the others in diligence and decorum, and although the palm was given to him by many, yet something was to be deducted because he was deficient in gravity; for as he added a grace to the human form beyond the truth, so he seemed not to have fulfilled the authority of the gods; and as he was said to have avoided the more important age, he presumed only to engage in lighter subjects. But the qualities wanting in Polycletus were given to Phidias and Alcamenes.* Phidias is said to have made gods better than men, his works in ivory are unrivalled, even if he had done nothing but the Athenian Minerva or the Olympian Jove in Elis, whose beauty seems to have added something to the received religion, so much the majesty of the work appeared to equal the divinity.

" Lysippus and Praxiteles, they affirm, approached nearest to the truth, for Demetrius is much reprehended as being a greater lover of exact resemblance than beauty."

As this compendious criticism is in perfect agreement with the ancient monuments of art still existing, there can be no doubt that it was composed by Quintilian from the writings of the ancient artists, whose MS. works he must have consulted equally with Pliny the naturalist, and there is sufficient reason also to believe that both these authors con-

* See Plates XIX. XX. and XXI.

sulted Greek artists at that time living and employed in Italy.

Sculpture rose to supreme eminence in the age of Phidias, by the additional attainments of the art, by the greatness of the works, and the sublimity of style. To establish our assertions, a transient view will be sufficient of the more celebrated productions in succession.

The Athenian Minerva, and the Olympian Jupiter by Phidias, both astonishing for greatness, but more so by the awful impression of divinity imposed on their innumerable beholders. In Jupiter, the Homeric divinity was personified with a beauty of majesty, beyond which human intellect did not extend. Minerva, the type of divine wisdom and power, both to the philosopher and common votary, manifested the charms of celestial youth with the expression of severe virtue. These determined the acknowledged apparent forms of these divinities, from which no painter or sculptor afterwards presumed to deviate. The countenances, figures, and attributes of all the other divinities in Homer were soon after decided by Phidias and his successors, whose laws became immutable, and were submitted to with willingness, until the darkness of polytheism was dispersed by the sacred light of the Gospel.

Yet with this pious reflection in our hearts, we cannot avoid pausing to dwell on the exquisite beauty of the ancient sculpture. The choice of the most perfect forms—countenances expressive of the most elevated dispositions of mind and innocence of character—the limbs and bodies, examples of manly grace and strength, or of female elegance—youth and beauty, in all their varieties and combinations in perfection : indeed, we must believe, when we look on those forms, so purified from grossness and imperfection, that if we could see angels and divine natures, they would resemble these.

The improvements of this and the following ages were not confined to determination of character, selection of form, harmony of proportion, or whatever else most perfect may be conceived in the individual divinity or hero ; they were extended through the various branches of association ; and the noble composition of Mycon, a sculptor and painter rather anterior to Phidias, of the fight between the Lapithæ and Centaurs in the Temple of Theseus,* with compositions by Phidias on the shield of Minerva, and on the throne of the Olympian Jupiter, embodied the Homeric theology and heroism, by examples which have generated or afforded principles for the subsequent efforts of painting and sculpture.

This will be the proper place to notice a subject which has caused much discussion, and which has generally been decided against the ancients, although a living author, M. Quatremère de Quincy, has defended the ancients with much learning and ingenuity, in an

* British Museum.

elaborate work. The practice here alluded to is colouring statues, and thus uniting painting and sculpture.

Without regarding the arguments that have been used on either side of this question, let us try the merits ourselves with unprejudiced minds, and decide from the conviction of natural evidence only.

We certainly know that the arts of painting and sculpture are different in their essential properties. Painting exists by colours only, and form is the peculiarity of sculpture; but there is a principle common to both, in which both are united, and without which neither can exist—and this is drawing; and in the union of light, shadow, and colour, sculpture may be seen more advantageously by the chill light of a winter's day, or the warmer tints of a midsummer sun, according to the solemnity or cheerfulness of the subject. These positions will be generally agreed to, but the question before us is, " How far was Phidias successful in adding colours to the sculpture of the Athenian Minerva and the Olympian Jove ?" which examples were followed by succeeding artists.

We have all been struck by the resemblance of figures in coloured wax-work to persons in fits, and therefore such a representation is particularly proper for the similitude of persons in fits, or for the deceased ; but the Olympian Jupiter and Athenian Minerva were intended to represent those who were superior to death and disease. They were believed immortal, and therefore the stillness of these statues having the colouring of life during the time the spectator viewed them, would appear divinity in awful abstraction or repose. Their stupendous size, alone, was supernatural; and the colours of life, in perfect stillness, increased the sublimity of the statue, and the terror of the pious beholder. The effect of the materials which composed these statues has also been questioned. The statues themselves (according to the information of Aristotle, in his book concerning the world) were made of stone, covered with plates of ivory, so fitted together that, at the distance requisite for seeing them, they appeared one mass of ivory, which has much the tint of delicate flesh. The ornaments and garments were enriched with gold, coloured metals, and precious stones.

Gold ornaments on ivory are equally splendid and harmonious, and in such colossal forms must have added a dazzling glory, like electric fluid running over the surface: the figure, character, and splendour must have had the appearance of an immortal vision in the eyes of the votary.

But let us attend to the judgment passed on these works by the ancients: we have already quoted Quintilian, who says, " they appear to have added something to religion, the work was so worthy of the divinity." Plato says, " the eyes of Minerva were of precious stones," and immediately adds, " Phidias was skilful in beauty." Aristotle calls him "the wise sculptor." An opinion prevailed that Jupiter

had revealed himself to Phidias, and the statue was said to have been touched with lightning in approbation of the work. After these testimonies, there seems no doubt remaining of the effect produced by these coloured statues; but the very reasons which prove that colours in sculpture may have the effect of supernatural vision, fits, or death, prove at the same time that such practice is utterly improper for general representation of the human figure: because, as the tints of carnation in nature are consequences of circulation, wherever the colour of flesh is seen without motion, it resembles only death, or suspension of the vital powers.

Let not this application of colours, however, in the instances of the Jupiter and Minerva, be considered as a mere arbitrary decision of choice or taste in the sculptor, to render his work agreeable in the eyes of the beholder. It was produced by a much higher motive. It was the desire of rendering these stupendous forms living and intelligent, to the astonished gaze of the votary, and to confound the sceptical by a flash of conviction, that something of divinity resided in the statues themselves.

The practice of painting sculpture seems to have been common to most countries, particularly in the early and barbarous states of society. But whether we look on the idols of the South Seas, the Etruscan painted sculpture and terra-cotta monuments, or the recumbent coloured statues on tombs of the middle ages, we shall generally find the practice has been employed to enforce superstition, or preserve an exact similitude of the deceased.

These, however, are in themselves perverted purposes. The real ends of painting, sculpture, and all other arts, are to elevate the mind to the contemplation of truth, to give the judgment a rational determination, and to represent such of our fellow-men as have been benefactors to society, not in the deplorable and fallen state of a lifeless and mouldering corpse, but in the full vigour of their faculties when living, or in something correspondent to the state of the good received among the just made perfect.

As the consideration of painted sculpture cannot really be entitled to any place in the progress of style, we will return to our legitimate subject.

The British Museum contains such noble relics of the Temple of Minerva, as enables us to understand the sublime conception of composition which filled the pediment, the heroic contest of the Lapithæ and Centaurs in the Metopes, and the animated men and horses in the Panathenaic procession of the frieze.

It is the peculiar character and praise of Phidias's style, that he represented gods better than men. As this sculptor determined the visible idea of Jupiter, his successors employed a hundred years on the forms of the inferior divinities. This must, therefore, be denominated the sublime era of sculpture.

Numerous were the painters and sculptors of renown, and numerous were their celebrated works between the time of Pericles and Phidias, and the death of Alexander the Great. During this time, the individual characters of the different divinities were not only represented in the supposed period of adult perfection, but also in infancy and youth, with all the varieties of countenance and form becoming their various offices and ministries.

I may instance the different forms in which Bacchus is represented, as an infant when he was delivered by Mercury to the nymphs; as a beautiful youth of almost feminine delicacy, supported by one of the Muses, and leader of the chorus; again, in a more masculine form, as a conqueror, or the giver of poetical inspiration; and lastly, as the venerable and bearded philosopher, in the sacred mysteries, teaching the immortality of the soul, transmigration, with the descent to Hades, or the lower world. Similar variations of character are seen in Apollo, Mercury, and the other deities, male and female.

During this era the Venus of Praxiteles* appeared, the most admired female statue of all antiquity, whose beauty is as perfect as it is elevated, and as innocent as perfect; from which the Medicean Venus seems but a deteriorated variety.

Whoever desires a more detailed account of the works of these ages will be gratified by consulting Pliny, Pausanias, and the published galleries and museums of ancient sculpture and painting.

* See Plate XXII.

In the times we speak of, every possible perfection that rival and accumulated talent could reach was added to the sister arts. In the character of countenance, every gradation from simple beauty to sublime dignity—the same gradation in form, from the most slender and elegant to the most powerful and massive—the attitudes the most choice, the movements the most easy, and the flesh seemingly yielding to the touch. The drapery in form and folds shewed or indicated the body and limbs most advantageously, by playing round the outline in harmony or contrast, or giving additional effect by the projection of strong shades.

The earlier productions of this era were distinguished by a Doric severity of style, which raised the subject above the level of general nature, and beyond its bounds. The geometrical simplicity of form was ideal; the character was decided, and the sentiment was single: of this class is the group of Niobe and her youngest daughter. A less severity of style is in the Apollo Belvidere. The most easy sway of motion, and the most delicate approaches to nature are observable in the statues of Venus, the Cupid, Faun, and Bacchus, of Praxiteles.

Busts and statues (portraits of individual persons) were not generally permitted, until near the time of the death of Socrates; and as this practice, once introduced, became popular and extensive under the successors of Alexander the Great, it was an additional stimulus to the study of the human figure in detail, and thus as the art departed from ideal sublimity, it partook of the peculiarities of nature. It descended to the intelligible, and became a stronger resemblance of the human race.

When Greece became provincial to the Romans, it indeed suffered a political subjection to its conquerors : but in return, the Romans were mental colonists to the Greeks, and received from them philosophy, science, literature, and arts. Grecian genius continued its admirable productions under the Roman emperors. The fine groups of Menelaus and Patroclus, Hæmon and Antigone, Pætus and Arria, Orestes and Electra, the Toro Farnese, or Zethus and Amphion tying Dirce to the bull's horns, and the Laocoon, were between the later years of the Roman republic and the time of the last Cæsars. To these may be added the beautiful examples of composition in basso-relievo, from Homeric mythology and ancient tragedy, among the latest productions of genuine Grecian sculpture. We shall not dwell on the pediments, arches, imperial statues, consular portraits, gems, and coins executed by the ingenious Greek, to swell the impious pride, and gratify the ignorant vanity of his rapacious master in the latter ages of the empire.

Then, sublimity and beauty, the essence of the ancient Grecian works, had, like Justice and Modesty, quitted the earth, and returned to the family of the immortals in heaven, to avoid the horrors of an iron age.

The Roman lust of dominion, avarice, and cruelty, had long provoked the remoter objects of their tyranny, the Goths, Vandals, Pannonians, Dacians, and Scythians, who at last poured the torrent of destruction back on the oppressors, levelling cities and their hosts in one fearful ruin, leaving only desolation and barbarism behind them. The schools of philosophy and literature in Athens ceased; those of Alexandria were destroyed and abandoned. The age of lead succeeded.

Painting and sculpture, under the Goths and Lombards, instead of exalting the intellect by the contemplation of beauty, heroic and divine, burlesqued the human figure by such clumsy and absurd forms, as could scarcely be supposed to be intended for man. Such was the state of art from the seventh to the eleventh century in Europe. The arts, however, were not to be wholly obliterated; for there is that inherent connection between the mind of man and progressive knowledge, that to deprive him entirely of the means of becoming wiser, and exercising his ingenuity, would be to take from him his rationality, and brutalize him at once. Besides, information and true science are given us as the means of rising from the ruins of fallen nature to higher intelligence and greater happiness: the preservation of arts and letters was therefore provided for in a wonderful manner, as appendages to religion, and as handmaids in the dispensation of the Gospel. When Constantine the Great transferred the seat of empire from Rome to Constantinople, the arts had much declined in the former city, although they still preserved a great portion of their vigour in Greece. The emperor employed the arts of painting and sculpture in an abundance of magnificent Christian decorations for his new capital, and the churches he built in it. This was the foundation for a stock of Christian art, which supplied the different countries of Europe after the barbarous inundations from the north had subsided, and assisted in raising the fallen arts of Italy, until the mighty genius of Michael Angelo shone forth in the unrivalled Sistine Chapel, whose interests and terrors, sublimity, beauty, and power of grouping, combined in the comprehension of sacred subjects, excels all we know, as a whole, in ancient or modern art.

LECTURE VIII.

DRAPERY.

AFTER considering the powers, character, and sentiment of the human figure, as expressed in its
forms, we may next proceed to its clothing, more
especially with a view to those plaits and folds whose
lines contrast or vary the lines of the body they
cover—twine round the limbs—hang in downward
curves from one projecting point to another—increase boldness of effect by additional projection—
or vary the undulations of the zig-zag edges, which
is understood by the term Drapery in the art of
design.

Drapery, as a medium through which the human
figure is intelligible, may be compared with speech,
by which ideas and thought are perceived. Dignity
is expressed by simplicity, grandeur, and quantity;
action by exertion and succession; grace by those
gentle and harmonious undulations peculiar to all
the efforts of this quality, and which are inspired
by the most grateful and soothing dispositions of
the soul. This consistency of the original image

with its outward appearance, is proper and decorous, and cannot be violated without inflicting the shock of absurdity and folly; for as the noblest thought would be degraded by low and unbecoming speech, so would the person of a legislator or a prophet by the dress of a buffoon or a bacchanal.

This introduction of our subject is intended to inform the younger student that drapery will form an important branch in his future study; it will add to the character of his figures, and give additional interest to sentiment and situation: it will not bear neglect, or slight, like articles of furniture or background, which, as they are utterly separated from the pathos of sublime composition, can scarcely deserve any share of his attention.

We will begin with an inquiry into the principles upon which the folds of drapery are formed; we will consider the difference of the finer and the heavier draperies—offer some critical observations on the clothing of different countries, as useful or advantageous to the human form—and produce examples to illustrate the discourse.

Drapery, like all other natural bodies, is subject to the laws of gravity and motion, by which it is affected according to its lightness or weight, strength or weakness, the repose or action of the wearer, and the force of wind: it is affected by these causes simply or complexly as it may be acted on by their separate or united force.

The most simple forms of drapery are produced

by the weight of the cloth itself, hanging from the
most projecting points of the figure, in a perpendicular fold : the next originates from two projecting
points of the figure and forms a pointed arch
reversed.* A succession of such folds, broken into
various lengths, and opposed in their diagonal forms,
are among the boldest and most beautiful effects of
drapery. These folds again become more complicated by twisting, and by which they will be partly
suspended from two points, and partly supported by
the body or limbs over which they are drawn. The
varieties produced in the folds, from suspension,
are multiplied and altered according to the portion
of the figure they pass over, and according to the
fineness and thickness of the cloth.

A full cloak, fastened round the neck, tied in
front, and falling without interruption from the
arms, will present nearly plain surfaces in every
view—a little flattened sometimes on the bend of the
back, and distinguished in front by the meeting of
the straight edges.†

The same garment, still fuller in its quality, under
the same circumstances, falls into a number of perpendicular folds. The same cloak,‡ raised by one
arm, will be divided by diagonal folds, inverted in
their arches, opposed in direction, and connected by
joints. The folds of this simplest of garments will
be further varied and complicated, by throwing one

* Plate XLII.   † Phocion—Muse Guestiniane.
‡ St. Philip. Plate XLI.

side of the cloak over the opposite arm, by various positions of the hands, and by every other circumstance of interruption and rest, opposed to the natural weight of the folds.

We will now consider the mechanical structure of the drapery by the simple lines of the folds as their principles.

1st. The perpendicular fold,* hanging from one point.

2nd. The succession of diagonal folds, falling from each other, hanging from two points, and which may be varied to infinity: for example, falling from the two points of the shoulders in the hollow of the back—from the two shoulders over the projection of the breast and abdomen—falling from one shoulder —and from the lower arm, making the principal folds below the elbow—and each of these again varied by every change of position and motion.

3rd. The cascade of diagonal forms produced by the edges when diagonally folded towards the extremity.

These three classes, although exemplified in the cloak, contain the principles of all folds, however produced, in all garments and draperies—modified by twisting—enlarging the direction to more circular forms, by the force of wind—or the succession of waving projections in the lower extremities of a garment, agitated by the motion of the feet in running.

We will now pursue the subject in an inquiry

* See Plates XLII. and XLIII.

concerning the modification of folds, in such garments as are closed, or fitted to the form of the body.

Those garments called tunics by the Romans,
nearly resemble the country or waggoners' frocks
in their form. Some are longer, reaching to the
ankles—some fuller, having an abundance of folds
—others scanty, discovering a more uninterrupted
outline of the figure, with more breadth of light and
shade, and fewer intersections of their own folds.
These have sometimes larger, sometimes smaller
sleeves—sometimes reaching the elbow,* sometimes
the wrist—and sometimes they are without sleeves.
When the tunic is made of thin woollen or calico,
its folds take their rise from the breast, and fall
directly to the feet, and there will be diverted into
different playful forms, as it rests on them, or is
altered by their motion.

If this garment is confined round the smaller
part of the figure by a girdle, the folds will be of the
inverted-arch kind, arising from the shoulders, and,
below the girdle, they will fall in perpendicular
masses of folds over the lower limbs, when the figure
is not in action, or preparing for action.

The sleeves, if full, will begin with folds falling
from the shoulders before and behind; but these
folds will be widened and changed into cross folds
at the bend of the arm, and continue crossing the

---

* Small figures on Aylmer de Valence's Tomb in Westminster
Abbey. Casts from them are in the Sepulchral Chamber of Sir
John Soane's Museum.

lower arm, more or less diagonally, to its termination at the wrist.

The folds become more or less diagonally spiral from the body if the arm is turned outward, and toward the body if the arm is turned inward. The folds on the back of the lower arm owe the upper portion of their direction to union with, or separation from, a projecting knobbed fold at the elbow. The same principles of folding on the arms will govern all coverings, from the fullest and most redundant, to the straitest and most exactly fitted to the limb— and, therefore, will preclude the necessity of saying more on this part of the subject.

Concerning the finer and more transparent draperies used by the ancients, their texture, and consequently their folds, strongly resembled our calico muslin, and are peculiar to the more elegant and delicate female characters of Grecian sculpture*—to the Nymphs, terrestrial, marine, and bacchanalian—Victories, Seasons, or Hours, and celestial female messengers.†

The more transparent of these draperies leave the forms and outline of the person as perfectly intelligible as if no covering were interposed between the eye and the object; and the existence of the veil is only understood by groups of small folds col_lected in the hollows between the body and limbs, or playing in curves and undulations on the bolder

* Herculaneum Tufa. Plate XLIII.
† See Plates XLIV. XLV. XLVI. and XLVII.

parts, adding the magic of diversity to the charm of beauty.

We will next consider the effect of motion upon drapery : such motion is here intended as the garment partakes of, or is propelled from the wearer's movement only.

As soon as a limb is moved from a perpendicular towards a horizontal direction, the drapery hanging on it changes the forms of its folds. The perpendicular folds bend by their weight into a curve, from the impulse of motion, or change from perpendicular to the inverted arch, the strongest portion of the fold depending from the stronger of the two supporters, whether it be that part of the person which is in rest, or that in motion. This is more particularly seen in the cloak or loose outer garment, but the principle is evident in all drapery worn by the human figure : as, for example, the lower portion of a tunic falls in perpendicular folds over the legs in a state of rest, but the instant one leg is advanced beyond the other in walking, the perpendicular folds, falling from the greatest projection in front of the figure, become curved, clinging in the lower extremities to the unmoved leg, until that limb is set forward, when the same change is produced on the other side : and this effect is still more evident in running violently, when the curved folds, at last, become horizontal, at right angles with the limbs.

Motion of the figure affects the whole mass of

drapery about the body; the folds are most interrupted and broken on the side moved in shortest
space, as the curves are most lengthened on the
side moved in a greater extent, and they are twisted
most diagonally where there is the greatest power of
motion.

Upon the legs, the folds change from downright
to long curves, in walking or running, alternately
as one leg or the other is set forward.* The
greater quantity of folds naturally falls in the hollow
spaces, and in quick motion the heavier portion of
folds are left behind the figure by their own weight,
in a diagonal curve, from the point on which they
are supported.

We will now consider a cause of motion in drapery
entirely independent of the figure by which it is
worn : this is wind, whose effects are more seen
in those parts of the garment extended beyond the
outline of the figure ; and to obtain the more
accurate idea of the manner in which it acts on
drapery, we should observe its effects on flexible and
fluent bodies in general.

The wind blowing on water, by pressure on a
small portion of the fluid nearest, forces it into a
wave, from resistance of a body of water, not affected
by the wind, on the other side of it : or thus, the
wind blowing obliquely on water, is resisted by
the mass beneath, until the surface is raised into a
wave, which, bending over the wave before it, falls

* Plate XLIV.

by the laws of gravitation into the surface again.*
There is a propensity to the same forms and
successions in clouds of the sky, and dust of the
ground driven before the wind; and from the same
causes.

The pendant, or streamer, hanging from the top
of a mast, is driven by the wind in the same direction,† and may be represented by the same section
as a succession of waves on the water.

Progressive movement of the figure changes the
perpendicular of falling folds into undulations. This
is more evident as the motion is quicker: but the
wind undulates all draperies; when moderate, the
undulation is diagonal, and when violent, it is
horizontal.‡

Effect of violent wind on cloaks.§

In the Gem of Callirrhoe‖ the drapery is shaken
and agitated to the utmost with the agonizing whirl
of the wearer.

A statue of Iris¶ descending from Ida to Olympus;
the flow of drapery filled like a sail, while the breeze
sports in the successive waving of its edges.

Examples might be easily produced far exceeding
our present purpose, which is to lay down the principles of study, not to circumvent the composer, or
tempt the unwary, by daring and far-sought exam-

---

* Plate XLII.　　　† Plate XLII.

‡ Example. Undulating downward folds, horizontal above in
profile. Sketch of Bacchanal, Plate XLIV.; undulations above
the feet.

§ Plate XLIV.　　　‖ Plate XLV.　　　¶ Plate XLVI.

ples, into a devious attachment to the preposterous and incredible. Simplicity, beauty, dignity, affection, and passion, employ the general contemplations and efforts of the sister arts with most success. We must remember, as in the Bacchic processions of antiquity, " Many carry the thyrsus, but few are inspired by the gods."

If any one, however, determines to go beyond his competitors in the extraordinary, the wonderful, or the sublime, let him first be assured he possesses powers equal to the undertaking, or the certain consequences will only be vapour and extravagance.

These Lectures have continually referred to examples of Grecian painting and sculpture for illustration, as to the most perfect productions of imitative art, and have never engaged in classical inquiry or criticism further than was absolutely requisite to understand our subject as painters and sculptors: the reason for which is plain—our studies and our employments are directed to the form and sentiment of the human figure; for this reason, therefore, we shall at present leave all inquiry concerning the names and forms of particular ancient garments to Montfaucon, Winckelman, the Notes on the Herculaneum Museum, and other professed writers of antiquity; whilst we notice only such garments as exhibit the human figure most advantageously— give dignity to its character—enrich its particular forms by flowing lines—or harmonize in its sentiment and actions.

Of all garments, the cloak is the simplest, being only a large square cloth laid on the person, or thrown round the figure, according to the wearer's convenience. It belongs to the most grave and dignified characters, philosophers, prophets, and apostles. Its simple form is well suited to such as give small attention to worldly objects, and whose thoughts are wholly engrossed by the cultivation of virtue and truth. The boldness of its folds adds an imposing grandeur to the venerable wearer; they agree with the profound research of the philosopher, or the irresistible mission of the evangelist or prophet. Of this class is the Greek pallium, worn by philosophers: the women also had a garment of this kind, made of a lighter cloth.

The military cloak of the Greeks and Romans was fastened with a button on the right shoulder; it reached little below the knees, and was not so full as the pallium.

The tunic of the Romans was called *chiton* by the Greeks: its form (as before observed) was like a waggoner's frock, and reached the ankles; but when the wearer prepared for labour, or a journey, he tied on his girdle, drew the upper part of his tunic over it, shortening it to the knee, and thus allowed free motion to the legs.

The tunic of the female reached the feet,* whether girded or not, the material of which it was made being more delicate than that worn by men. It

* See Plate XLIII.

produced a display of folds diagonally arched downward below the throat, and a variety of flowing forms, of varied directions above the zone, according to the quantity of material, the bend of the body or the manner of adjusting the vestment. A prodigious and beautiful variety in this part of the drapery may be seen on the painted vases.

Sometimes we find small garments laid over the tunic, not reaching to the zone, in female figures, which add folds of a different direction to those in the tunic. Sometimes the tunic is doubled over at the top, and open at the side.* This, however, is not simply a tunic; it was called *diplos* by the Greeks, or a doubled tunic.

The peplos, or veil,† was an outward female garment, like the cloak or pallium, but of a finer texture, worn by Homer's female divinities and heroines, and frequently seen on the statues. It is this garment, of a transparent material, in which the nymphs are clothed, as before observed.

This brief enumeration contains all those garments which afford the most beautiful specimens in ancient art. We will conclude with such general observations on clothing as seem most conducive to the painter's and sculptor's views and researches.

Clothing, like other conveniences and requisites, must be accommodated to the local situation and habits of man. In hot climates little clothing is required, and in cold countries the warmest skins

* See Plates XLV. XLVI. † Plate XLVII.

and furs of animals are scarcely sufficient to enliven the body with a genial warmth.

In the more barbarous states of society, plumes, necklaces, and bracelets of bone and teeth, are displayed by chiefs and leaders in the pride of distinction. Their war dresses and cloaks are formed of such stubborn materials, as serve the double purpose of covering and of defensive armour.

As regular habits of industry succeed, the short tunic is adopted as a dress convenient for the labours of agriculture and manufacture. The cloak or pallium, in this state of society, becomes a habit of dignity to the priest* or magistrate, which will be found generally prevalent, except in those warm countries like India and Egypt, where a narrow shawl or handkerchief supplies its place; and in the colder regions, pantaloons, sometimes made of skins, were worn on the lower limbs. This system of clothing seems to have been nearly universal before the Roman empire, and continued with little alteration for twelve or thirteen centuries afterwards, if we except the vagaries of fashion in Rome, Constantinople, and a few other metropolitan cities. In Rome, fashion was indeed active among the ladies very early; for a short passage in one of the comedies of Plautus "complains that a fashion does not last a year," and enumerates about twenty-three articles of female attire, all of which might perhaps be comprehended under the heads of cloaks, hand-

* See Plate XL.

kerchiefs, and gowns: but their names and etymo-
logies have puzzled the commentators beyond the
possibility of explanation. But notwithstanding an
occasional instance of this kind occurs in courts and
vortexes of dissipation in the eighth century, the
western provinces universally wore the Roman military cloak, and the eastern provinces generally the
pallium and tunic.*

Charlemagne and his successors, down to St. Louis,
are represented in the same dress in all the mosaics,
monumental statues, and illuminations of those
times.

The first deluge of various fashions came into
Europe with the Crusaders: the princes of the
West seem to have vied with each other in motley
importations from Constantinople, Antioch, and
Damascus.

In France and England before this time, the only
covering for the head, worn by men, was a cap like
that of Paris, and that of the Italian sailors; but
after the Crusades, turbans, hats, and hoods of
different patterns became general.

The cloak and tunic were cut into different forms,
and ornamented with different baubles of tassels,
scallops, and toys, until no trace remained of the
original garments. To sum up the childish passion
for novel absurdity, the common playing cards represent the court dresses of France and England,
between the reigns of our Edward IV., Henry VIII.,

* See Plate IV.

and Elizabeth. The kings, queens, and knaves, have actually the state dresses of sovereigns and courtiers at that time.

Perhaps this part of our subject may now be supposed to have attained its climax, and that every purpose of extravagance and absurdity was answered, when the courtier's taste for elegance was exemplified by a waistcoat half black and half yellow, a red stocking on one leg, and a green one on the other;—when a great prince's hall of audience was filled with the figures of mountebanks, harlequins, and playhouse imps: but the tale is not yet told, nor is the measure full. To what was monstrous and disgusting to look on, was added, studied inconvenience. Ruffs so large the head could scarcely turn in them, the middle of the figure rendered so bulky as to be contained by no arm-chair, and the waistcoats so stiff, pointed, and narrow, that they must have impeded digestion, and restrained the functions of life.

Shall we not be induced to inquire, to what causes could be attributed such an accumulation of absurdities? we may perhaps account for them in the spirit of the times,—the wars, and their military distinctions—the alternate dissipations, and particularly masquerades — and above all, those military and party dissensions — those extensive and violent theological and political contests, which ferment the general mass beyond the control of reason, humanity, and common sense.

These instances of useless variety and absurdity
in dress will naturally lead to the reflection that
there is a reasonable propriety in dress, as in all
other concerns, and that this propriety will be
governed by climate and character; light draperies
being agreeable in summer, warmer and thicker in
winter ; graceful and gay attire becomes the
youthful, more grave is proper for the aged. The
magistrate bears such distinctions as denote his rank
and dignity in society. But in these and all other
cases, the drapery will be more becoming and
expressive, as it harmonizes with the proportions,
sympathizes with the character, and is consistent
with the requisites of the wearer. Any offences
against these rules will naturally produce dis-
satisfaction and contempt; for mere dress cannot
make the old young, the ugly handsome, or the
mean dignified.

The only difference must be confined to a transient
glance, for real qualities are inherent in the man,
and depend not upon outward accidents.

We may conceive the effect of dress and appearance, on the judicious spectator's mind, from a
comparison of the following characters.

The lower Emperors of the East retained their
inordinate love of magnificence after their power was
broken ; and their state dress was apparently covered
with jewels, even when their poverty obliged them
to eke out the splendid mass with false pearls and
paste : these were attached to a scanty, ungraceful

мantle, which, being closed round the figure, presented the insipid resemblance of an Egyptian
mummy incrusted with gems. How different from
the prophets of Michael Angelo, the apostles of
Raffaelle and Albert Durer,* or those of Henry the
Seventh's Chapel!† *Their* countenances are determined by their divine commission; and the patriarchal simplicity and grandeur of their persons bear
testimony to their sacred character.

Michael Angelo's Patriarch sleeps!—but when he
wakes, we are assured he will declare a prophecy or
holy vision, received from his attendant angel.

* Plate XLI.   † See Plates VII. VIII.

LECTURE IX.

———+———

ANCIENT ART.

WHEN we look at any portion of the natural land-scape, if the objects are few, a rock, a plain, or a tower, they are understood at once, and without effort; but if they are numerous and complicated, they must be considered attentively, to distinguish woods from mountains, the form and extent of buildings or cities, the winding of rivers, and the expanse of the sea or sky, in order that we may understand the several parts of the view; and it is thus we must conduct our inquiries in art and science: beginning by a search for their natural principles, we must make ourselves acquainted with their relations to. and dependence upon, other branches of knowledge, and we should assure our-selves of their purposes and ends. To render our present inquiries the more effectual, and to obtain all the advantages experience can afford, we must avail ourselves of the studies and practice of the most celebrated artists, in such a compendious view of ancient and modern sculpture as may be expected in the compass of these lectures.

Time would be lost for the purposes of our institution, were we to seek out an accurate history of the early steps by which the march of art was directed in its first and most barbarous efforts. Those who desire information on this subject will be abundantly supplied by Pliny's 'Natural History,' Pausanias's 'Tour of Greece,' and Winckelman's 'History of Art.' But the great object of every student must be, to copy nature most perfectly, and for this purpose to possess himself of unerring rules for the government of his practice. The most likely way to obtain these advantages will not be to consider sculpture by attention to dates and trifling incidents, but rather to divide its history into ages or periods, each characterized by styles of art expressive of its advancement.

The arts of design have their origin in the disposition to imitate, which guides us in our earliest attainments, and assists us in the most perfect of our finished works. The attempt to imitate the human figure is found in all countries, even the most barbarous, and according to the barbarity of the people such is the grossness, the disproportion, and the feebleness of the imitation. Such is the sculpture of the ancient Germans, the Tartars, Mexicans, and the people of the South Seas.

The Egyptian sculpture was more perfect than that of any other ancient nation before the Greeks,

because they were assisted in execution by principles of science* not possessed by any other people
until a much later period; they had made some progress in geometry, proportions, and in the structure
of the human figure.

Some very early remains of Grecian sculpture †
resemble the Egyptian so strongly, that we cannot
resist the testimony of those writers which inform us
they received sculpture from that people.

This at least is certain, that the sculpture of Greece
was equally rude with that of their barbarous neighbours, until they had excelled them in the advancement of knowledge, the improvement of science, and
the establishment of political institutions.

We may distinguish the ancient art of Greece as
three ages :—the heroic age, the philosophic age, and
the age of maturity or perfection.

By the heroic age we understand the state of
society described in the poems of Homer and Hesiod,
in which the land was cultivated, and cattle fed to
supply the wants of life; but whose most important
business was predatory war. To this age we may
refer the earliest productions of Grecian art—of this
age are two lions † over the gate of Mycene—of this
age, from a similarity of style, we may also believe
many small bronze and stone statues to have been
the production.‡   Perhaps, though rude and ill-
formed, they were domestic divinities : early in the
progress of idolatry, so far as we may venture an

* Denon's Egypt.   † See Plate XIV.   ‡ See Plate XVI.

opinion upon this class of art, the endeavour was limited to the single figure, naked, and in few and simple attitudes. It is nevertheless likely, before this age passed away, the artists became more bold, and adorned their earthen vases with subjects of three or four figures, such as frequently occurred in their habits of life, a conversation, a battle, or a procession : the designs of these compositions appear like profiles of their statues, and unconnected with each other ; scarcely more than the labour of their hands, in which the superintendence of the mind was little concerned, the first rude attempts at imi-ation.

The second " age of art," which we shall denominate the philosophic, commenced when the seven sages or wise men flourished in Greece, about 700 years before the Christian era; when the mental faculties were expanded, and when, by contemplation and science, man was elevated from savage life to the dignity of a rational creature. In this period Solon and Lycurgus reformed the laws of preceding legislators, and rendered the system more salutary in the correction of crime, and the security of justice to their fellow citizens.

The seven sages, by the example of their own heroism and virtue, enforced the moral and political order which their wisdom and prudence taught.

In the school of Pythagoras, mathematics, astronomy, geometry, arithmetic, and music, were diligently cultivated; the structure of animals was

studied, and the contemplations of philosophy elevated the mind above the grosser allurements of
sense: the improvement of civil and political security afforded additional leisure for all ingenious and
liberal pursuits, while the advancement of science
supplied means for nearer approaches towards perfection.

In the institutions of Greece, the five gymnastic
exercises of boxing, running, wrestling, leaping, and
throwing the spear, at the same time that they increased the strength and agility, exhibited all the
various beauty of the human figure, diversified by all
the difference of motion the several exertions could
produce, with the multiplicity of anatomical changes
in action and remission occasioned by each exertion
of body and limbs.

It cannot be denied that the religion of ancient
Greece was gross polytheism; but this was the religion of the multitude – that of the philosopher was
much more pure. It allowed, indeed, the ministry
of subordinate divinities, angels, and heroic souls,
but all directed by the unerring wisdom and providence of the one Omnipotent. The graces and perfections of these celestial intelligences and ministers
are so described in the ' Dialogues ' of Plato, and by
the Pythagoreans, as to lead the artist to the choice
of supreme natural beauty for the object of his imitation throughout the numerous ideal orders of the
Grecian theology, and elevated the real persons by
the noblest traits of limb, feature, and character.

The first essays of Grecian art, in the heroic age, prove they were neither stronger nor swifter in the race than other nations ; but the improved imitation of nature, founded on the sure principles of science, left their competitors at a distance not to be recovered ; and the ability and zeal with which they pursued their advantage, gave them possession of the palm beyond dispute.

The Greeks, in this age, added the cultivation of letters to their discoveries in science and improvement of philosophy. Hipparchus is said to have first made the Athenians acquainted with Homer's Rhapsodies (and from which that people received their system of theology) : these were recited in the Panathenaic solemnities, and became so popular that they were continually quoted in the Dialogues of Plato, and by succeeding writers.

The poems of Hesiod, Sappho, Anacreon, and Simonides, are also believed to have been collected in a public library at Athens in this time.

Thus was infant art inspired by the spirit of poetry, and the effects of this inspiration are seen in the councils of the gods in the friezes of the Parthenon, and the Temple of Theseus,* besides innumerable Homeric subjects on the painted vases and Greek basso-relievos of after ages.

Geometry enabled the artist scientifically to ascertain forms for the configuration of bodies—to determine the motion of the figure, in leaping, running,

striking, or falling—by curves and angles, whilst
arithmetic gave the multiplication of measures in
proportions. The anatomical observations of Thales,
Pythagoras, and Alcmeon, prepared the way for the
more connected inquiries of Hippocrates. Thus by
the gradual advancement and connection of art and
science, painting and sculpture obtained sound principles to insure a certain and felicitous practice,
which introduced the age of perfection or consum-
mation in the time of Pericles and Phidias.

This third age of art may be said to have been
called into practice by the destruction of those
enormous fleets and armies prepared by the Persians
to annihilate Grecian freedom.

This illustrious achievement, performed by a comparatively small band of patriots, increased the
estimation of Greece, and especially of Athens, in proportion to the terrific power of the vanquished, and
the glory of delivering their country from a foreign
yoke. These successes in war stimulated their exertions in peace—they rebuilt the temples destroyed
in the war, with increased magnificence—their
pediments and friezes were decorated with synods
of gods and heroes, from their history, both real
and mythological. They raised sacred statues,
which for their colossal size, richness of materials,
and embellishment, future ages ranked as wonders of
the world. Nor were the statues of smaller dimensions less deserving attention for exquisite beauty of
feature, form, proportions, character, dignity, sim-

plicity, and elegance. Their groups possess the united interests of action and passion, sentiment elevated and heroic, consistent with the persons engaged.

The basso-relievos are epic and dramatic compositions, containing great variety in the subjects, combination and diversity of lines, with whatever, in the distribution and opposition of light and shadow, produces the most powerful and agreeable effect in the relief of figures from a back-ground, or that department of sculpture the most nearly allied to painting.

But as our subject becomes more extensive in its progress, it will be rendered more simple by considering each class of sculpture separately, under the following heads:—

1. Colossal statues. 2. Smaller statues. 3. Groups. 4. Basso-relievos and the Grecian schools of sculpture.

The largest colossal statues of the Egyptians were seventy-five feet in height, and therefore the Greeks excelled them in the magnitude as well as the beauty of those enormous monuments.

Many colossal statues are enumerated by the classical authors (particularly Pliny and Pausanias), which have long since ceased to exist, and of which any memorials beyond their names are unknown at present. It is, notwithstanding, not only possible, but even probable, that antiquarian industry may still recover recollections of them from gems, the reverses of coins, and small bronze statues, in which the celebrated works of antiquity were so frequently copied. But as the mere repetition of names and measurement would afford information of little use either to the painter or sculptor, to avoid the misapplication of time in uncertain conjecture, we will direct our attention to the three most celebrated of these works, the most copiously described by authors, and illustrated by ancient copies of smaller size.

The statue of Olympian Jupiter,* sixty feet in height, was the most renowned work of ancient sculpture, not for stupendous magnitude alone, but more for awful majesty and sublime beauty: it was adorned with all the charms poetic vision could bestow, embodied by labours which have been the wonder, and the school, of all succeeding ages. It is thus described by Pausanias, who saw it in meridian splendour :—

" The god sat on a throne of ivory and gold, his head crowned with a branch of olive—his left hand presented a Victory of ivory and gold, with a crown and fillet; his right hand held a sceptre beautifully distinguished by all the different metals, on which an eagle sat; the sandals of the god were gold, so was his drapery, on which were various animals, with flowers of all kinds, especially lilies; his throne was refulgent with gold and precious stones. There were also statues—four Victories alighting,

* See Plate XX.

were annexed to the feet of the throne, those in front rested each on a sphinx that had seized a Theban youth—below the sphinxes the children of Niobe were slain by the arrows of Apollo and Diana."

After mentioning some statues of victors in the Olympic exercises, standing on the foot of the throne, Pausanias also describes the pictures (by Panæneus, brother of Phidias) which were on the sides of the seat. Among these were " Atlas supporting heaven and earth, Hercules near him, about to relieve him from his burthen; Theseus and Pirithous; and the figures representing Greece and Salamis, the latter bearing the rostra of a ship in her hands; the combat of Hercules with the Nemæan lion; Ajax and Cassandra; Hippodamia, the daughter of Œnomaus, with her mother; Prometheus chained, and Hercules preparing to kill the eagle which prayed on him. The last of the pictures are Penthesilea dying, supported by Achilles, and Hesperian nymphs bearing fruit." On the recess for the throne, above the head of the statue, are the three Graces on one side, and on the other the three Hours, or Seasons. On the base of the statue are golden lions, with the battle of Theseus and the Amazons. On the sub-plinth, which supports the whole are emblems in gold. The Sun, Jupiter, and Juno ascend in a car. Near them is Chares, whom Mercury embraces, and Vesta, Mercury, and Love receive Venus rising from the sea, to whom Persua-

sion brings a crown. Apollo, Diana, Minerva, and
Hercules are present. On the lowest part are Neptune and Amphitrite, with the Moon exciting her
horses to the race. This great work, which raised
the fame of Phidias above all the sculptors of antiquity, has numerous imitations still existing in
marble and bronze, and on coins of Alexander the
Great and his successors, also on the Emperor Domitian's medals in large brass.

In the Acropolis of Athens * was a Minerva by the
same sculptor, twenty-six cubits high, also formed of
ivory and gold. In the right hand was a Victory,
four cubits high; the left hand rested on her shield.
The goddess was clothed in a tunic reaching to her
feet; her helmet was adorned with horses and gry-
phons; on the round side of the shield was the fight
with the Amazons; on the concave side, the battle of
the Gods and Giants; on her sandals, the contest of
the Lapithæ and Centaurs; on the base was the birth
of Pandora in the presence of thirty divinities.
Memorials of this statue are preserved on Athenian
coins, of which there are engravings in the vignettes
of Stuart's 'Athens.'

The Colossus of the Sun,† in the Island of Rhodes,
is allowed by Pliny the Elder to have excited more
astonishment than all the other colossal statues he
has mentioned, on account of its height, which was
105 feet: it was made by Chares, a Lindian, the
disciple of Lysippus. The statue was thrown down

* See Plate XIX.   † See Plate XLVIII.

by an earthquake, after standing fifty-six years.
When lying on the ground this work appeared
miraculous. Few were able to embrace the thumb,
and the fingers were larger than many statues. Vast
caverns yawned in the broken limbs, and within
were seen great masses of stone, by whose weight it
was supported. Twelve years were employed in the
execution of it, and the cost 300 talents, about
£60,000 English. The same author observes, there
were, in the same city, an hundred lesser colossal
figures, each of which did honour to the place where
it stood; besides five colossal statues of divinities by
the sculptor Bryaxis.

Heads of the celebrated Colossus are repeatedly
seen on the bronze coins of Rhodes, and small figures,
with radiated heads, are sometimes found on the
coins of this island, which possibly were intended to
represent the whole figure.

The most numerous class of ancient statues was
about the height of nature, or approaching to seven
feet, which has been distinguished as the heroic
size.

Statues were anciently appropriated to divinities.
Portraits of men were not executed unless for some
illustrious cause which deserved perpetuity.

First were the victorious contests in the sacred
games, chiefly those of Olympia, where the custom
was for all the conquerors to dedicate their statues,
and those who were thrice victors had exact portraits of their persons. It was thought the Athe-

nians first placed statues to Harmodius and Aris-
togiton, the Tyrannicides, the same year the kings
were expelled from Rome. " This," says Pliny,
" was afterwards universal; and now the forum of
every municipal town begins to be ornamented with
statues to prolong the memory of men, and to have
the honours of the age inscribed on their bases, lest
they should be read only on their sepulchres. In
the course of time this has been done abroad, in
public courts and private houses. Thus clients have
determined to celebrate their patrons."

After the custom was adopted of bestowing this
honour on distinguished merit, every battle increased
heroic memorials; the porticoes, libraries, museums,
and walks were filled with the statues of legislators,
poets, philosophers, and all whose public spirit or
rare qualities had raised them to general notice and
esteem.

The practice so universal in Greece passed with
the conquerors into their colonies; and the successors
of Alexander the Great added to the sacred sculpture of Egypt and Syria the memorials of Grecian
valour and wisdom. The same practice was fol
lowed in Sicily, Magna Græcia, Naples, the principal
cities on the coast of Italy, the Etruscan states, and
wherever their colonies or commerce gave them
intercourse. The remains of sculpture found in all
these countries frequently bear this indisputable
testimony of Grecian origin—that they are stamped
with the beauty, grace, purity, and perfection which

are to be found in the works of that country alone, of all nations in the ancient world.

This increase of sculpture, extending over so considerable a portion of the globe known to the ancients, will account for the number of statues brought to Rome after the conquest of Greece.

Marcus Scaurus, when Ædile, decorated his temporary theatre with three thousand statues. Two thousand were taken from the Volscians. Mummius, after the conquest of Achaia, is said to have filled the city. Lucullus brought many. Three thousand came from Rhodes—not fewer from Athens or Olympia—more are believed to have come from Delphi; "but," says our author, "what mortal can follow them? or what is the use of knowing?"

It will be sufficient for our present purpose to comprehend in two sentences what remains of this part of our subject: after the terrific repetition of those conflagrations which destroyed the noblest monuments in Rome, it was said that the city contained more gods than men!

The equestrian and pedestrian statues, trophies and triumphal arches, which adorned the Roman forum, and the forum of Trajan—the innumerable sculptures in the imperial palace—in the baths of Dioclesian and Caracalla—the Mausoleum of Augustus, and that of Hadrian—the files of patriots and heroes which lined the Flaminian way—were objects to fill the imagination, and occupy the mind. But neither the multitude of them nor their magnificence will produce any great impression on the painter or sculptor. He will keenly search out the rare specimens of excellence from among the hundreds of ordinary beauty; upon these he will fix his attention, and from these he will deduce his principles.

We shall now return to our more immediate object, the pursuit and study of excellence, by noticing some of the noblest examples which the ravages of time, and the destructive hand of barbarism have spared.

Besides the works of Phidias already mentioned, duplicates of smaller statues by him have come down to us: the Amazon called "Euknemon," from her fine leg, of which there is a print in the 'Museum Pium Clementinum,' in the library of our Royal Academy. Two Minervas are mentioned by Pliny, one of which had the surname of Callimorphes, expressive of her fine form. Perhaps this might be similar to the statue of the goddess in Mr. Hope's Gallery, as it strongly resembles a Minerva on an Athenian coin among the vignettes in Stuart's 'Athens.'

Perhaps, in this place, a remark may be offered, without impropriety, concerning the group of a hero governing a horse, which stands opposite the Papal palace, on Monte Cavallo, in Rome. This group is said to stand nearly on the same spot it occupied (with its companion) when they guarded the entrance to the baths of Constantine. "The work of

Phidias " was inscribed on the pedestal, as we may see at the present time. In illustration of this group, three Roman coins may be adduced, one struck in the reign of Nero, another under Hadrian, and a third by Commodus, all bearing this group on the reverse, representing Bellerophon about to mount Pegasus, for the purpose of destroying the Chimæra. These coins were struck in the city of Corinth, where Bellerophon was much honoured. The attitude of the hero, as well as that of the horse, resembles a bas-relief on the Parthenon ; and for that reason, in addition to the style and spirit of the work, is likely to have been executed under the direction of Phidias.

Alcamenes,* the scholar of Phidias, was celebrated for his Venus (Aphrodite). Many small statues of bronze and marble represent the goddess pressing the water from her hair, and by their elegance are probably copies from that statue.

Praxiteles excelled in the highest graces of youth and ideal beauty. His Venus of Cnidos,† which is said to be more perfect than any other, is known from the descriptions of Lucian and Cedrenus. It is on the reverse of a bronze medal of Caracalla and Plautilla, in the king of France's cabinet.

The drawing introduced in this Lecture was from a statue said to have been found in a vineyard, about thirty years since, in Rome, and was the property of

* See Plate XXI.   † See Plate XXII.

Duke Braschi, nephew of Pius the Sixth. Sketches from it were made at that time.*

Among the celebrated statues by Praxiteles, of which copies have come down to us, are his Satyr, his Capid bending his bow, and Apollo the lizard-killer. Casts are in this academy, for which we are indebted to the munificence of his present majesty George the Fourth; to which may be added Bacchus leaning on a faun, although this latter properly belongs to the class of groups.

Polycletus of Sicyon, the scholar of Ageladas, was celebrated for his statue of Diadumenus, a youth binding a fillet round his head, of which copies are seen occasionally on bas-reliefs. It was valued by the ancients at 100 talents, rather more than £18,000 English money. His Doryphorus, or spear-bearer, from which sculptors copied the rules of art, is known to us only from Pliny's description.

The Discobolus by Naucydes is universally admired for the heroic form and retreating motion preparatory to the force and weight of the person requisite to project the disk.

The Discobolus† by Myron is ascertained by an antique gem, and the description of Quintilian, who apologizes for its forced attitude, (perhaps that of some particular man distinguished in this game). There is an ancient example of this statue in the British Museum.

* A full account of this statue has already been given in the Lecture on Grecian Sculpture.   † See Plate XXIV.

A wounded man, the famous work of Ctesilaus, is perhaps the same as that called the "Dying Gladiator," but more properly a herald or hero.

Prints of the wounded Amazon of Ctesilaus are not uncommon in the volumes of antique statues.

Pliny mentions the Nine Muses of Philiscus of Rhodes, and the Muses brought by Fulvius Nobilior to Rome. From one or both of these series, the Muses in the Vatican were probably obtained, as they appear to be the work of different hands. Casts from them are in the Council-room. The Comedy is remarkable for juvenile grace of person, and elegance of drapery. The Tragedy for solemnity and heroic grandeur.

The Apollo Philesius, by Canachus, has many repetitions.

Ganymede borne in the eagle's talons is exactly described by Pliny. A print of it may be seen in the 'Museum Pium Clementinum.'

The Apollo Belvidere is believed by the learned Visconti to be the Deliverer from Evil, the work of Calamis, set up in Athens in memory of a plague which raged in that city.

Sublime in his beauty, and terrible in his anger, it has been considered as the Phoebus Apollo of Homer, destroying the Greeks. It has also been looked upon as a variation from a statue by Phidias.

The Hercules Farnese was evidently one of the first favourites of antiquity, from its frequent repetition in bronze and marble, on gems and coins. It is worthy of remark, that some statues of Hercules, in the same attitude of repose with that surnamed Farnese, but of much earlier date, have the proportions of comnon men, and that a series of them may be found in the various collections, gradually increasing to the terrific strength of Glycon's statue. The head of this formidable hero bears a noble resemblance to his father Jupiter. The anatomical detail in the body and limbs is more distinct than in any other work of antiquity.

The Ancient Groups next claim attention.

Laocoon and his sons is a work composed in a noble concatenation of lines, in the three principal views. The children's appeal to the father, and the father's to the gods, are highly pathetic. The convulsed rise of the youngest from the ground is the most electric circumstance in the whole sentiment. It was the work of Apollodorous, Athenadorus, and Agesander, of Rhodes.

Zethus and Amphion tying Dirce to the bull's horns—an example of filial vengeance in behalf of a persecuted mother. The conception is heroic, and the execution vast. The marble is at Naples, but, like many other noble works, it has been miserably restored.

Hercules raising Antæus in his arms is in the Pitti Palace, Florence.

The group of Atreus bearing a dead son of Thyestes, Orestes and Electra, Ajax supporting the dead Patroclus, and that of Hæmon and Antigone, are all examples of fine form, heroic character, and sentiment.

Niobe and her youngest daughter, by Scopas, is an example of heroic beauty in mature age. The sentiment is maternal affection. She exposes her own life to shield her child from the threatened destruction. The statues of the several children all possess the same heroic beauty, mixed with astonishment, terror, dismay, and death. That fine example of anatomical study, of a difficult but harmonious composition, the Group of Wrestlers, was found in the same excavation with, and has been supposed to belong to, the family of Niobe.

The group of Cupid and Psyche, interesting from the beauty of youthful male and female forms and harmony of lines, is an allegory of the Pythagorean philosophy, representing the union of desire and the soul.

We may now take some notice of the antique basrelievos, particularly those in the British Museum. The metopes which formerly adorned the Parthenon of Athens, which contain the combats of the Lapithæ and Centaurs, are distinguished by simplicity and heroic exertion. Some casts from them are placed in the model academy. The procession of chariots, horsemen, maidens bearing sacred baskets and candelabræ, animals for sacrifice, and sacred instructors in the Celebration of Minerva and the Assembly of the Gods, are admired by all for simplicity of composition, breadth of general effect, the elegance and delicacy of the heads and draperies, and the life and spirit of the horses.

The casts (in the same collection) from the temple of Theseus. The metopes represent his heroic deeds, and the frieze within the temple councils of the gods. The style of these is more like the metopes on the Parthenon than the broad masses in the procession within that temple.

The whole of the sculpture in the temple of Theseus is bold, varied, and full of action. The fragments of statues and groups which were in the pediment of the Parthenon are executed with great effect; but, as all the Athenian marbles in the Museum have been seen and universally admired, additional description would be useless.

The contention for the body of Patroclus, in the pediment of the temple of Jupiter Panhellenius at Egina, is a fine composition, of which there is a beautiful etching by Mr. Cockerell, who assisted in restoring this specimen of ancient art to the world.

The battle of the Amazons and Athenians, from the temple of Apollo Epicourus, is also in the British Museum.

Those already named are among the ancient works of chief excellence, and most worthy of the student's contemplation and imitation in bassorelievo.

Others, however, may be mentioned, of great beauty, the study of which will be highly important in the progress of the student. Of this number are the beautiful compositions of Perseus and Andromeda, and the Endymion, casts of which are in the Royal Academy; to these may be added the basso-relievos on the Trajan column—on the arches of Constantine and Marcus Aurelius—and, above all, the ancient sarcophagi, which present a magnificent collection of compositions from the great poets of antiquity, Homer, Hesiod, Æschylus, Euripides, and Sophocles—the systems of ancient philosophy, with Greek mysteries, initiations, and mythology. The study of these will give the young artist the true principles of composition, with effect, and without confusion, to produce the chief interest of his subject by grand lines of figures, without the intrusion of useless, impertinent, or trivial objects. By carefully observing them he will accustom himself to a noble habit of thinking, and consequently choose whatever is beautiful, elegant, and grand, rejecting all that is mean and vulgar: by thus imbibing an electric spark of the poetic fire, he will learn to choose fit subjects for the employment of his talents, and to convert the beauty and grace of ancient poetry and genius to the service of the morals and institutions of our own time and country.

In the comparatively few antique statues, groups, and basso-relievos here mentioned, the attention has been called only to such as have been esteemed the most, by the united consent of ancients and moderns; the rest, which are very numerous, must be sought for in the various collections of antiquities, Montfaucon, the ' Museum Pium Clementinum,' ' Museum Romanum,' ' Florentinum,' ' Giustiniani,' ' Borghese,' and many other works of the same kind, most of which are in the library of our academy.

The principal schools of sculpture appear to have been Athens and Rhodes : in the first the school of Phidias was established ; and we learn from Pliny that his emulators were Alcamenes, Critias, and Nestocles, and, twenty years after, Agelades, Callon, Polycletus, Phragmon, Gorgias, Lacon, Myron, Pythagoras, Scopas, and Perillus. This catalogue, we may reasonably believe, contains the sculptors whose labours adorned the temple of Theseus and the Parthenon; and from them also the successive pupils descended, whose works embellished the Roman empire, until the northern irruptions spread universal destruction in the west, and the Saracens and Turks conquered and wasted the eastern provinces.

The other school of sculpture, namely, Rhodes, is likely to have sprung from that of Athens. We have already observed that the Roman conquerors took 3000 statues from thence. To this school of Rhodes we owe the two noble groups, the Laocoon, and Zethus and Amphion, both mentioned by Pliny with extraordinary praise.

The sculptors of Sicyon and Ægina appear to have been chiefly employed on works of bronze, although Corinth, Delos, and other cities, have a just claim to reputation on the same account.

To this general view of ancient sculpt re, a few remarks may be added concerning the practical advantage it may afford—by guarding against error and false systems, so frequently ruinous impediments in the path of talent and industry, by which the inexperienced mind is first entangled in doubt, and ultimately turned from the course it had taken, without any sure guide to the desired object.

It is a sound maxim, that " the same cause will always produce the same effect;" therefore, if we would attain excellence in art, we cannot proceed by a more certain course than that by which it has been attained before.

The arts of Greece astonished and delighted the world in their own times, and they have continued to do so through the lapse of many ages; and now, in their fragments and mutilations, demand the same just homage from the beholder, and afford the same example of excitement, admiration, and instruction to the artist; and in this lecture has been shewn, not according to chimerical notions, or mere supposition, but according to the testimony of contemporary authors, supported by the ancient works of art, the progress of sculpture in Greece from the first rude beginning common to all countries, by the various gradations of improvement, until it arrived at that perfection which has not been equalled in modern times, except perhaps in some very few instances, and never excelled.

In the former part of this discourse, we nave seen

that the Greeks, in their uncivilized state, did not excel their barbarous neighbours in the arts; that religion gave the first impulse to sculpture; that philosophic improvement furnished the artist with rules; that legislation, by determination of moral and civil rights, reduced society to a more settled state, and thereby afforded a more tranquil leisure for the cultivation of liberal studies; that the institution of gymnastic exercises exhibited the naked figure in all views, actions, and motions for the study of the artist; the anatomical school of Hippocrates, and the more extended knowledge of that science in the school of Alexandria, gave more exact details of the parts of the human figure; and lastly, the dialogues of Plato on beauty, its origin, cause, and effect, from the mind upon the body, completed the general principles of information for the ancient sculptor; and as it was a summary of the gradual progress by which the excellence of Grecian art was accumulated, so in its perfection it became the course of study by which every individual artist rose to eminence.

LECTURE X.

MODERN SCULPTURE.

THE preceding lecture contained a very general and summary sketch of ancient sculpture, as introductory to a similar review of modern sculpture. In that lecture it was observed that no attempt would be made to give a regular history of the art in its commencement by the Egyptians, in all the particulars of its progress and perfection by the Greeks—at what point its course had been arrested among the Syrians, Persians, and Babylonians—what portion of the colonial arts of Greece, found in Sicily and Italy, might be considered the undoubted property of the mother-country, and in what respects they could be claimed by the people to whom they were originally exotics: all these topics are doubtless necessary to a complete history of the arts of design, and all of consequence to the antiquary. But in the number of these topics we must, as artists, distinguish between such as are requisite to history, and those passages most important to us of the ancient authors which supply profound maxims and principles indispensable to a sound theory and successful practice of the arts.

Whenever a more extensive knowledge is required, application must be made to the various writers on the subject, ancient and modern.

The first objects in this institution are the principles of art, as must be evident in every branch of the establishment; as a valuable library has been formed, and lectures appointed for the communication of whatever in science and literature the artist may find most useful; and he may try the rules he acquires, by comparing his own studies with the finest specimens of ancient sculpture, and the works of the most esteemed painters of the fifteenth century, or the great criterion of all art—nature—in the schools of this institution.

It is subservient to this wise and liberal plan of education that these Lectures have been conceived; in which I have endeavoured to present a comprehensive view of the means by which ancient art obtained its unrivalled excellence, and that by the same means, and by application to the same studies, modern art rose again to excellence in the fifteenth century.

Thus the student of the present day has the most satisfactory assurance that the ancient arts of Greece were carried to perfection, and the modern arts of Italy restored, by the same system of education established in this institution; and we may with certainty predict that a race of painters and sculptors will be produced by our Royal Academy whose merits will secure the admiration of their own time, and of future ages, as effectually as their great predecessors have done; with this proviso, that on their part they bring with them to the arts they intend to practise, minds truly liberal, debased by no sordid or unworthy motives,—a disposition so devoted that any other employment would render life miserable,—a ready inclination to overcome all difficulties by indefatigable labour,—and above all, a comprehensiveness of mind, an acuteness of perception, and a soundness of judgment capable of attaining the various acquirements of science, literature, and the study of nature, required in the profession. We shall now proceed with the subject of Modern Art.

It is a fact known to all, that the successive irruptions of barbarians into the provinces of the Roman empire, both East and West, from the fifth to the tenth century of the Christian era, spread universal devastation, even to the rendering great tracts of country desert, where an abundant population had flourished in magnificent towns and cities.

In these dismal times, when the violence of fanaticism increased the horrors of barbarous invasion—when the works of ancient genius in painting and sculpture were buried under the ruins of temples, forums, and palaces, which they had adorned to the fifth century—there were accounts of the Olympian Jupiter, and the Venus of Cnidos; but at that time their history ends in the common destruction and darkness of the times. The spirit of violence and warfare did not cease, but was continued by the feudal successors to the Roman provinces long after the tenth century, with the same baneful influence, unabated, upon arts, learning, and civilization. In the city of Rome, the architectural monuments of antiquity were converted into fortresses by the contending barons; and in the beginning of the fifteenth century, the city was so encumbered with ruined buildings and lesser forts, that two horsemen could scarcely pass abreast in any principal street or open place. Wherever excavations have been made in later times, to clear the basements of columns, arches, or buildings, in the Roman Forum, the Forum of Trajan, and other distinguished parts of the city, the ancient pavement has been always found from ten to sixteen feet lower than the present; and the whole of the mass between, formed from the rubbish of ruined structures, mixed with fragments of statues, bassorelievos, capitals, columns, &c. We need but one instance more, which is within the compass of our own knowledge or inquiry, to demonstrate the general ruin which accompanied the destruction of the works of art during the barbarous irruptions in the great cities of the Roman empire—the instance referred to was in our own country. In London, several magnificent mosaic or tesselated pavements and fragments of ancient art have been found, covered by a mass of burnt rubbish, from ten to twelve feet deep below the present pavement.

Similar instances have occurred in most of the cities of England, proving the destructive progress of the Saxons and Danes in our country not to have been less furious than those of the Goths, Vandals, Huns, and Lombards in Italy, or of the Saracens and Turks in the East.

But from the vengeance of barbarians, stimulated by prey, and provoked by oppression, we shall willingly turn our view to the re-establishment of social order, and the restoration of arts and letters.

After the entire destruction of the Roman power in the West of Europe, Italy was divided into republics and principalities, the chief of which, Venice, Genoa, and Pisa, possessing the advantage of extensive sea-coasts, were the first to enrich their countries by commerce, and improve their knowledge by voyages. The Venetians, situated in the neighbourhood of Greece, were induced to emulate the Church of St. Sophia at Constantinople, in the building and decoration of St. Mark's in their own city. The plan of this church is a Greek cross, and the mosaic pictures, from sacred history, which adorn the interior, are from Greek paintings of the same age. The present church was consecrated, A.D. 10⁹5.

The republic of Pisa had a naval force so considerable previous to this period, that they had beaten the Saracens in Africa, Sardinia, Majorca, Minorca, and Sicily, besides taking from them immense treasure, with which they built the Cathedral of Pisa, begun in 1063, finished 1092.

The building of these cathedrals was followed by those of Verona, Modena, Pistoia, and several others in Italy.

Schools of painting and sculpture, as well as architecture, were formed and established in the eleventh and twelfth centuries; and the distinguished talents produced in them were cherished and employed in the cause of religion.

It will be found on a careful inquiry, that the elements, as well as the perfection of the arts, have always been received, either immediately or intermediately, from the Greeks, by Western Europe, although this has been denied by Vasari; and, as far as concerns the Greek Christian paintings, does not seem to have been even suspected by Winckelmann. To this part of our subject, therefore, a short but satisfactory illustration is required.

The germ, or first beginning of modern art, is not to be so absolutely reckoned from the commencement of the eleventh century, when society began to be settled in Europe, as from the reign of Constantine, seven centuries earlier, when Christianity became the established religion of the empire; then it was that painting and sculpture ceased to be employed on the pagan gods, and their powers were engaged to adorn the churches built by Christian emperors, with the persons and events of sacred history. The portrait of our Saviour,* with those of some of the Apostles, particularly

* Vide Arringhi's Roma Subterranea, Plate XLIX.

S. Peter and S. Paul, appear to have been known in Galilee either during their life, or shortly after their death.

The Emperior Tiberius was desirous of having the Messiah admitted among the gods of the empire, out was refused by the Senate. Alexander Severus nad the statue of Jesus Christ among his household gods.

Even during the reigns of those emperors, by whom the Christians were cruelly persecuted, when they were obliged to perform their sacred worship in subterrains and sepulchral chambers, they ornamented those retreats with sacred portraits and subjects from Scripture. But when the churches of St. Sophia and the Apostles were built in Constantinople by Constantine and his successors, they were embellished with mosaics and statues.

Bosius, in his 'Roma Subterranea,' exhibits many Christian sarcophagi sculptured with scriptural subjects from the Old and New Testament in basso-relievo.

Monier,* in his History of Painting, Sculpture and Architecture, gives large quotations from the Christian Fathers concerning the excellent paintings of sacred subjects in the Eastern churches, from the fourth to the eighth century, and the powerful effects produced by them on the beholders. Indeed, there are still remaining in the libraries of the Emperor of Austria and King of France, Greek paintings

* Monier, page 60.

executed in the middle ages, of great beauty; but above all the Greek painting and sculpture now existing which particularly deserve notice, are the Nativity,* the Transfiguration, the Crucifixion, the Resurrection, and the Glorification, because they were the examples universally followed by the Italian artists, until after Raffaelle and Michael Angelo.

Andrea Tafi, a Florentine, contemporary with Cimabue, studied under the Grecian artists in St. Mark's Church, Venice, while they were employed in decorating the interior with the principal subjects recorded in the Old and New Testaments.

Apollonius, a Grecian painter, returned from Venice with Tafi, and assisted him in the mosaics afterwards executed in St. John's Baptistery at Florence. Cimabue was also instructed by Greek artists. These facts being acknowledged by the Italian writers, there remains no cause for surprise that the Greek Christian compositions should assist the restoration of painting, more than that their paintings and basso-relievo should have supplied the principles of ancient art.

The Cathedral of Pisa, built by Buschetto, an architect from Dulichium, was the second sacred edifice (St. Mark's in Venice being the first) raised after the destruction of the Roman power in Italy. It has received the honour of being allowed by posterity to have taken the lead in restoring art :

* Plates XXXV. and XXXVI

and indeed the traveller, on entering the city gates, is astonished by a scene of architectural magnificence and singularity not to be equalled in the world. Four stupendous structures of fine marble in one group—the solemn cathedral, in the general parallelogram of its form resembling an ancient temple,* which unites and simplifies the arched divisions of its exterior; the Baptistery, a circular building, surrounded with arches and columns, crowned with niches, statues and pinnacles, rising to an apex in the centre, terminated by a statue of the Baptist;— the Falling Tower (which is thirteen feet out of the perpendicular), a most elegant cylinder, raised by eight rows of columns surmounting each other, and surrounding a staircase;—the Cemetery, a long square corridor of elegant pointed architecture, 400 by 200 feet, containing the ingenious works of the improvers of painting, down to the sixteenth century. This extraordinary scene in the evening of a summer's day, with a splendid red sun setting in the dark-blue sky, the full moon rising on the opposite side over a city nearly deserted, affects the beholder's mind with such a sensation of magnificence, solitude, and wonder, that he scarcely knows whether he is any longer an inhabitant of this world or not.

To describe the numerous works of painting and sculpture with which the restorers of art laboured to adorn these magnificent edifices during 500 years would require time equal to that allowed for the

* A Latin cross.

Lectures on Sculpture during one season. Fortunately for the student, fine prints from the paintings in the Campo Santo, with outlines of the sarcophagi in the same corridor, may be seen in the library of the Royal Academy.

The general effect of this group of buildings deserves to be dwelt on, for these two reasons in particular, first, because noble ideas, finely executed, cannot fail to produce an irresistible effect on the mind; and, secondly, this assemblage of buildings contains a more regular series of those labours by which the restoration of art was effected, than is to be found within the same compass in any other place.

We shall now proceed to notice the restorers of sculpture in Italy, with the same brevity as the first improvers in Greece.

It is not unlikely that Buschetto, the Greek, who built the Cathedral of Pisa in the eleventh century, established the schools of architecture and sculpture at the same time in that city (although we have no historical proof of the fact), because we know it was not unusual with those early artists to practise painting, sculpture, and architecture at the same time, and because there are rude statues on the cathedral coeval with the building; and it is acknowledged by the Pisan writers, that there were sculptors in that city before Nicolas and his son John, whose works became famous throughout Italy in the middle of the thirteenth century. These sculptors executed most magnificent marble pulpits, enriched with basso-relievos and statues, in the cathedrals of Pisa, Pistoia, and Sienna, also in the Baptistery of Pisa: a series of sacred subjects from the Old and New Testaments, by them and their scholars, are seen on the west front of Orvieto Cathedral. There are also by John Pisano some elegant statues of the Virgin and Child. Nicolas and John improved sculpture, by study of the antique basso-relievos in the Campo Santo; in their own works the compositions are simple and intelligible; the female figures are frequently elegant in their movements and their drapery. In them are occasionally seen an originality of idea and a force of thought seldom met with when schools of art are in the habit of copying from each other.

Andrea Ugolino Pisano, from the school of these sculptors, designed and executed in bronze the oldest gate of the Baptistery in Florence, the compartments of which represent the life of S. John. The compositions have a Gothic and simple grandeur. He also executed some statues in marble, but they were rather inferior to the productions of Nicolas and John.

The next distinguished restorer of sculpture was Donatello, the Florentine. Some of his works, both in bronze and marble, might be placed beside the best productions of ancient Greece without discredit. In the 'Opera del Duomo' of Santa Maria del Fiore, the Cathedral of Florence, there is an alto-relievo of

two singing-boys of extraordinary beauty in sentiment, character, drawing, and drapery. In the
gallery of Florence there is a bronze statue of a lad
(perhaps a Mercury), so delicately proportioned, and
so perfectly natural, that it is excelled only by the
best works of antiquity, in certain exquisite graces
peculiar to the finest monuments in Greece, but not
to be attained or expected from the endeavours of
lately resurgent genius. His marble statue of St.
George, on the exterior of Or San Michael, is an
example of sentiment, simple and forcible; he stands
upright, equally poised on both legs, his hands
resting on his shield before him. Michael Angelo,
after admiring this statue some time in silence, suddenly exclaimed, "March!" His basso-relievos of
the life of Christ, on the pulpit of Saint Lorenzo's
Church, abound in noble conceptions, but they were
the works of his advanced age, and finished by his
scholars. He was a man of modesty and principle :
whatever work he engaged in, his chief concern was
to make it the most perfect possible. The contemporaries of this artist are not to be forgotten, although
perhaps, on the whole, inferior sculptors to him.
Brunelleschi executed a crucifix in wood, now in the
Church of Santa Maria Novella, which represents the
suffering Saviour, in a manner not to be looked on
with indifference. He afterwards engaged in architecture, and built the much-admired Church of Santa
Maria del Fiore.

Lorenzo Ghiberti, the other illustrious contempo-

rary of Donatello, has immortalized his memory by
the bronze gates of St. John's Baptistery, called " the
Gates of Paradise," from Michael Angelo's compli-
ment.   This is a beautiful and laborious work.   But
the criticism of Sir Joshua Reynolds was one indisputable proof of that great man's judgment in the
sister arts.   His observation amounted to this, that
" Ghiberti's landscape and buildings occupied so
large a portion of the compartments, that the figures
remained but secondary objects, entirely contrary to
the principle of the ancients."   Ghiberti, likewise,
made a statue in bronze of S. Matthew, on the exterior of San Michele; but his talents were better
suited to the elegance and delicate finishing of
smaller works.   His S. Matthew wants the severe
chastity of the apostolic character, and the head is
inferior to those in the spandrils of his gates; the
attitude also is affected and the drapery unnatural.

We may, without neglecting our great purpose
(the principles of art), pass over the intermediate
names between Donatello and Michael Angelo, as
having added little to the value of modern sculpture.

We now arrive at a great and venerable name,
without an equal in the three sister arts.

Michael Angelo, according to the testimony of
Vasari (his biographer and kinsman), was descended
from the Counts of Canossa, a Lombard family, possessed by conquest, and imperial gift, of Lombardy,
Tuscany, and Lucca, and allied by marriage to the
blood of Charlemagne.

Certainly, if superior genius, enlightened by poetic inspiration, regulated and purified by philosophy and religion, can attest an illustrious descent, few names are recorded in history whose pretensions are better founded than his of whom we are speaking. But it is also possible that a noble mind may be compatible with an humbler descent, and we know that the cultivation of mental powers, moral virtues and knowledge, are the results of fortitude and perseverance ; and these were the qualities by which Michael Angelo became the wonder and example of his own and succeeding ages. His early attachment to the arts at last overcame his father's prejudice against a profession which he fancied disgraced the nobility of his family, and he was placed under Domenico Ghirlandaio, the best painter of his time. He afterwards studied in the Museum of Ancient Sculpture, formed by Lorenzo di Medici in the garden of St. Mark, where Bertoldo the sculptor, a disciple of Donatello, was employed by the magnificent founder of the school to instruct the pupils. Here Michael Angelo's diligence and ability distinguished him above the other students, as they had previously in Ghirlandaio's school of painting. As Michael Angelo was patronized by Lorenzo, and ate at his table, he became acquainted with Politian and Marsilius Ficinus, and with such of the learned Greeks as had sought refuge in Italy previous to the taking of Constantinople by the Turks. From the society and conversation of these distinguished philosophers and scholars, he could not fail to obtain a general clue to the connection between ancient literature and the arts, and a knowledge of the passages in Vitruvius relating to proportions, geometry, and perspective, together with portions from those ancient physicians who had revived the study of anatomy. Because conversations of these kinds were usual only at the table of Lorenzo; and as one of his darling endeavours was to raise a great school of art in Florence, his friends and visitors would naturally pay their court to him, by communications of whatever was likely to forward his patriotic wishes on this subject.

Michael Angelo commenced his career by various works of sculpture, a sleeping Cupid, a Bacchus and young Faun, the colossal David, and a group of Pietée, or a sitting Madonna bearing the dead Christ on her knees, which raised his fame above all his modern predecessors in the art. Fortunately, however, this success did not wholly overcome his love for painting, of which there is a most beautiful example in the Florentine gallery of a Holy Family, with a number of small figures in the background representing S. John baptizing the multitudes in the River Jordan.

Thus had the ceaseless study and unwearied labours of Buonarotti raised him so high in public estimation, that he was appointed to paint a portion of the great hall in Florence, on which Leonardi da Vinci was already employed; and it is to a competition of such talent as but rarely occurs in the history of the world, that we are indebted for that surprising composition, the Battle of the Standard, which Rubens imitated in four admirable hunting scenes; and it is most likely that it is to the lesson Michael Angelo received from this design that he was more particularly led to that study of complicated grouping in which his " Last Judgment " is unrivalled.

Though this great man was afterwards employed on works of sculpture, imposing and admirable from their originality and power, yet his noblest productions are in colours.

The " Ceiling of the Sistine Chapel," and the " Last Judgment," taken together as two portions of one whole, are unparalleled in the history of art, ancient or modern, in the vastness of the idea—the grandeur of the subject, comprehending the entire scheme of divine revelation—the dignity of the characters, among which, our reason is convinced, are those which cannot be represented. Nevertheless, if the whole is considered with the great elevation of mind which accompanies the observation of visible objects, each part is so harmoniously sublime and extraordinary, that the beholder believes he is admitted to a vision of " Light separated from Darkness," the " Benediction of the Waters," and the " Creation of the Human Race."

The groups of patriarchal families, which border the composition of the ceiling are choice selections of piety and love, in sentiments and forms unknown to the ancients, and unattempted by the moderns before his time; the naked figures are new and admirable—the prophets, sibyls, and the four corners of the ceiling, taken separately, will afford matter for contemplation and study not to be found in whole galleries by other masters.

The "Last Judgment" is indeed a consummate work; as sublime and terrific to all beholders in relation to the most important interests of humanity, as it was novel and astonishing to contemporary painters when first exposed to the public, and has been since to all admirers of the noblest productions of genius. This work has been so powerfully described, and so admirably commented on by the great professor of painting in this academy, that little more need be said at present. Perhaps, in justice to the originality of conception, it may not be impertinent to observe, that Lucas Signorelli, a painter of great merit, some years before Michael Angelo became eminent, painted a "Last Judgment" in the cathedral of Orvieto—represented by a multitude of figures standing upright on the fore-ground, waiting conveyance to their final destinations by angels or demons in the air above them. Michael Angelo's composition is the actual accomplishment of the Judgment. The Divine Son in the midst of saints and apostles, has the books opened by the angels before Him, from which every one is judged according to his works. The Christian charities and the deadly sins,* with the struggles of good and evil, are most strikingly expressed † in characteristic groups immediately below the angels, whilst the dead are rising from their graves in the earth : thus confining the ultimate horror of the scene to a smaller space in the lower part of the altar-piece.

Michael Angelo's two great compositions in the Pauline Chapel must not be forgotten : they were, it is true, the productions of his old age, but they are the works of a mighty veteran. In the "Conversion of Saul," the groups of angels surrounding the descending Saviour, whilst calling His apostle, are luxuriantly ecstatic, and offer an internal testimony that Correggio's ideas of the celestial ministry, in his celebrated "Nativity," were probably awakened by the sight of some sketches from this picture. The terror and flight of the horses from the fallen Saul bear evidence to the miracle.

The Martyrdom of S. Peter is a scene of solemn gloom congenial with the occasion, where his Christian brethren descend with slow and sorrowing steps into the excavation, in which the cross is fixed, to receive the dying apostle's benediction.

The character of Michael Angelo's sculpture is too lofty and original to be dismissed without farther notice, although we must acknowledge it has been criticised with severity, because it rarely possesses the chaste simplicity of Grecian art. True ; but although Michael Angelo lived long, he did not

* Plates XXXIII. and XXXIV. † See Plate XXXVII

live long enough to give absolute perfection to all his works: yet the pensive sitting figure of Lorenzo di Medici, in the Medici Chapel, is not without this charm; and the Madonna and Child on the north side of the same chapel is simple, and is endowed with a sentiment of maternal affection never found in the Greek sculpture, but frequently in the works of this artist, particularly in his paintings, and that of the most tender kind.

The recumbent statues in the monument of Julian di Medici, in the same chapel, of Daybreak or Dawn, and Night, are grand and mysterious: the characters and forms bespeak the same mighty mind and hand evident throughout the ceiling of the Sistine Chapel, and Last Judgment.

The monument of Julius the Second, according to Michael Angelo's sketch, was magnificently conceived, and characteristic of this haughty pontiff; but the composition was reduced to one quarter of the first intention by succeeding popes, and the statues were executed by inferior sculptors, excepting Moses. Two slaves, in the original design, were done in marble; these are now in the Louvre, admired for disposition and anatomical perfection.

The character and works of Michael Angelo have been dwelt on at greater length, because, as his mental and bodily powers continued far beyond the usual period of human life, his diligence attained to so much greater perfection in the principles of art. Anatomy—the motion and perspective of the **figure**

—the complication, grandeur and harmony of his grouping—the advantages and facility of execution in painting and sculpture—his mathematical and mechanical attainments in architecture and building, exhibited in the many and prodigious works he accomplished, demonstrate how greatly he contributed to the restoration of art.

After the works of the great man just mentioned, John of Bologna's "Venus coming from the Bath," both standing and kneeling, are remarkable for delicacy and grace. His Mercury rising to fly is energetic and original; his groups are harmoniously incatenated.

Benvenuto Cellini deserves praise for his group of Perseus and Medusa; but the succeeding sculptors in the seventeenth century must be looked on as having debased, rather than contributed to the restoration of art. Even Bernini, whose reputation was so great in his time, can be praised only for his Apollo and Daphne, and for the ease and nature of his portraits. His larger works are remarkable for presuming airs, affected grace, and unmeaning flutter.

Towards the close of the seventeenth century, however, better knowledge of principles and science, more attention to ideal beauty, and more careful and profound study of nature, raised the productions of this art again to a promise of future success, unknown since the times of ancient Greece.

By this sketch it will be seen, that the arts rose to the highest elevation in the free states of Greece—

that they were destroyed and buried by the inroads of barbarism and ignorance—and, that they were restored in the free states of Italy by the same means which gave them birth, and reared them to maturity in their native land.

Painting and sculpture had been practised and generally admired in Italy from the eleventh century ; but at that time they were without determined proportions for the human figure; without anatomy, perspective, or the principles of motion.

In the beginning of the fifteenth century, the increasing power of the Turks had reduced the eastern empire to little more than the city of Constantinople, when such of the learned Greeks as dreaded the dominion of this barbarous people sought shelter in Italy, and brought with them copies of the ancient classics in science and polite literature ; as they were perfect masters of these in their own language, they communicated them to the Italians in Venice, Rome and Florence.

Leonardo da Vinci at this time made studies of anatomy from the horse, and afterwards a complete series of anatomical designs from the human subject, assisted in the dissections by the celebrated anatomist Marc Antonio della Torre. Rather before this time, Michael Angelo engaged in a most diligent course of this study. Both these great men were most likely encouraged to undertake a careful application to this science, by the publication of John Guinter of Anderon, one of the masters of Vesalius, in the year 1536, "the only anatomist before Vesalius who gives an accurate and full description of the muscles."

Leon Baptista Alberti had, some years before, found the necessity of geometrical knowledge in painting, which Paolo Uccello pursued until he brought perspective to a perfection that bewitched several of his contemporaries. In justice to the ancients, however, it must be acknowledged as an improvement only (though an exceedingly valuable one) on Euclid's optics.

The use of perspective in fore-shortening the human figure has given a marvellous grandeur and truth to the groups of Michael Angelo. A drawing by this great master is extant of a figure measured in the same manner as Vitruvius informs us was practised by the Greeks, and which has since been generally used.

Of all the advantages which the sister arts derived from the restoration of Greek literature, nothing seems more extraordinary than the following coincidence, and few circumstances relating to the subject deserve a more serious attention.

Previous to the time of Phidias, the Grecian sculpture, both gods and men, had the same ordinary outline of body, limbs, and countenance usually found in common nature; and it has been remarked, that the ancient statue of Minerva in the Villa Albani was characterized as the goddess of wisdom, by an aged countenance.

Phidias, however, began the reformation. He gave dignity to Jupiter from Homer's description. Succeeding artists continued to refine and elevate the different orders of divinity, until each personage of the mythology received the appointed portion of ideal beauty from selected nature and abstracted reasoning.

We must remember that Phidias and Plato were nearly contemporaries; and considering the astonishing influence of this philosopher's discourses and writings, particularly concerning the power of the soul's energies in the configuration of the countenance and person, according to established habits of virtue or vice—his distinction of the spiritual orders—his accurate investigation of the good, the perfect, and the beautiful itself—when we consider the high and extensive veneration in which these discourses were held, little doubt can be entertained of their influence in directing the artist's mind in his choice of subjects, and the expression of qualities for the perfection of beauty.

The coincidence, then, alluded to above, was that, in the very zenith of the restoration of the art, in the time of Michael Angelo, Leonardo da Vinci, and Raffaelle, the magnificent Lorenzo di Medici formed a society of Platonic philosophers, consisting of the most celebrated scholars of his time and country, and caused the philosopher's dialogues to be translated and commented on by Marsilius Ficinus; and as this work was highly esteemed by the Medici family, the pontiffs Leo the Tenth, Clement the Seventh, and Julius the Third, as well as by the learned and ingenious generally, there can be little doubt that Plato's reasoning on the beautiful and its characteristics, supplied as happy assistance in the determination of sublime and spiritual characters to the restorers of art in Italy, as it had done to the ancient Greek artists.

As a brief sketch has been offered of the restoration of art, and some of the circumstances noticed which contributed to this end, the following question naturally presents itself : from what complication of causes did literature and the arts remain in such a state of concealment and darkness for the long period of a thousand years, from the fifth to the fifteenth century?

Though the answer to this question is sufficiently given in the general history of the times, it is so much interwoven with the nature of our subject. that it may not appear impertinent to introduce an illustrative paragraph, to preserve the connection of argument.

Whilst the northern people overran Europe in the seventh century, the Saracens invaded the east, and established themselves in Egypt, Persia, and a portion of Greece, where they soon became sensible of the advantages that Christians derived from science and letters, particularly in commerce and medicine.

Two successive Saracen princes, Haroun Al Raschid

and Al Mamon, to obtain the same benefits for themselves and their subjects, employed Syrian Christians to translate the Greek authors of highest reputation into the Arabic language, after which they caused the original MSS. to be burnt; thus endeavouring to secure all the philosophy, mathematics, medicine, anatomy, geography, history, and poetry which they had found among the conquered people, and by the destruction of the MSS. to reduce the Greeks to the same state of ignorance as that in which they were themselves previously involved. This conduct of the Saracens, as they intended, deprived the Christians of a considerable portion of the remaining light, which former calamity and destruction had spared. Greek authors translated by Syrians into Arabic, that is to say, from one language foreign to the translators, into another equally foreign, produced copies abounding in mistakes, and, wherever the subject was abstruse, misconception or ignorance frequently rendered the passage unintelligible. In this state of things, the conquests of the Saracens had enabled them to found universities in Europe and Asia, in which they alone assumed the privilege of instruction. The confusion and perversion the ancient authors had suffered by translation, rendered philosophy the instrument of the Koran, and infected Christianity with its poison far and wide. Whilst science remained torpid, painting and sculpture ceased to be practised, as the representation of the human figure was forbidden by the Mohammedan law; and architecture as practised by the Arabians and Saracens became an imitation, in the larger masses and columns, of the declining architecture of the lower empire, with capitals formed of unmeaning flourishes, or dug into numerous small cavities, because that was more easily effected by unskilful workmen than a decoration of foliage, from which that style improperly called Gothic is believed to have originated in Europe.

Thus were the arts and their principles lost for so long a period, in addition to the other miseries of a darkened and afflicted world, until providentially restored in the fifteenth century by men especially endowed, to whose genius and indefatigable labours we must always look with respect and gratitude.

In considering the impediments that prevented an earlier manifestation of the progress of modern art, and which were (by some) believed to be insurmountable, the following opinion, prevalent among the classical admirers of art previous to the time of Winckelman and afterwards, deserves particular notice. This was, that the Christian religion afforded subjects less favourable to the painter or sculptor than the Pagan mythology: although we hope this prejudice is diminished, yet it is not so entirely passed away as to render an inquiry into its merits wholly useless. We will first, therefore, consider the question in respect to beauty; next, in respect to the moral systems; and, lastly, we will consider what has been done, in relation to what is possible to be done.

In the first place, the ancient theory of personal beauty is, that it consists in a body and limbs accommodated to perform the various functions and offices of life, under the government of the best principles of intelligence and will: in this definition the generality of moderns agree with the ancients. Here, then, we see that the artist is equally bound by the modern, as by the ancient practice, to make himself acquainted by physiological inquiry and philosophical reasoning, with the most perfect union of form and sentiment for his studies.

Beauty is to be considered as pertaining to two orders of creation—the supernatural and the natural. In the Pagan mythology, the supernatural order consists of superior and inferior divinities, beatified heroes, and purified spirits. These have been represented by the ancients with a grandeur, perfection, and distinctness of character, by which we as immediately distinguish Jupiter from Hercules, or Mercury, as we distinguish Cicero from Demosthenes, or Socrates from Zeno. The most elevated orders are dignified in their characters, forms and attitudes, whilst the younger deities are more remarkable for beauty in the bloom of youth, and a corresponding lightness of figure and sprightliness of action; to these might be added an enumeration of distinctions both celestial and terrestrial.

But the arts of design may exert their utmost

efforts, could they call even the genius of Phidias and the grace of Praxiteles to employ their most exalted conceptions in the most lively execution, without the reasonable expectation of being perfectly satisfied with their own productions, if employed on the personages and events of Divine revelation.

The gradations of celestial power and beauty in the orders of angels and archangels, the grandeur and inspiration of prophets according to the difference of mission, and the sanctity of apostles, have produced examples of grace, beauty, and grandeur of character, original in themselves, and not to be found in such variety among the remains of antiquity, as in works by the restorers of art in the fifteenth century.

If we compare the moral systems of Paganism and Christianity, we cannot fail to wonder that society was not exterminated in an empire which sacrificed 20,000 gladiators every year, in the amphitheatres for public diversion. This is but one instance of the public character of the Romans. Even the Athenians, so justly admired for arts and letters, in their moral habits tolerated the most frightful offences. Besides that contradiction to the love of liberty in which they defended their country against foreign invaders, that at the time Athens contained 12,000 free citizens, it contained also 120,000 slaves, or ten slaves to every free citizen.

But enough of this. We will console ourselves

with the cheering reflection, that some sense of piety and mutual duty was kept alive by the spirit of philosophy, under Pagan systems, and felicitate ourselves upon the enjoyment of that perfect Dispensation which enjoins moral practice to secure the happiness of all—allowing an extent of political freedom beneficial to all, at the same time that it guards the just rights of every one—which protects knowledge and science, and bestows on the arts a moral purity and a perfection of sentiment, arising from the various duties and charities which belong to Christianity, and are not to be found under any other code. These advantages were well understood by Leonardo da Vinci, Raffaelle, and Michael Angelo. The Holy Families only, by these great masters, would form a gallery of the greatest beauty —the most tender and interesting sentiment, totally unlike any ancient work, and entirely novel in subject, composition and character. The same may be said of those noble compositions by Raffaelle, the Cartoons, which for expression of Divine and exalted character, grand and extraordinary grouping, may be compared with the noblest remains of ancient art.

Michael Angelo's merits have been frequently and ably insisted on by your excellent professor of painting: but we may be still permitted to observe, that in the Sistine Chapel, the sublimity of subjects and characters, the several patriarchal groups of incomparable interest and beauty, all original, and unlike any production of antiquity, with that wonderful altar-piece of the Last Judgment, form together a labour that seems scarcely the work of man, and stands without a rival in ancient or modern art.

When we consider what was done by the restorers of art in the fifteenth century, what incredible improvements were made in a comparatively few years, and remember that these works are still before us for our instruction, and that we possess, besides, the invaluable principles and rules used by those distinguished persons for conducting their works. In addition to these advantages, great numbers of the finest examples of ancient art, including the Herculaneum collection of paintings and the Greek painted vases, which were hidden in the earth when Raffaelle and Michael Angelo lived in Italy, have since been extracted from the oblivion in which they lay, and have shed additional light on the arts of design. With these assistances from ancient art and ancient wisdom, in addition to the beautiful and novel works of the fifteenth century, and the continual improvements in every branch of science, which give much more facility to labour, shall we not say with Dr. Young, in his 'Essay on Composition,' that considering all these advantages of principles from so many preceding ages, with the innumerable works of genius by which they are illustrated and we are instructed,—that we are properly the ancients, because these our mental riches are more abundant than have ever been enjoyed before, and possess us with advantages the ancients had not? We can employ our imaginations in the sister arts, on the sublime, the heroic, the severely beautiful personages and events of the venerable Homer and Hesiod's poems; we may venture on the terrific or afflicting scenes of the Greek tragedians; or we may relax our fancy with the innocent simplicity of the pastoral poets; but we have subjects also, which, although unknown to the Greeks and Romans, will employ the greatest powers with the greatest advantage to the best faculties and dispositions of man, to his happiness both present and future. It will be at once understood that the book which supplies these subjects is the Holy Bible.

Some have thought, that so many compositions have already been made, that nothing new can now be found in it for painting or sculpture; but it should be remembered that the compositions have been little more than selections from the common historical subjects, with few or none from the Prophecies and Psalms, which offer an abundance of the most sublime and splendid, as well as most simple and affecting subjects for design. Besides, when we consider that every subject may be represented in three striking points of time, the commencement of an action, the heat of the action, and the conclusion—and also that every action may be represented in four or five different manners, especially if it comprehends several figures—under all these circumstances, we may then safely affirm, without danger of exaggeration, that many hundred subjects are to be found in the sacred writings, which, being ably designed, would be new to the beholder.

In the number of original subjects, of the noblest class, derived from revelation, we must remember the immortal poem of 'Paradise Lost,' by our countryman John Milton; concerning which Dryden wrote familiarly to the Earl of Dorset:—" This man has out-cut us all, and the ancients too." A learned Italian (the Marquis Manto) said of the author, in a Latin distich, that " Greece boasted her Meonides, Rome her Virgil, and England her Milton, equal to both." Dr. Johnson, to whom we are indebted for the inimitable Preface to Shakspeare, has also done justice to the genius of Milton, and, though his adversary in religious and political opinions, has honestly and magnanimously pronounced an encomium on the 'Paradise Lost,' not cursorily and generally, but particularly; accompanied by reasons on each occasion which flash conviction on the mind of the reader, and which, by sagacity of observation and power of expression, evince the most extraordinary discrimination of excellence, and of preference, ever offered to the epic muse.

And yet, it is to be believed, that this Poet, abounding in subjects and characters of the most extraordinary kind, has been almost entirely neglected in the arts of his own country, whilst his merits have been vindicated and illustrated by the liberal mind and genius of a foreigner !*

In future, let us, conscious of the means we possess, not be negligent in exerting ourselves for posterity in the same proportion as we feel our own obligations to former ages.

---

* Fuseli's 'Milton Gallery.' Several of the pictures were engraved for Du Roveray's edition of 'Milton's Paradise Lost,' 1802. Westall and Martin have, since that period, illustrated the immortal work.

TWO ADDRESSES

DELIVERED AT

THE ROYAL ACADEMY

ON THE DEATH OF

THOMAS BANKS, R.A., 1805,

AND ON

ANTONIO CANOVA, MARQUIS OF ISCHIA,

WHO DIED AT VENICE, OCTOBER, 1822.

BY

JOHN FLAXMAN.

AN ADDRESS

TO THE

PRESIDENT AND MEMBERS OF THE ROYAL ACADEMY

ON THE

DEATH OF THOMAS BANKS,

SCULPTOR,

SIR,

It is with feelings of deep regret that I address you and the several distinguished members of the Royal Academy this evening. One whose virtues and talents have been familiar to me for forty years, has just been separated from this institution for ever: such is the condition of humanity, whether we are allied by blood or affection, endeared by rare worth or eminent endowments. Time and death burst the bonds and tear the parties from each other, while this mortal scene of change and fluctuation still continues. A little space shows the father followed by the son and grandson, he again by his children, until all are swallowed in the gulf of eternity; hence the frequent lamentations on the shortness of life. But let us beware we do not charge on Infinite Goodness and Wisdom that which properly belongs to the misapprehension of man: we are assured, on the best authority, that this world is only a state of trial preparatory to a more perfect final existence in happiness or punishment. If then the term of human life is sufficient by *mis-application* to load ourselves with misery, or by virtue to prepare for everlasting bliss, we ought to be well contented with the dispensations of Providence, and go on cheerfully towards the better prospect before us. Even in the progress of human knowledge the length of life seems better suited to great productions than we are aware of at the first view, for the labours of Aristotle, Bacon, Newton, and other luminaries of science, might incline us to believe that each of them had lived some ages, if we did not know how many years old they were at the time of their decease. In the arts of design, the works of Michael Angelo in painting, sculpture and architecture, seem more than could possibly be performed during the lives of two or three men, and some of the Greek sculpture which we admire and imitate at this day, seems the accumulated perfection of centuries, rather than the production of individual men; thus, although human life may appear short when considered in some points of view, yet the industrious and energetic have left works which evince the excellence and extent of the mind, at the same time that they secure the respect and affection of posterity.

The worthy man of whom we propose to speak, deserves well to be placed in this class,—his best works may be considered as standard in sentiment and execution; his memory, therefore, deserves the respect of this society, and a share of public gratitude. But in proceeding, I shall quote the following passage from Mr. Rollin's Introduction to the Arts and Sciences, in which he describes the rank and value of this kind of merit:—" The history of arts and sciences, and of the persons who have most eminently distinguished themselves by them, to speak properly, is the history of the human genius, which in some sense does not give place to that of princes and heroes, whom common opinion places in the highest degree of elevation and glory. I do not intend, by speaking in this manner, to strike at the difference of rank and condition, nor to confound or level the order which God himself has instituted amongst men. He has placed princes, kings, and rulers of states over our heads, with whom He has deposited His authority, and after them generals of armies, ministers, magistrates, and all those with whom the sovereign divides the cares of government; the honours paid to them, and the pre-eminence they possess, are no usurpation on their side. Divine Providence itself has assigned them their high stations, and demands submission, obedience and respect for those that sit in His place.

" But there is also another order of things, and if I may be permitted to say so, another disposition of the same Providence, which, without regard to the first kinds of greatness I have mentioned, establishes quite a different species of eminence, in which distinction arises neither from birth, riches, authority, nor elevation of place, but from merit and knowledge alone. It is the same Providence that regulates rank also of this kind, by the free and entirely voluntary dispensation of the talents of the mind, which it distributes in what proportion, and to whom it pleases, without any regard to the quality or nobility of the person. It forms, from the assemblage of learned of all kinds, a new species of empire, infinitely more extensive than all others, which takes in all times and nations, without regard to age, sex, condition, or climate; here the plebeian finds himself on a level with the nobleman, the subject with the prince, nay, often his superior."

As the foregoing quotation gives a fair comparative view of that class of character to which Mr. Banks belongs, so it affords a just appreciation of the following particulars of his life and works.

Thomas Banks was born December 29, 1735; at the age of fifteen he was placed under Mr. Barlow, an ornament carver, who lived near the late Mr. Peter Scheemaker, the sculptor. Young Banks, by means of his acquaintance with Mr. Scheemaker's pupils, obtained a sight of the studies, and was so struck with the collection of models and casts, that he determined to become a sculptor also; and notwithstanding he was constantly employed from 6 o'clock in the morning till 8 at night for Mr. Barlow, such was his enthusiasm, that having obtained permission, he drew or modelled in Mr. Scheemaker's study every evening, from 8 till 10 or 11. Having completed his time with Mr. Barlow, at the age of twenty-three he began his studies from the life at the academy in St. Martin's Lane; and his determination to follow sculpture was strengthened by the premiums offered in the society for the encouragement of arts, manufactures, and commerce : three of these rewards he obtained—for a basso-relievo of the death of Epaminondas, in Portland stone ; another, of Hector's body redeemed, in marble, and a figure of Prometheus with the vulture, in clay, the size of life; as far as memory may be depended on, this figure was boldly conceived, the composition was harmonious and compact, the character was natural, and on the whole it was a fair earnest of his future productions.

In 1770 he received the gold medal of the Royal Academy for a basso-relievo of the rape of Proserpine, and in consequence was sent to Rome, at the academy's expense, in 1772. He studied in Italy seven years, three years on the academy's account and four years on his own : during this time he executed a basso-relievo in marble, of the death of Germanicus, now in the possession of Thomas Coke, Esq., of Holkham ; another, of Caractacus before Claudius, now at Stowe ; another basso-relievo in plaster, of Thetis rising to comfort Achilles ; and the statue of a Cupid four feet and a half high : upon the three last-mentioned works I shall presently trouble you with some further observations. In 1779 he returned to England, finished the statue of Cupid, and not being much employed, he embarked for St. Petersburgh in 1781, and took this statue with him, which was purchased by the Empress Catherine for £380 sterling, and placed in a grotto in the gardens of Czarscozelo.

In 1782 he returned from Russia. His merit now beginning to be felt and acknowledged, he was immediately engaged in Bishop Newton's monument for Bow Church in the City; and to the honour of Mr. Dance, the architect, he strongly recommended Mr. Banks to execute the monument of Sir Eyre Coote, for Westminster Abbey, in which he was accordingly employed by the East India Company. About this time he produced his statue of Achilles in the Royal Exhibition, which, besides receiving the general approbation of the public, was so much admired by the academy, that the artist was elected an Associate. Some years after, when chosen an Academician, he presented to the institution that fine statue of the Falling Giant which is placed in the Council Room.

It is not the present intention to relate a complete chronological catalogue of all this industrious man's labours; such a collection would be as difficult to ascertain, as it would be tedious and unintelligible in the recital, unless we could refer to a repository present, for drawings, or models, of the several works.

It will be more to the present purpose that we

should point out his most celebrated performances and their situations, that the hearer may see and admire them at his own leisure.

After those already mentioned I shall add the following—

Shakspeare between Painting and Poetry, a colossal alto-relievo, on the Shakspeare Gallery in Pall Mall. The trophies on the back front of Somerset House. The monument of Miss Boothby at Ashburne, in Derbyshire; this is a beautiful statue of a girl reposing on a bed. A monument to Mrs. Petree, in Lewisham Church, Kent; it is a large basso-relievo of the lady dying, supported by Faith, and attended by Hope and Charity; her son sits by absorbed in grief; the marble was exhibited in the Royal Academy, 1788. The statue of Lord Cornwallis, sent to Madras, the model of which is in Mr. Banks' study The national monument of Captain Burgess, in St. Paul's Cathedral; the Captain is represented receiving a sword from Victory; the pedestal is adorned with naval trophies and figures of captives.

In private life Mr. Banks' moral conduct was exemplary; he was a good and beneficent son, an excellent husband, a kind and gentle master, faithful and just in all his engagements; he was modest concerning his own merits, and generous in his praise of others, wherever they appeared to deserve commendation; he freely gave professional advice and instruction to beginners in the arts, and thought on all occasions, that forming and directing the rising generation in the right way, was a duty of too much importance ever to be neglected. As a member of this academy he was active and independent; he obeyed its laws, attended diligently in its offices, and supported its rights, while his eminent qualifications made him a perfect judge of its true interests, and his integrity promoted them to the utmost of his power.

Such was the academician whom this institution has lost, and when the character of the man, and the merits of the artist are considered, it must appear, that it will be no easy task worthily to fill up the vacancy.

But in order to form a just estimate of the benefit which sculpture has derived from his talents in England, it will be necessary to take a cursory view of this art in Europe previous to the time when Mr. Banks' studies commenced, and to observe its progress with a little more accuracy in our own country.

In Rome (the centre from which the arts have emanated for centuries past), about 150 years since, the taste of Bernini, the Neapolitan sculptor, infected and prevailed over the Florentine and Roman schools. He had studied painting, and seems to have been enamoured with the works of Correggio, who, to avoid the dryness of his master, Andrea Mantegna, gave prodigious flow to the lines of his figures, and redundance to his draperies; of which Bernini's statues are only caricatures. totally devoid of the painter's ecstatic grace and sentiment. Before he was twenty years old, he not only composed but completed a marble group, the size of nature, of Apollo and Daphne, at the moment the nymph is changing into a laurel-tree; the delicate characters of the figures, the sprightly expression, the smooth finish of the material and the light execution of the foliage, so captivated the public taste, that M. Angelo was forgotten, the antique statues disregarded, and nothing looked on with delight that was not produced by the new favourite. It is true, Bernini showed respectable talents in the group above mentioned, and had he continued to select and study nature with diligence, he might have been a most valuable artist; but sudden success prevented him, and he never improved; the immense works crowded on him made him spurn all example, and consider only how he might send out his models and designs most speedily. The attitudes of his figures are much twisted, the heads turned with a meretricious grace, the countenances simper affectedly, or are deformed by low passions; the poor and vulgar limbs and bodies are loaded with draperies of such protruding or flying folds, as equally expose the unskilfulness of the artist and the solidity of the material on which he worked; his groups have an unmeaning connection, and his basso-relievos are filled up with buildings in perspective, clouds, water, diminished figures, and attempts to represent such aerial effects as break down the boundaries of painting and sculpture, and confound the two arts. Pope Urban the Eighth was patron of this artist, and so passionately did he admire and promote his works, that not contented with spending immense sums upon them, he took the ancient bronze ornaments from the roof in the portico of the Pantheon, to the amount of 186,000 pounds, for Bernini to cast his bizarre and childish baldachin for St. Peter's, and then published their mutual shame in a boasting Latin inscription, affixed to the building he had robbed so shamefully. Thus the pope and the sculptor carried all before them in their time, and sent out a baneful influence, which corrupted public taste for upwards of one hundred years afterwards.

Mocho, Bolgio, Quesnoy (commonly called Fiamingo), and the inferior sculptors of the time, adopted the popular taste, which their scholars continued, and its last puny and insipid efforts are to be seen in the statues at the Fountain of Trevi, and monument of Benedict the Fourteenth, executed by Bracci and Sibylla, in St. Peter's Church, about fifty years since.

Nearly the same taste in the arts of design which prevailed in Italy prevailed also in France, as the latter country was supplied with art, or artists, from the former; thus when Louis the Fourteenth invited Bernini to come into France, Bernini answered, "that he had no need of him, whilst he had such a sculptor as Puget." Puget's works were somewhat more dry and detailed than Bernini's; Gerardon's (his contemporary) were more heavy ; but they were all of the same school. The opinion of Bernini con firmed the monarch, and the same bad taste was cultivated in France with as much zeal as it was fostered in Italy, as we see by the works of Bouchardon, Boucher, &c., who continued it to the same time which extinguished its last feeble efforts in both countries.

Spain, Germany, and the other nations of Europe receiving their supplies of fine art from the two countries above mentioned, were consequently influenced by the same motives and trammelled in the same taste, which was at this period become so degraded, as to be at the point of utter dissolution, had not some controlling circumstances arisen which assisted in its revival.

The King of Naples had, in part, cleared the ruins of Herculaneum and Pompeii, which exposed to view streets, dwelling-houses, temples, theatres, baths, and public places, nearly in the same state as when they were inhabited 1700 years before; these discoveries brought back to the light of day, as it were by miracle, 700 ancient paintings, and a prodigious number of bronze statues and busts, of the finest Greek sculpture.

The success of these discoveries, and the interest they excited, stimulated the popes, Roman nobility, and antiquarians, to make excavations wherever there was a probability their labours would be rewarded. These researches fortunately recovered from oblivion innumerable pieces of exquisite sculpture: many of the most precious formed the Clementine Museum; many enriched the Borghese, Albani, and other collections; several passed into Germany, Holland, Sweden, Russia, France and Spain. England was not insensible to the opportunity, and several intelligent and spirited individuals profited by this profusion of ancient treasure. Such acquisitions roused attention from all quarters; they were eagerly visited, greedily examined, dissertations and memoirs were written concerning them, and systematic inquiries into their principles published.

During all this research and analysis, frequent comparisons were made with the modern works, the remains of the bad taste above mentioned, and which were found so deficient in every excellence, that they were universally abandoned to contempt. The interested antiquarian, with sordid cruelty, and to raise the price of his own commodity, whispered, that modern talents were unequal to the meanest of these productions, and sometimes he found a senseless purchaser, whose only measure of intelligence was the abundance of his wealth; who would pay dearly enough for anything that was called ancient, to be received into the number of the cognoscenti and join in the outcry against modern ability.

All this however brought in a new and severer mode of study among the artists, with a more diligent attention to nature and the antique, and has enabled some of them to exhibit performances much more on a level with the merit of those works, than the insensible can feel or the interested choose to own.

Having marked these phenomena in the hemisphere of art, we should now turn our thoughts more particularly to England, and see in what manner our own country was affected by their influence.

Previous to the Reformation, although Italian artists were employed in ornamenting our churches and tombs, yet in the old histories, records, and contracts of public buildings, there are abundant names of English painters and sculptors, who appear to have been considered able masters in their time, perhaps not inferior to their Italian fellow-workmen. But after Henry the Eighth's separation from the Church of Rome, Elizabeth, proceeding in the Reformation, destroyed the pictures and images in the churches; strictly forbidding anything of the kind to be admitted in future, under the severest penalties, as being Catholic and idolatrous. This entirely prevented the exercise of historical painting, or sculpture in this country; at the very time Raffaelle and Michael Angelo had brought those arts into the highest estimation on the Continent. The Rebellion in 1643 completed what the Reformation had begun; the fanatics defaced whatever they could, that the former inquisition had spared; they broke painted windows and tombs, carried away the monumental brass, and church plate, crying, " Cursed be he that doeth the work of the Lord deceitfully." Thus the artist, terrified by the threats of the sovereign, the denunciation of death or perpetual imprisonment from the law, and scared by fanatical anathemas, found that his only hope of safety rested upon quitting for ever a profession, which enclosed him on all sides with the prospect of misery and destruction.

From this time, and from these causes, we scarcely hear of any attempt at historical art by an Englishman, until it was again called forth by the benign influence of the present reign.

When the liberal spirit of Charles the First desired to adorn the architecture of Whitehall with the graces of painting, he was obliged to seek the artist in a foreign land; he had no subject equal to the task. Rubens and Vandyck were employed, and when the King's bust was to be done, Vandyck painted three views of his face, a front, a side, and a three-quarter, which were sent to Bernini in Rome, by whom it was executed in marble. If our kings and nobility had continued to inhabit castles, as in the feudal times, painting and sculpture would have been but little wanted; for if the walls of the buildings were sufficiently strong to resist battery or shot, and contained retreats to secure the inhabitants from the enemy, the end of that kind of dwelling was answered; but in the times succeeding Charles the First, the improved state of society and knowledge had induced the great to build commodious villas and palaces, in which the architectural distribution made the sister arts absolutely necessary to uniformity and completion. Still ingenious foreigners were employed for this purpose, whilst the native was treated with contempt, both at home and abroad, for his inability in those arts which law and religion had forbidden him to practise.

As this suppression of ability was extremely impolitic and dishonourable to the country, let us inquire for a moment on what scriptural authority the prohibition which occasioned it was supported. Painting and sculpture were banished from the churches, that they might not be idolatrously worshipped; and this is just; the Divine law orders they shall not be worshipped, but utters no prohibition against the arts themselves : on the contrary, Divine precept directed images of cherubim to be made, whose wings should extend over the ark of the covenant, and cherubim to be embroidered on the curtains which surrounded it. This decision in favour of the arts being employed for proper purposes in sacred buildings is so clear and strong, that it could only be overlooked, or opposed by infatuated bigotry.

A succession of foreign artists, as has been observed, were employed in almost every work of importance, from the time of Charles the First until within forty years of the present day. The painters, Vandyck, Lely, Verrio, Kneller, and Casali, succeeded to each other; as did also the sculptors, Cibber, Gibbons, Scheemaker, Rysbrack, Bertocini, Roubiliac.

This variety of artists (sculptors are more particularly meant) from different countries, French,
Flemings, and Italians, sometimes brought the taste
of John Goujon or Puget, sometimes a debased imitation of John of Bologna and the Florentine
school, and sometimes the taste of Bernini; but
never a pure style and sound principle.

After the Reformation, the chief employment of
sculpture was in sepulchral monuments, which
during the reigns of James the First and his son
Charles, were chiefly executed by Frenchmen or
Flemings, scholars of John Goujon, still regulated
by the principles their master had acquired from
Primaticcio, the pupil of Raffaelle. Some of these
works have great merit, particularly the tombs of
Sir John Norris and Sir Francis Vere,* in the same
chapel with Roubiliac's monument of Lady E.
Nightingale in Westminster Abbey.

The rebuilding of London, in the reign of Charles
the Second, gave some employment to sculpture.
Cibber's works are the most conspicuous of that
period; his mad figures on the Bedlam gates have a
natural sentiment, but are ill drawn; his bas-relief
on the pedestal of London Monument is not ill
conceived, but stiff and clumsy in the execution; his
clothed figures in the Royal Exchange strut like
dancing-masters, and have the importance of cox-
combs. But with all his faults, what he left is far
preferable to the succeeding works. The figures on

* See Plate LI.

St. Paul's Church, and the Conversion of the Saint in the pediment, partake strongly of Bernini's affectation; and from that time to the establishment of this academy, we must expect to see every piece of sculpture more or less tinctured with the same bad taste, especially the sepulchral monuments, to which, after the statues and basso-relievos last noticed, we must chiefly look for the progress of sculpture amongst us.

It will be proper here to remark, that all the Grecian sculpture was arranged in three classes: the group of figures; the single statue; and alto- or basso-relievo. The first two classes were suited to all insulated situations, and the latter to fill panels in walls. These classes not only serve all architectural purposes, but adorn, harmonize, and finish its forms; every attempt to make other combinations between sculpture and architecture will be found unreasonable, and degrading to one as well as the other. After the statues and basso-relievos last noticed, we must return again to sepulchral monuments for the progress of sculpture, and here the taste of Bernini (whose character and works we have already noticed, and who seems to have thought that he had the privilege of equally subverting art and nature in his works,) again obtrudes itself. I shall mention the following instances, although I am afraid their extreme absurdities will prevent such of those from believing the descriptions as have not seen the things themselves. In the area before the

Church of Santa Maria Sopra Minerva, he raised a
bronze elephant on a pedestal, and on the elephant's
back placed an Egyptian obelisk : the architecture of
the east window in St. Peter's Church he has loaded
with many tons weight of stucco clouds, out of
which issue huge rays, intended for light or glory
of the same materials, but long and thick enough for
the beams of a house.

Extravagances of this kind, and many others that
he has committed, have fortunately had little effect
upon us, because some have been necessarily connected with Catholic churches, and others introduced
in fountains, which are frequent in hot countries :
we were, however, the dupes of his school until
native genius gained sufficient judgment and strength
to correct its errors, and supply a better style of art.

Before the time of Bernini, two kinds of sepulchral
monuments prevailed, one from the highest antiquity,
which was a sarcophagus, either plain or covered
with basso-relievos, with or without the statue
of the deceased on its top. The other kind was
introduced by Michael Angelo, in the Mausoleum of
Julius the Second, and those of the Medici family, in
the Chapel of St. Lorenzo at Florence. In these the
sarcophagus, as in the former kind, was suited to the
niche or architecture against which it was placed,
and surmounted or surrounded by statues of the
deceased and his moral attributes.

Both these practices were rational and proper,
the one for plainer, the other for more magnificent

tombs. This branch of sculpture was of too much importance to be neglected by Bernini; he stripped it of its ancient simple grandeur, leaving it neither group, statue, basso-relievo, sarcophagus, or trophy, but an absurd mixture of all, placed against a dark marble pyramid, and thus sacrificing all that is valuable in sculpture to what he conceived a picturesque effect.

The pyramid is, from its immense size, solid base, diminishing upwards, a building intended to last thousands of years : how ridiculous, then, to raise a little pyramid of slab marble, an inch thick, on a neat pedestal, to be the background of sculpture belonging to none of the ancient classes, foisted into architecture, with which it has neither connection nor harmony, and in which it appears equally disgusting and deformed! The first monuments he raised of this kind, were two in the Chigi Chapel, in the Church of Santa Maria del Popolo, in Rome : this novelty soon found its way into every country in Europe; our Westminster Abbey is an unfortunate instance of its prevalence. Rysbrack and Roubiliac spread the popularity of this taste in England; but, as the first of these sculptors was a mere workman, too insipid to give pleasure, and too dull to offend greatly, we shall dismiss him without farther notice. The other deserves more attention. Roubiliac was an enthusiast in his art, possessed of considerable talents. He copied vulgar nature with zeal, and some of his figures seem alive; but their characters are mean, their expressions grimace, and their forms frequently bad: his draperies are worked with great diligence and labour, from the most disagreeable examples in nature, the folds being either heavy or meagre, frequently without a determined general form, and hung on his figures with little meaning. He grouped two figures together (for he never attempted more) better than most of his contemporaries; but his thoughts are conceits, and his compositions epigrams. This artist went to Italy, in company with Mr. Pond, an English painter: he was absent from home three months, going and returning, stayed three days in Rome, and laughed at the sublime remains of ancient sculpture!! The other sculptors of his time were ordinary men: their faults were common, and their works have no beauty to rescue them from oblivion.

Thus we have seen the nobler efforts of painting and sculpture driven out of the country by reforming violence, and puritanical fury; sculpture reduced to the narrow limits of monument-making, and by these means degraded to a sort of trade; and this department supplied from the corrupt source of Bernini's school, and not unfrequently through the worst mediums.

In this state the art continued, until the establishment of the Royal Academy settled a course of study both at home and abroad, which developed the powers of English genius, till then unknown to the natives, and denied by foreigners.

Such was the low state of the arts when Mr. Banks began his studies, which, although not regular under any sculptor, were attended with some peculiar advantages. He was instructed in the principles of architecture, and practised drawing under his father, who was an architect; this enabled him soon to form a correct taste in that art, and displayed itself in the beauty and propriety of his architectural forms in the works he has left; it besides taught him how to introduce and combine sculpture with architecture, advantageously to both. Being placed under an ornament carver gave him a facility in his own ornamental sculpture, which may be observed in some flat foliage on Dr. Watts' monument in Westminster Abbey. Another advantage, and perhaps not the least, was that, having his opinions unbiassed from the sculptors of that time, he escaped being tinctured with the predominant manners of their work. He studied nature diligently for himself, and copied the antique to form his taste; his constant attention to the Admiranda and Stuart's Athens, had initiated him in the Greek style and composition, to which his academic drawings and models had added an extensive knowledge of the human figure and its conformation, parts, proportions and perspective, under the different circumstances of position, action, light and shade. During his residence in Rome, the ancient groups and statues, the basso-relievos, and the works of Michael Angelo in the Sistine Chapel, roused every faculty of his soul,

and urged him on to labour night and day, in a noble
emulation of those miracles of art and wonders of the
world : what was the consequence we shall see in
our examination of the two basso-relievos and the
statue of Cupid before us, which are specimens of
ais employments in Italy.

The Cupid catching a butterfly on his wing, is
rendered highly interesting to the mind by its philosophic allusion to the power of love, divine or
natural, on the soul; nothing can be more graceful
than the attitude; the outline is finely varied in the
different views; the softness of the form, the character of the face, and the adjustment of the hair,
are classically beautiful. The basso-relievo of Caractacus before Claudius, is composed on the principle
of those on the ancient sarcophagi, of which many
are to be seen in Rome, and other parts of Europe;
the subject is historical, but the characters are heroic,
and a dramatic gradation of passion is expressed in
a few figures : from the patriot's undaunted attitude,
you perceive he is saying, " Nor wouldest thou have
disdained to receive me with articles of peace, because
I am descended of noble progenitors, and I have
ruled over many warlike nations," whilst the emperor
listens with attentive respect.

The basso-relievo of Thetis rising to comfort
Achilles,* is of the epic class; (to follow our enlightened professor of painting in the application
of Aristotle's poetics to the arts of design) the sen-

* 1–359. " She rose from the dark sea like mist."

timent and character are beautiful and pathetic: the composition is so unlike any work ancient or modern, that the combination may be considered as the artist's own. The harmony of composition in the parts, which strengthens the unity of sentiment, is striking in these two, as well as several other works of this artist, and may be reckoned among the acquisitions which *our* sculpture has received from his talents and industry; nor is this our only obligation; he laboured in every department, and the whole art of sculpture has profited by his means. Before his time only one English sculptor (Mr. Nollekens) had formed his taste on the antique, and introduced a purer style of art; since then, sculpture has been gradually emerging from its state of barbarity, simple emblems have supplied the place of epigrammatical conceits, and imitations of the fine heads and beautiful outlines of the antique statues have succeeded to lifeless blocks, or caricature copies of common nature.

Another work by Mr. Banks deserves particular attention from its intrinsic merit, which, like the two above mentioned, is unequalled by similar productions of the present day in France or Italy, and may rank with this class of sculpture among the works of antiquity: I allude to Mrs. Petree's monument in Lewisham Church. It was exhibited in this academy in 1795, under the title of "The death of Eloisa;" the composition has been described above, and it 's to be regretted that an idea can only be given here by a slight sketch, which conveys but little of its merit. As the situation represented is the most important to humanity, so the expression is most powerfully penetrating; the dying woman is piously resigned, and the theological virtues which surround the bed are such as you might expect to see—the departed good, eminent for those qualities in a better state of existence: the son is an admirable human figure absorbed in grief. This basso-relievo is affixed on one side of the organ, companion to one on the other side, both being so placed as to be panels, and consequently regular architectural decorations to the wall; by which means, together with the excellence of the work, the church becomes a museum of sacred sculpture.

This example is worthy to be followed; architecture and sculpture should always be united in this manner. The monumental encouragement given to sculpture in England affords noble occasions for the artist to exercise his powers. I should deserve but little credit for saying the subjects of Holy Writ are the finest that can be treated. Michael Angelo and Raffaelle have long since proved them to be so. The Last Judgment, the Patriarchal Families, the Prophets, the Conversion of S. Paul, and the Crucifixion of S. Peter, by the former, and the Cartoons of the latter, are the first of human productions. These are fit subjects for the sculptor's employment, which ranges through whatever is great or good in the natural or intelligible worlds, extending beyond the limits of time and space, and comprehending all orders of created beings. But what man shall be equal to the task? We may however exert all our faculties in the most delightful and profitable manner by such exercises in our art; we may honour our Creator, and make ourselves and our fellow-creatures happier and better.

AN ADDRESS

PRESIDENT AND MEMBERS OF THE ROYAL ACADEMY,

DEATH OF SIGNOR CANOVA,

MARQUIS OF ISCHIA.

———————

THE arts of design, when considered in an extensive view, will be seen in continual fluctuation, like all other human concerns, for as states and empires gradually rise to power by the wisdom of institutions, the equity of laws and the union of interests, and are overthrown by the opposite causes; so by the same process of rise and decay or fluctuation, the history of painting, sculpture and architecture may be described, and their excellence or depression, progress or extinction, accounted for. The painter or sculptor, however, is little more concerned in the general fluctuations above mentioned, as connected with political history or the general disposal of human affairs, than any other member of the great family of mankind; he is much more interested in the productions of particular periods, and such maxims and studies of particular men as may be useful in forming his own: the diligent will not be slow in seizing the means to advance himself in the road he is going, by the maxims and practice of those who have gone before him : by those who have gone before him, are meant the venerated dead, from whom our most important instructions have been obtained by the schools they have established, and the rich treasury of accumulated works they have bequeathed to posterity, valuable for the double purpose of instruction and stimulation. Such benefits must be always remembered with grateful acknowledgments, and those from whom they were received looked up to with a pious regard.

Such reflections were suggested by the recent departure from this life of the celebrated sculptor, ANTONIO CANOVA. But, notwithstanding this distinguished man is now removed from us by the course of earthly events, in accordance with the dispensations of Providence, we are consoled by the recollection that his genius added rays to the lustre of his own time, and his virtues equally with his works will claim the admiration of succeeding ages.

Signor Canova was so generally celebrated and esteemed throughout Europe, as well as by the members of this academy, that it may be presumed not only that no apology need be offered for the introduction of his name, but on the contrary, not to have offered some eulogy on the solemn occasion, would have been disrespectful to the feelings of the Royal Academy, and unjust to the memory of the illustrious deceased.

This sculptor, in addition to his other distinguished and amiable qualities, has a claim to the affectionate regard of Englishmen in particular, not only by his strong attachment to the institutions and manners of our country, but by his polite and careful attentions to our countrymen in Italy, of whom I believe it may be truly said, that no English traveller ever sought a reasonable service from Signor Canova in vain.

The members of this academy, I know, retain a lively remembrance of the zeal, activity, and industry with which Canova procured and forwarded several scarce groups and statues in the noble collection of casts lately bestowed on the schools of this institution, by the munificence of his Majesty King George the Fourth.

In consequence of the mutual friendly regard subsisting between the President and Members of the British Academy, and the late President or Prince of the Roman Academy, I shall presume to lay before you a compendious sketch of Signor Canova's life as a sculptor and a man.

Antonio Canova was born in the territory of Bassano, in the Venetian State; his family was employed in agriculture, and he was placed under a sculptor in the neighbourhood, from whom he learned the rudiments and manual labour of his profession; this was all that was requisite for a beginning to the career of young Antonio, his own ardent spirit and indefatigable industry supplied every deficiency. After staying a few years with his master, he sought

improvement in the galleries and museums of Roma
A group of Dædalus and Icarus gave the first
indication of his talents, and another of Theseus and
the Minotaur procured his engagement, first for the
monument of Pope Ganganelli, in the Church of
the St. S. Apostoli, and afterwards for that of Pope
Rezzonico, in St. Peter's Church. Whilst engaged
in these works he also produced statues of Cupid and
Psyche, and a Magdalene—the latter was presented
to a church in Bassano; a group of Cupid and
Psyche, in the possession of Lord Gwydir; a group
of Hercules casting Lycus into the sea; a Theseus
and Centaur; with other works of inferior note.
During the time Bonaparte governed France, Signor
Canova was called to Paris to model his portrait, as
an exemplar for two colossal marble statues, one of
which is at Apsley House, in the possession of his
Grace the Duke of Wellington. While he remained
in Paris, one day he attended Bonaparte in the
Museum of Antiques, and they were both admiring
a fine bust of the Emperor Antoninus Pius, when
Bonaparte inquired how it happened that there
were found so many busts of this emperor? Canova
replied, he was a good and just prince, therefore
everybody loved him, and for this reason his busts
are found in all the cities, towns and villages of his
dominions. Such was the respect the French ruler
entertained for the sculptor's honesty, as well as his
talents, that he was permitted to speak with more
freedom than the mareschals of the imperial court.

There will be no need, on the present occasion, to detail a correct list of his works; prints of them all may be seen in the collections of the metropolis; yet we must not deny ourselves the gratification of noticing some of the more distinguished. Of this description is the group of the Three Graces in the Duke of Bedford's possession, and a beautiful recumbent statue of a Nymph, executed by order of his present Majesty King George the Fourth.

In the number of monuments by this distinguished sculptor, the most considerable is justly the most esteemed; it was erected at the expense of the present Emperor of Austria to his sister, an archduchess. The design is simple, and nobly expressive; a pyramid raised on three steps presents an entrance to the tomb; the widow, the aged, and the helpless child in tears, are bearing flowers to the shrine of their benefactress, while the Genius of the Empire sits on the steps in sorrow.

We are sanctioned by the high authority of our president's opinion, for believing this to be one of Canova's most successful productions.

In considering the style of this artist's sculpture, we shall at once acknowledge a poetic fancy which gave a luminous interest to his conversation, equally with his compositions; his figures are graceful, his forms grand, muscle, tendon or bone most naturally distinguished, and the flesh seems yielding to the touch, by an execution as powerful as delicate.

It has been observed by some that in Canova's

sculpture, we sometimes seek in vain for the severe chastity of Grecian Art; this may indeed not be destitute of some foundation in truth, but we must not look for complete perfection in the works of imperfect man; he is most perfect in whom the fewest faults are discoverable.

Canova, in early life, must have received a strong bias from the imposing and luxuriant paintings of the Venetian school, but many and great excellencies counterbalance, and as it were annihilate, trivial and venial faults.

Canova the sculptor is known to all, but the great qualities and moral virtues of Canova are known to comparatively few; yet we cannot fail to dwell on these also with equal delight and profit : his indefatigable industry and entire devotion to his art, at the same time that they supplied his most agreeable occupation, and increased his rich legacy of valuable works bequeathed to posterity, afforded him the more ample means of gratifying his benevolence and generosity; he was provident for his relations, liberal to his friends, and extensively charitable to the poor; his kindness to his family was equally becoming the Christian and the philosopher; he rendered such assistance as increased their comfort, without raising them above the sphere of life in which they were most useful to society. Canova's mind possessed an acute perception, a vivid imagination, a ready decision, and a strong sense of right, which, together with those mental qualities more

immediately engaged in his profession, he cultivated
to the utmost of his power; and in order to make
the greatest possible advantage of his time, some
person generally read to him while he was at work,
and by this means he became acquainted, not only
with all the best Italian literature, but also the best
classical authors, philosophers, poets, and historians,
together with many eminent productions of modern
Europe. Such a stock of knowledge enlightened his
views in general intercourse or private contemplation,
matured his studies, and gave an additional charm
to his conversation.

We must not pass over an heroic act of service
to his country which deserves to be recorded with
the great actions of any age. When it was determined that the magnificent collections of ancient
sculpture should be returned to Rome, Signor
Canova was despatched to superintend the package
and conveyance, and although he was opposed by
every artifice and discouragement, and repeatedly
threatened with assassination, he persevered with so
much spirit and resolution that he surmounted all
opposition, and sent them all back in a week. On
this occasion he pathetically blessed the generosity
of the English nation, without whose powerful
assistance and effectual patronage he acknowledged
those collections would never have been returned
to Italy. Upon Signor Canova's return to Rome
after the redoubted achievement of re-establishing
her divinities and heroes in the station they had

held so many ages, he was welcomed by the Roman people with universal applause and festivity: the Sovereign Pontiff received him with honour and gratitude : he created the sculptor Marquis of Ischia, and to enable him to support his new dignity, gave him a pension of three thousand crowns. Canova returned his dutiful thanks for the patent of nobility, but concerning the pension, he declared, like a disinterested patriot, "that he had always maintained himself by his labour, and he trusted with the Almighty's support he should continue to do so as long as he lived ; he should therefore apply the whole 3000 crowns per annum to the purposes adopted in the papal academy, for the encouragement of painting and sculpture, and for the assistance of young men in their studies."

As Signor Canova had never married, and consequently had no children looking to him for provision, he indulged the pious desire of building a church in his native country, which he intended to decorate with sacred subjects of statues and basso-relievos in his latter years, and thus dedicate his last efforts to Him that gave him being. For this purpose he determined the architectural design, and calculated the expense of the building at about £12,000 sterling. In the progress of the work he took a journey to see the state of its forwardness, in which his expectations were disappointed ; to which was added the cruel mortification that double the money he had calculated to lay out would be required to complete the church—a sum, perhaps, not in his power to command. However that might be, the digestive powers ceased in his system; medicine was tried, but afforded no relief; he prepared for his end with resignation and fortitude, and passed in Christian hope to a better life.

I have thus presumed to produce before you a compendious sketch of a man distinguished by rare talents and rare virtues, as little clouded by defect or failure as is generally to be found among the worthiest of the sons of men.

Such a character will be contemplated with equal pleasure and profit by the Members of this Academy. Our time will not be lost in the study of talents and qualities which rendered their possessor the delight and pride of his country, and whose example affords valuable materials towards forming distinguished men in the rising generation.

INDEX.

LONDON : PRINTED BY WILLIAM CLOWES AND SONS, LIMITED,
DUKE STREET, STAMFORD STREET, S.E., AND GREAT WINDMILL STREET, W.

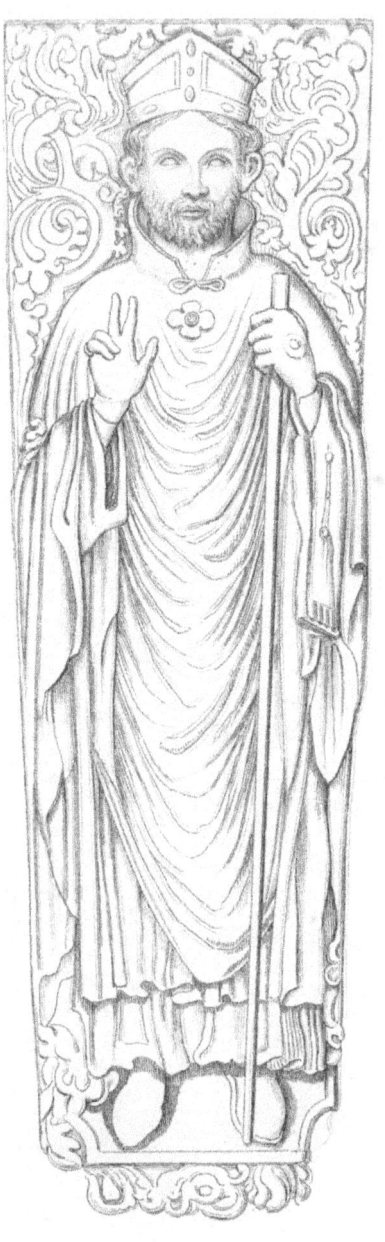

Pl. 1.

Bishop Wulstan. Worcester Cathedral.

PLATE II.

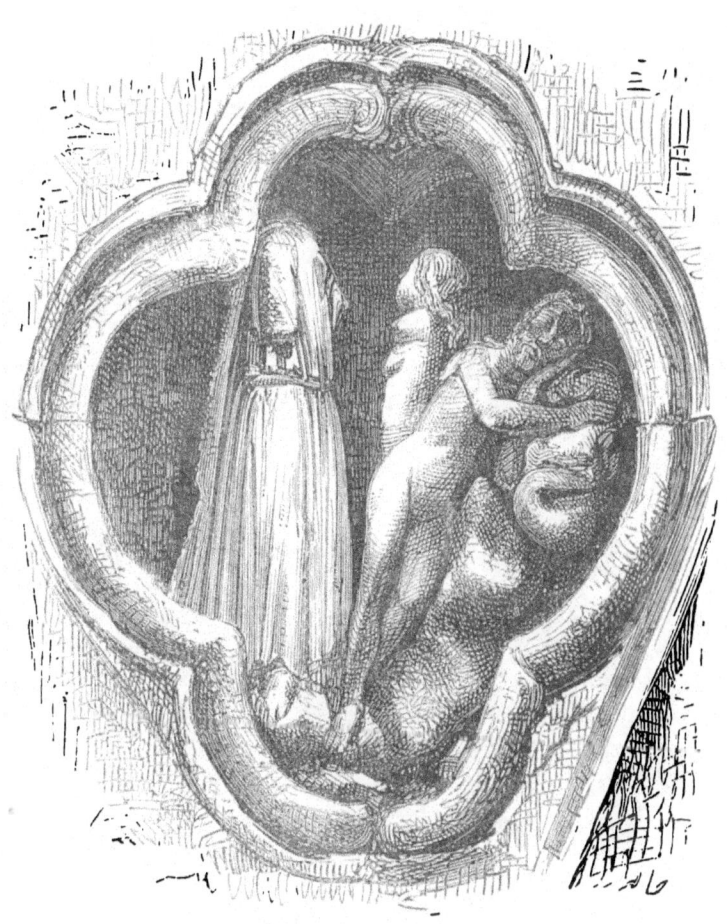

CREATION OF EVE—WELLS CATHEDRAL.

PLATE III.

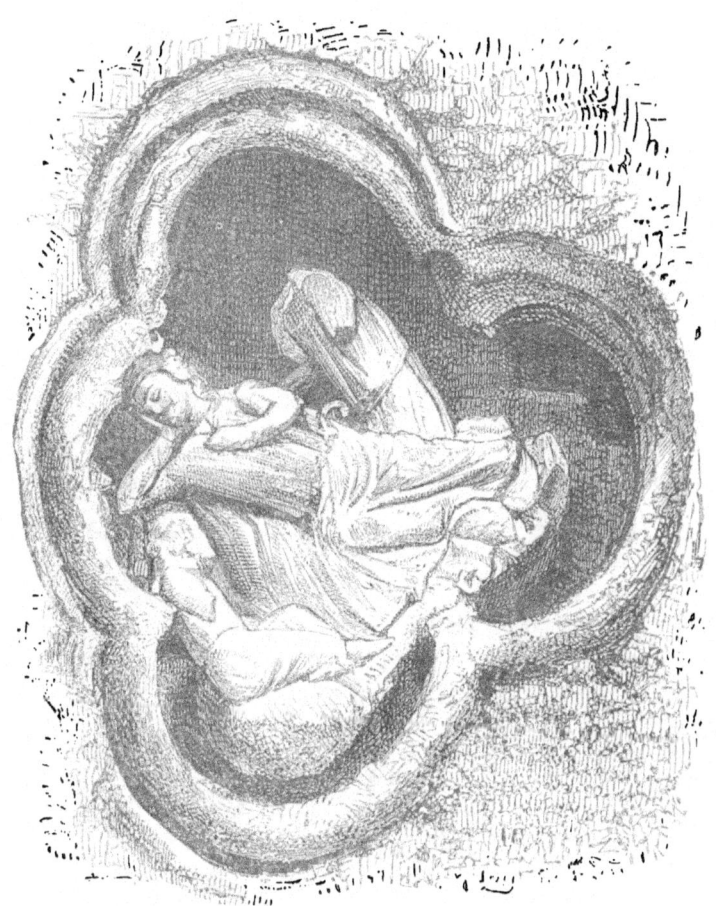

DEATH OF ISAAC—WELLS CATHEDRAL.

PLATE IV.

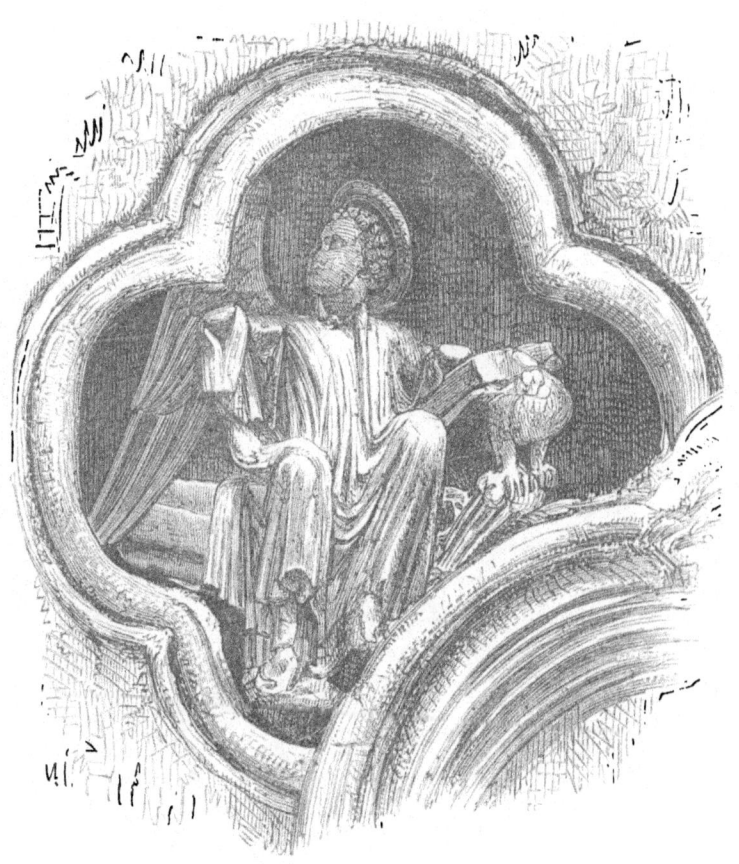

ANGEL—WELLS CATHEDRAL.

PLATE V.

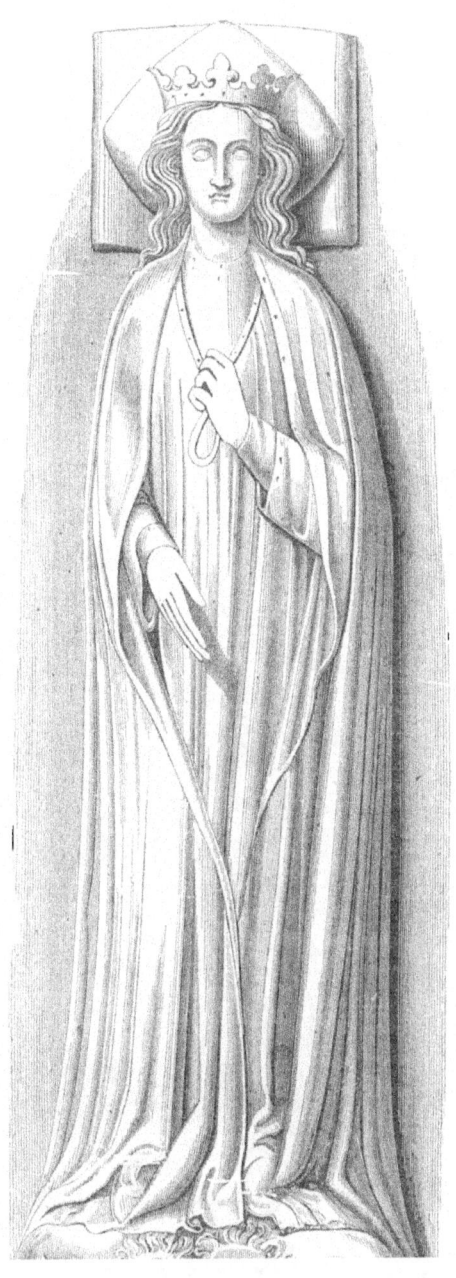

Pl.6.

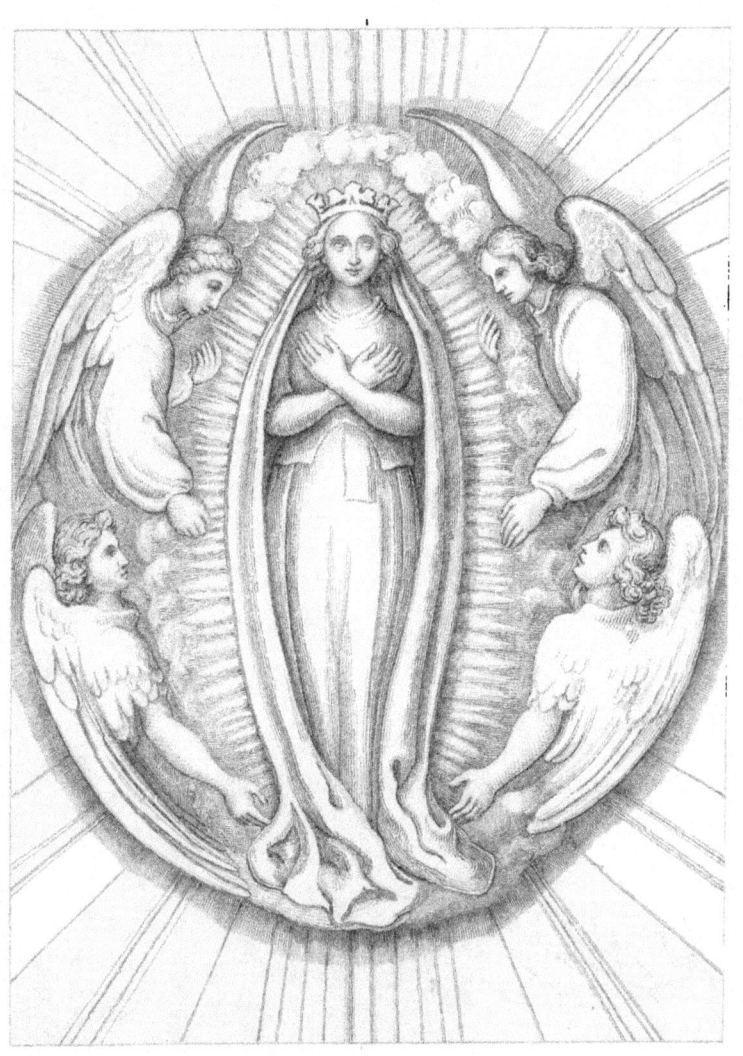

Virgin and Angels York Cathedral.

PLATE VII.

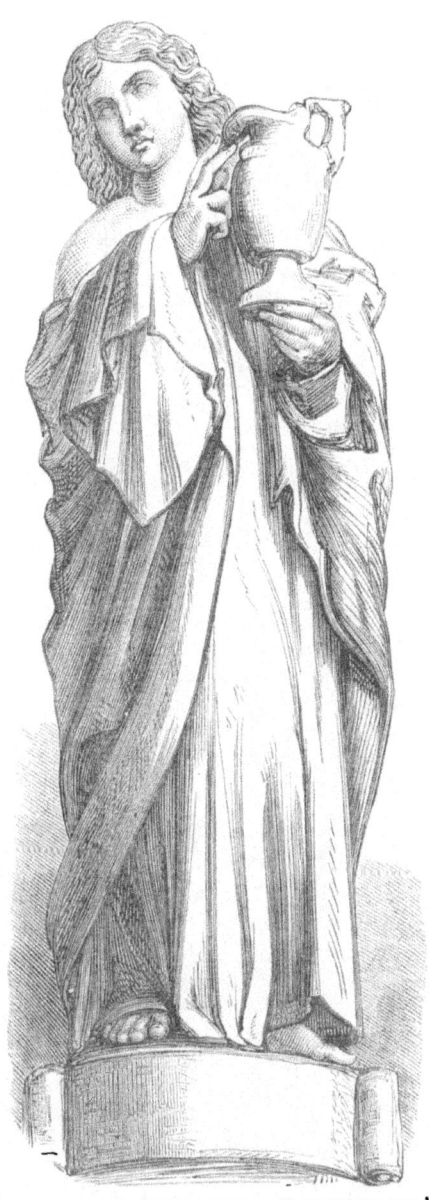

A STATUE IN ONE OF THE NICHES IN HENRY VII.'S CHAPEL,
WESTMINSTER ABBEY.

PLATE VIII.

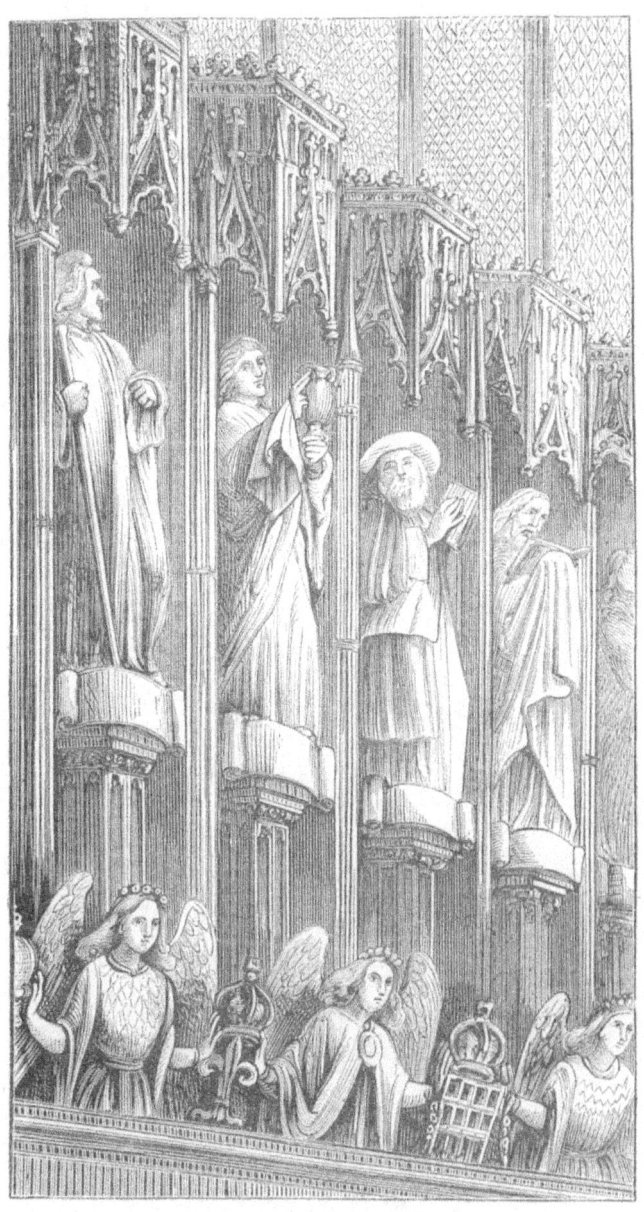

STATUES IN THE ARCHITECTURE OF HENRY VII.'S CHAPEL,
WESTMINSTER ABBEY.

PLATE IX.

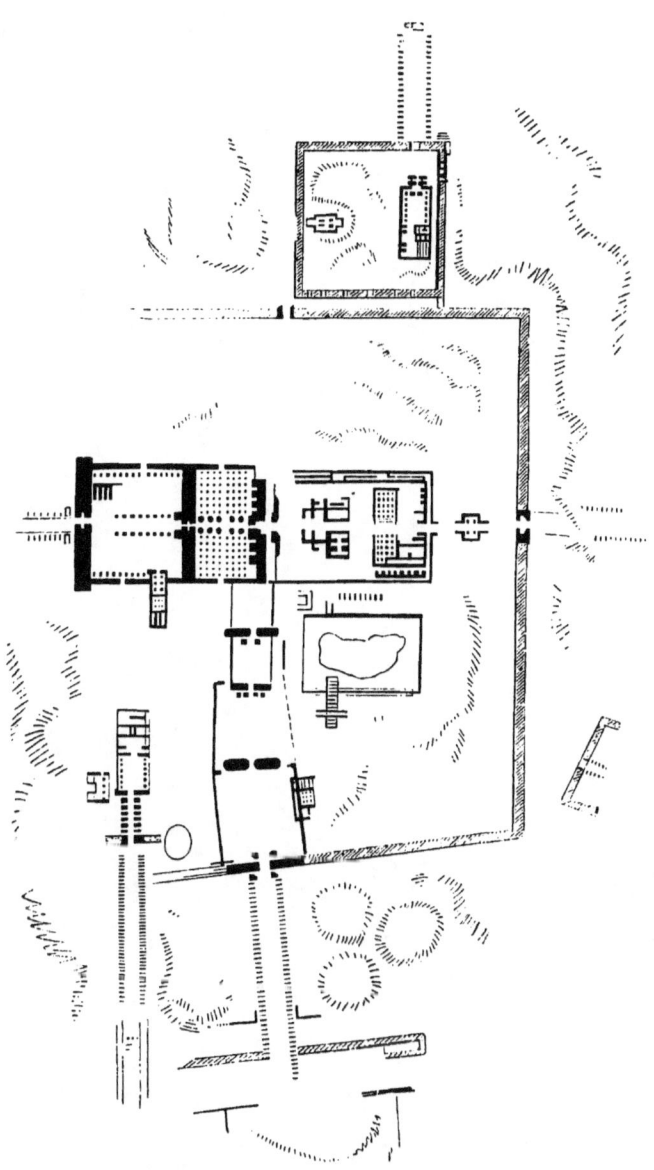

PLAN OF THE PALACE OF CARNAC.

PLATE X.

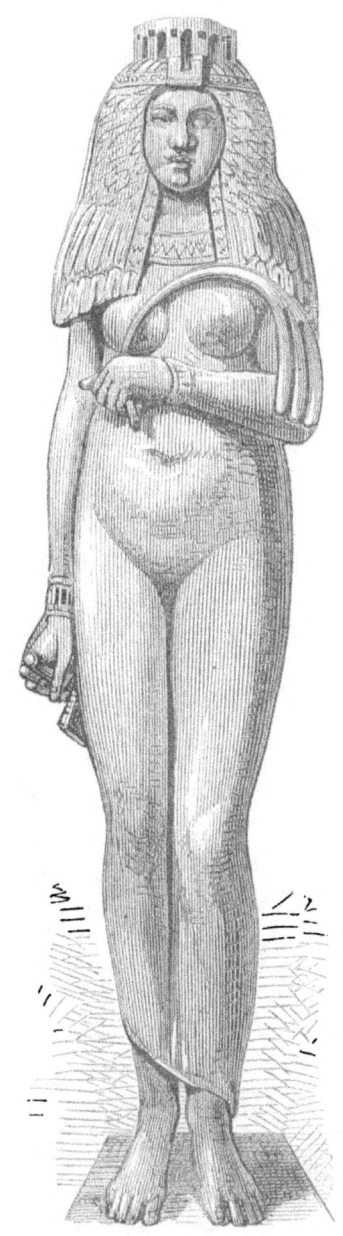

FIGURE OF BUBASTE, OR ISIS.

PLATE XI.

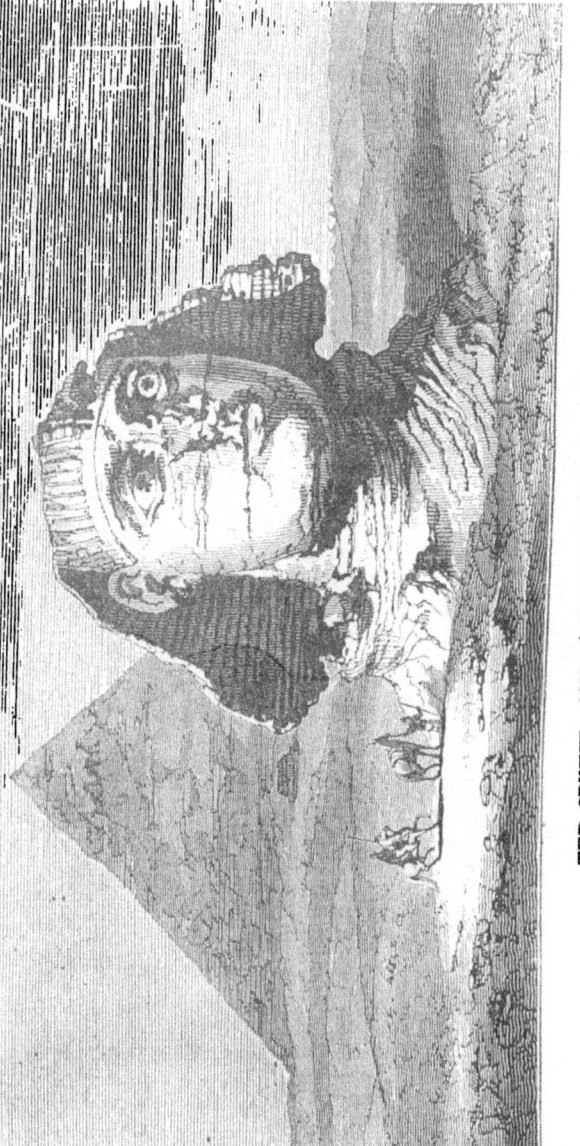

THE SPHINX, AND GREAT PYRAMID OF MEMPHIS.

PLATE XII.

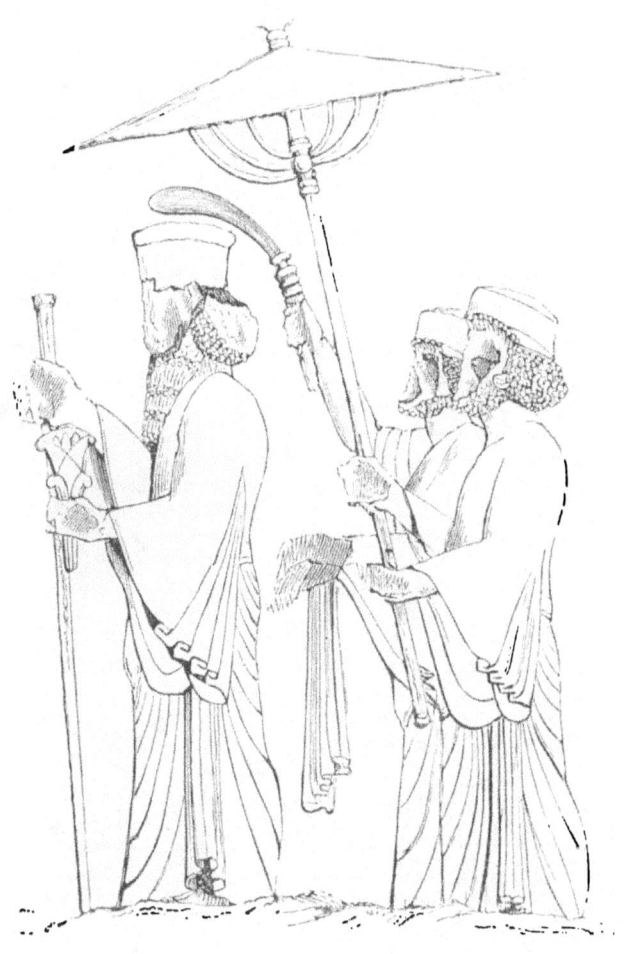

SCULPTURE FROM PERSEPOLIS.

PLATE XIII.

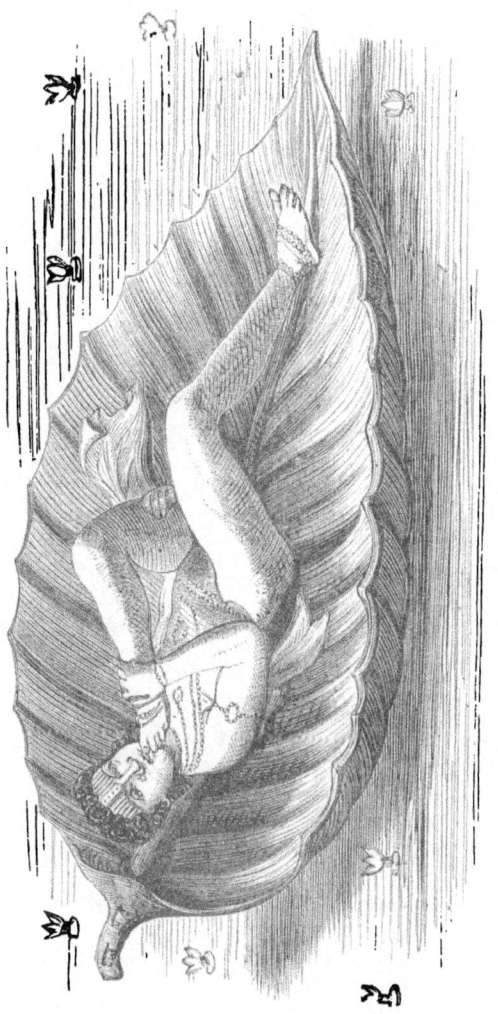

VISHNU.

Plate XIV.

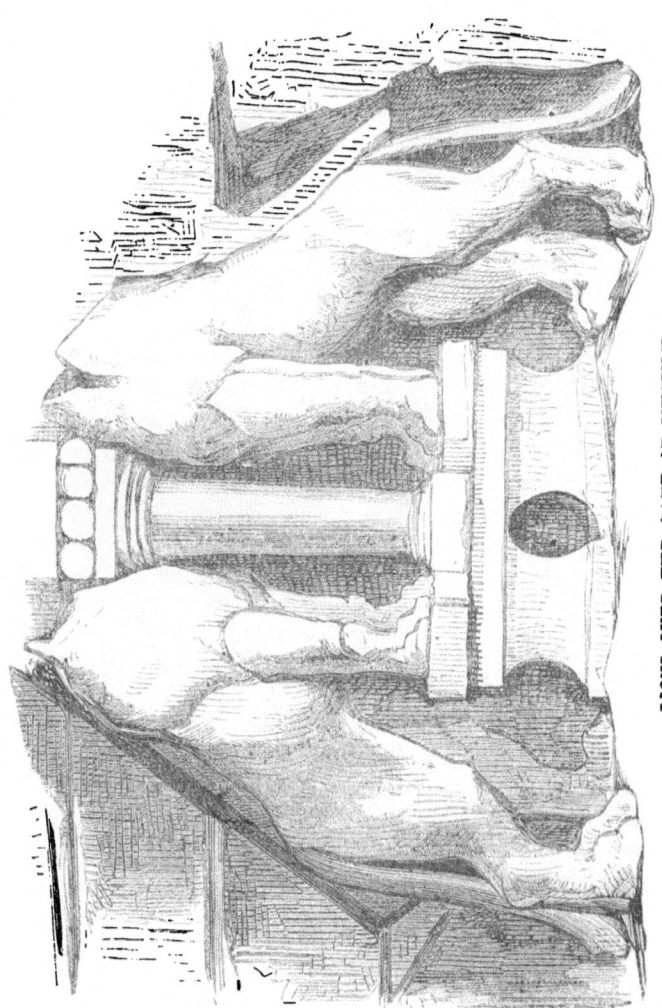

LIONS OVER THE GATE OF MYCENÆ.

PLATE XV.

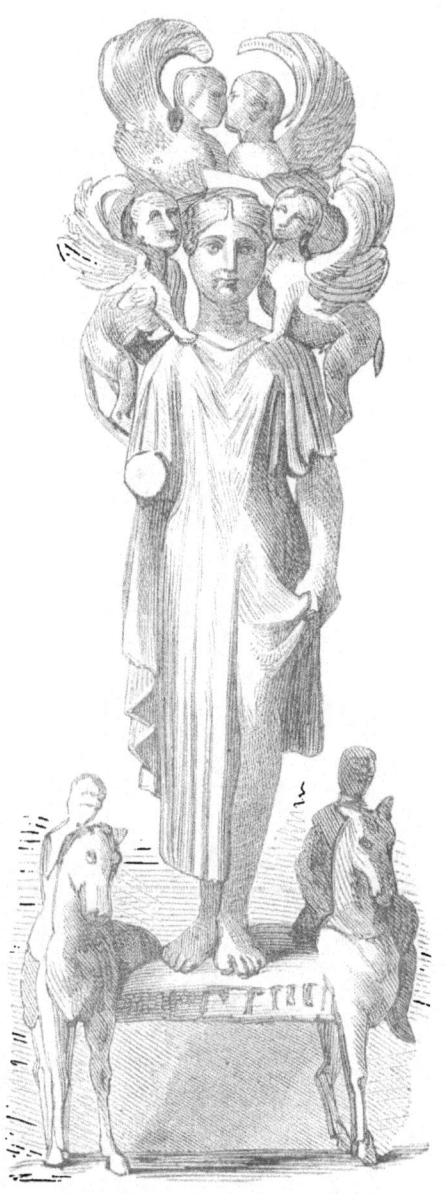

A BRONZE STATUE OF MINERVA.

Plate XVI.

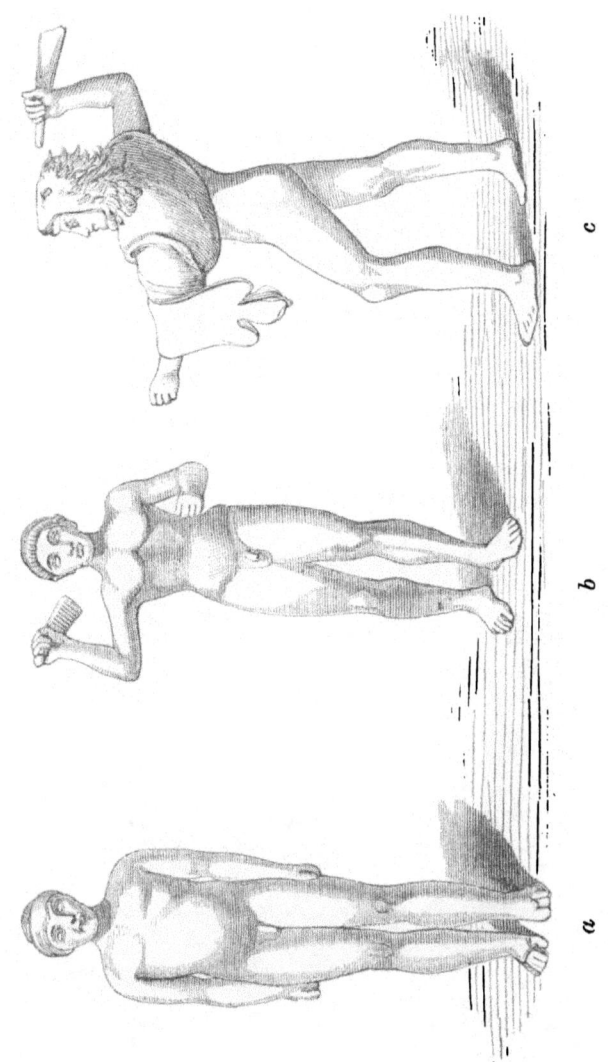

a   *b*   *c*

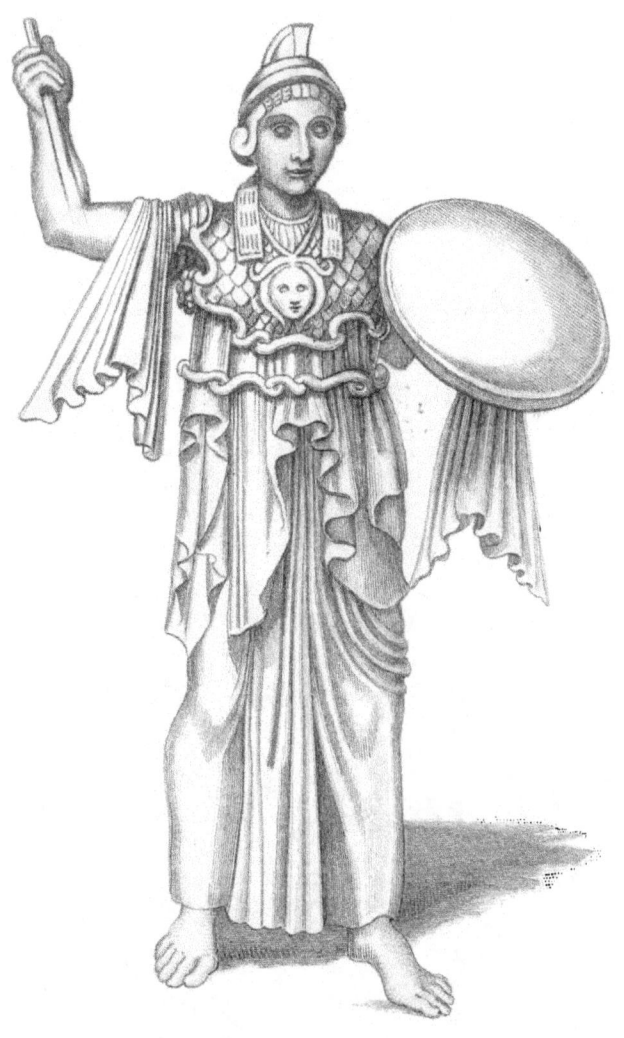

Minerva of Dipœnis & Scylles.

PLATE XVIII.

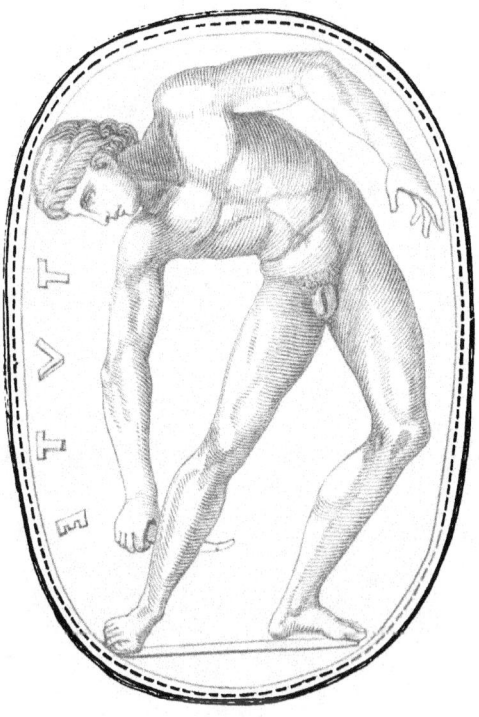

TYDEUS.

PLATE XIX.

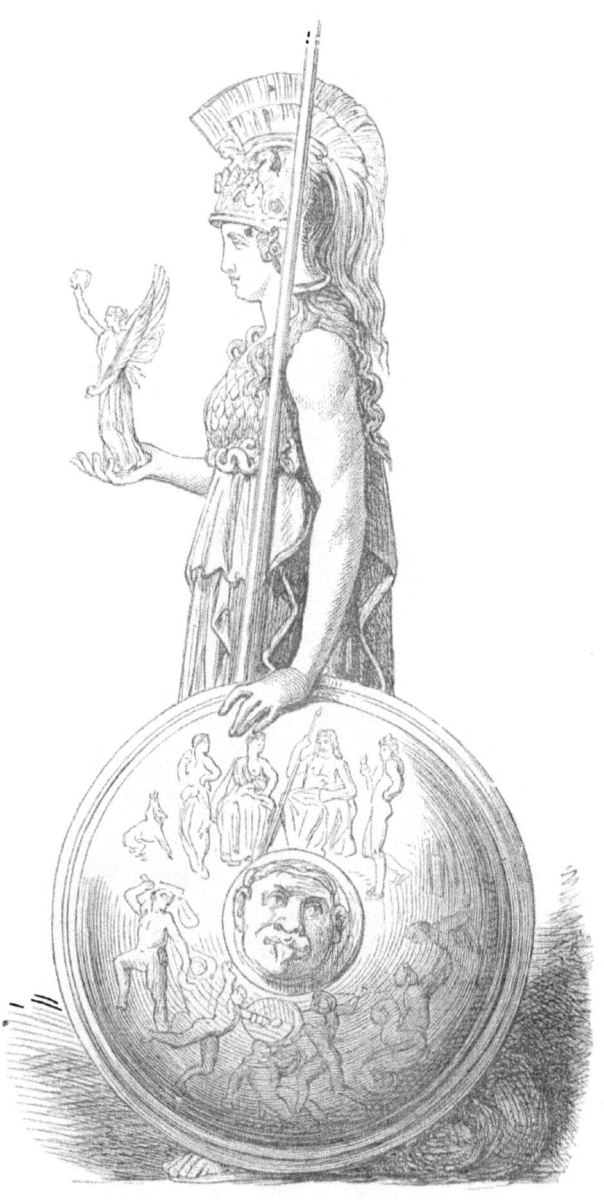

MINERVA, 39 FEET HIGH—PHIDIAS.

PLATE XX.

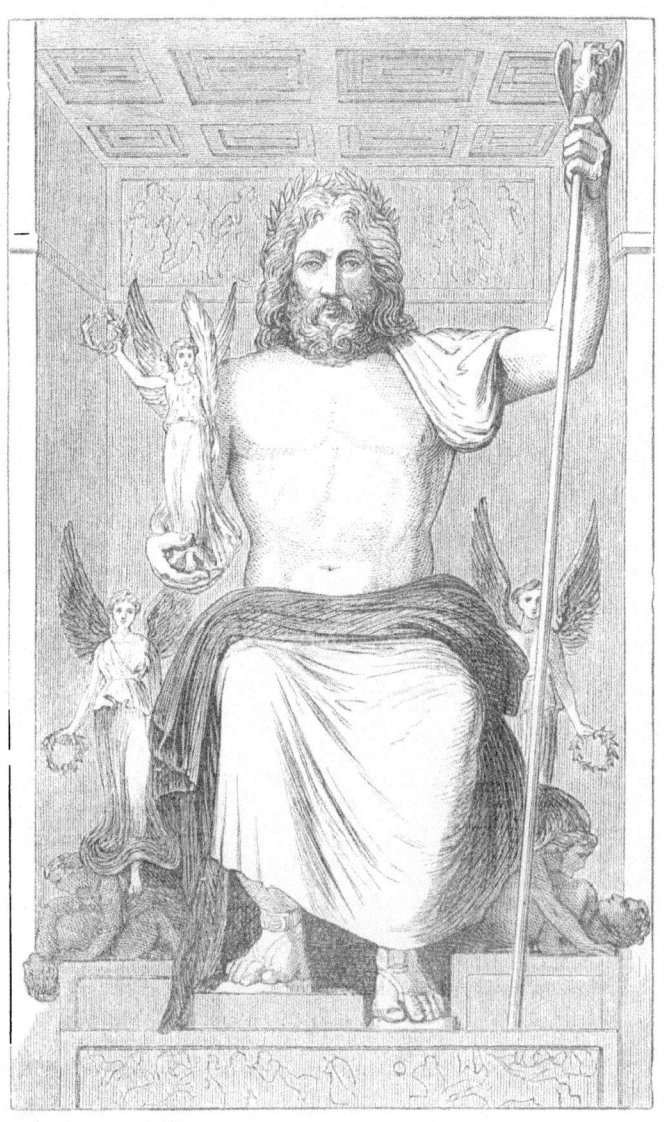

JUPITER OLYMPIUS, AT ELIS.

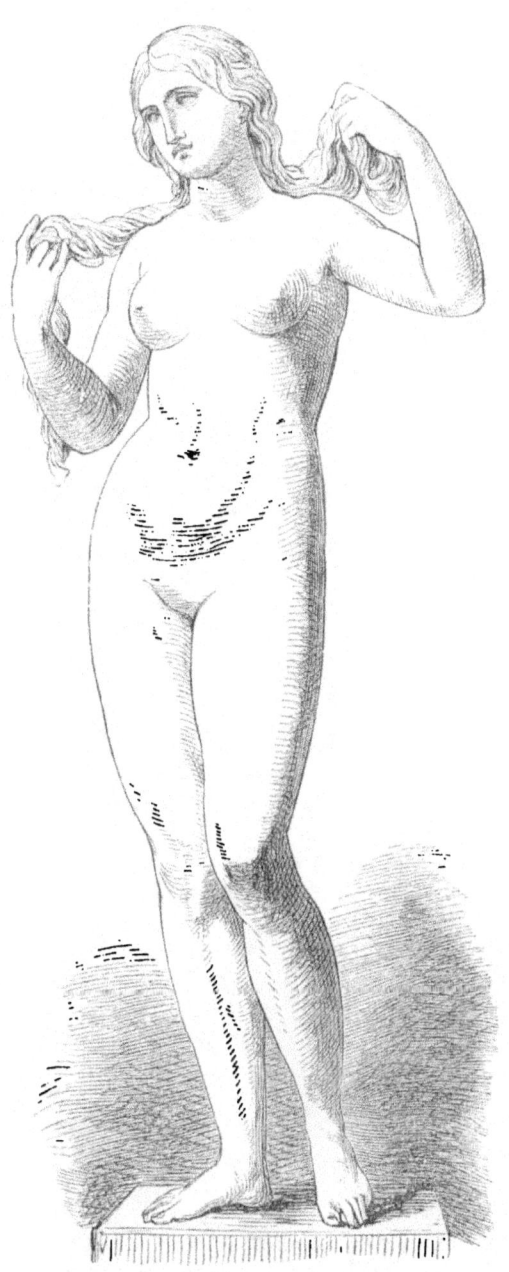

VENUS APHRODITE— ALCAMENES.

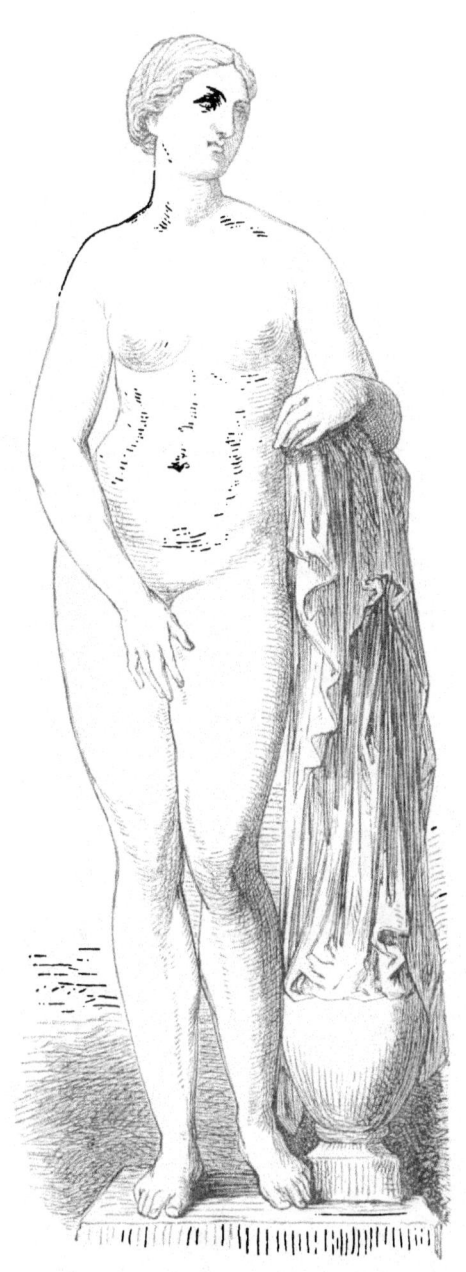

VENUS OF CNIDOS—PRAXITELES.

Pl. 23

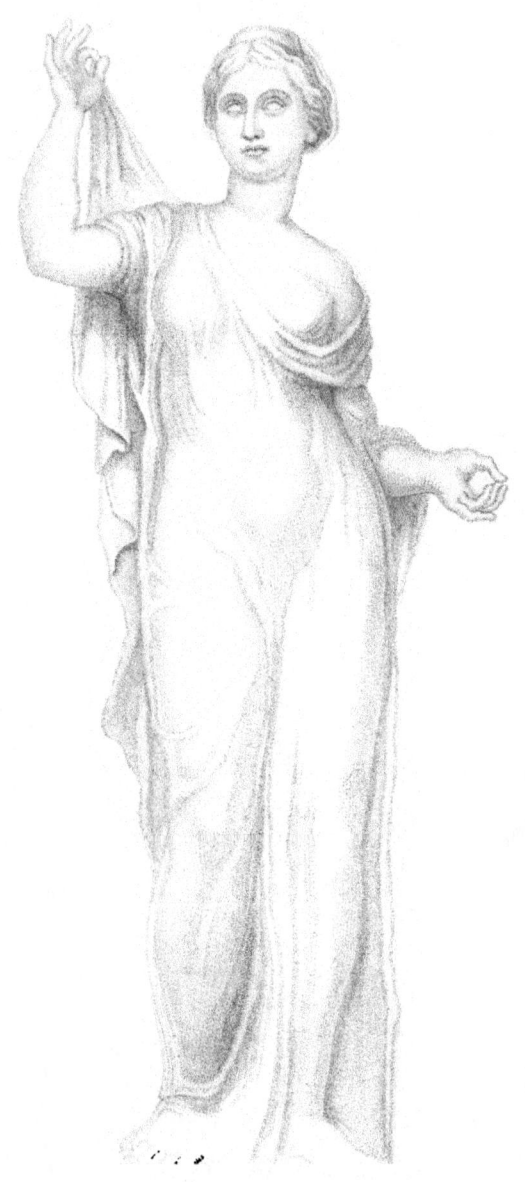

PLATE XXIV.

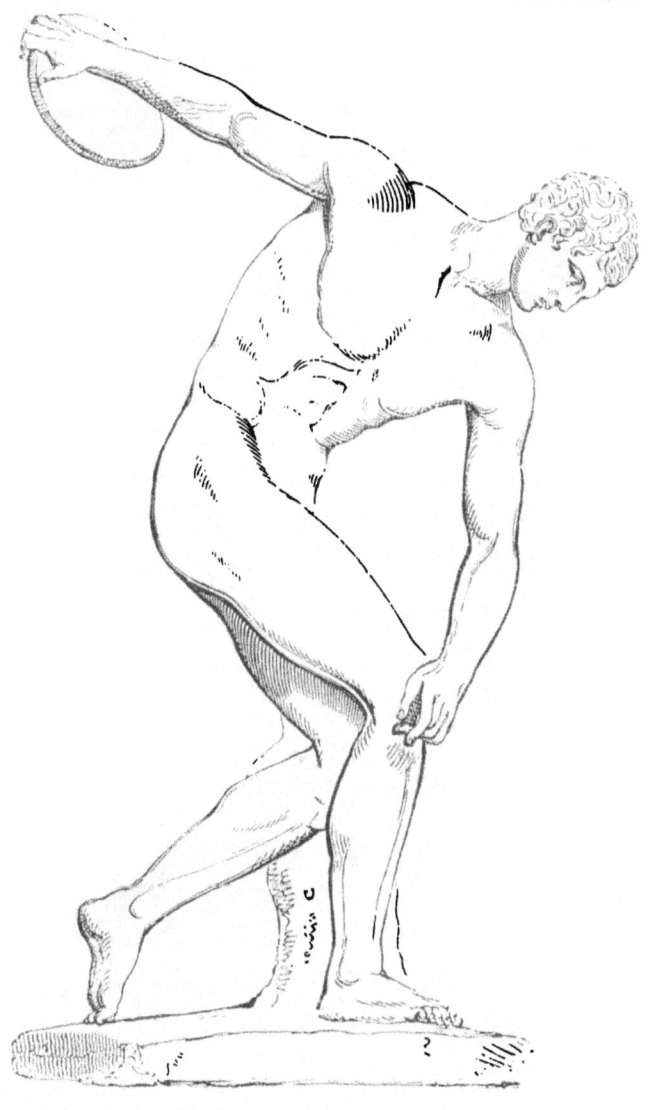

DISCOBULUS—BRITISH MUSEUM.

PLATE XXV.

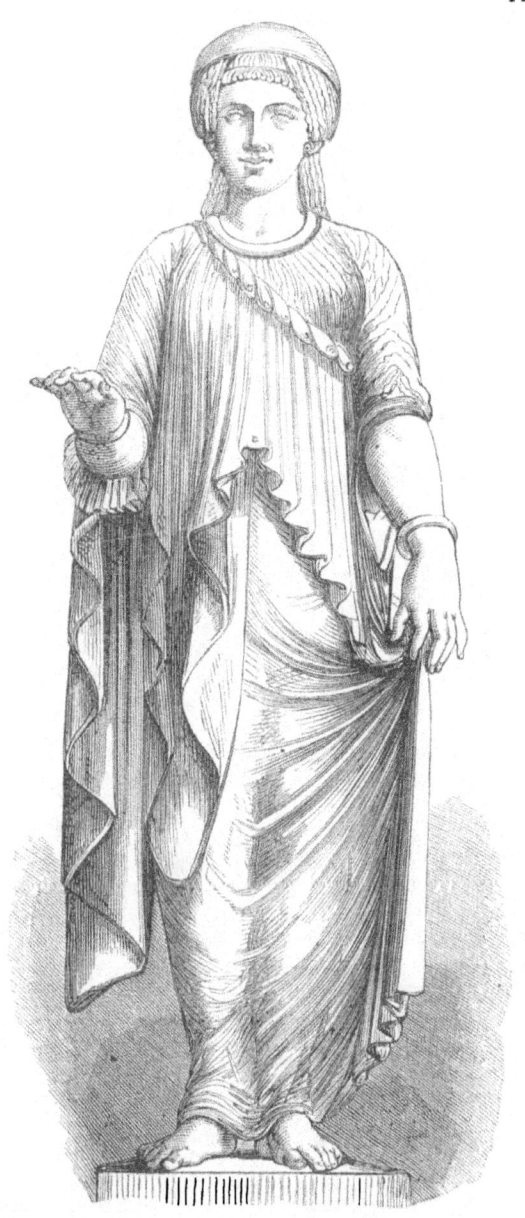

ONE OF THE FIGURES ON THE PEDIMENT AT EGINA.

PLATE XXVI.

PROPORTIONS.

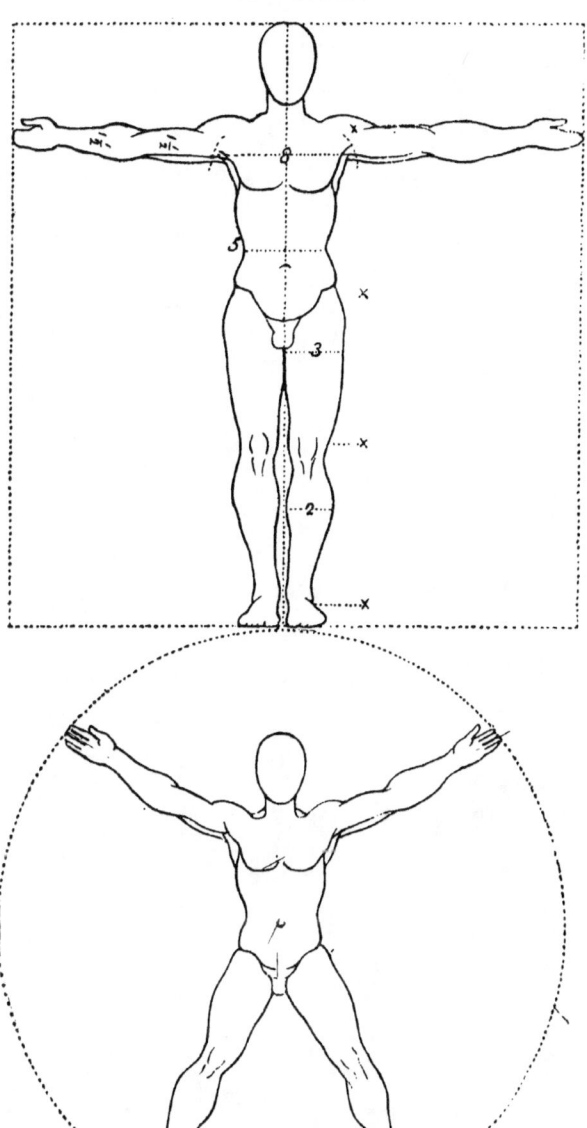

PLATE XXVII.

EXTENT OF MOTION IN THE SKELETON.

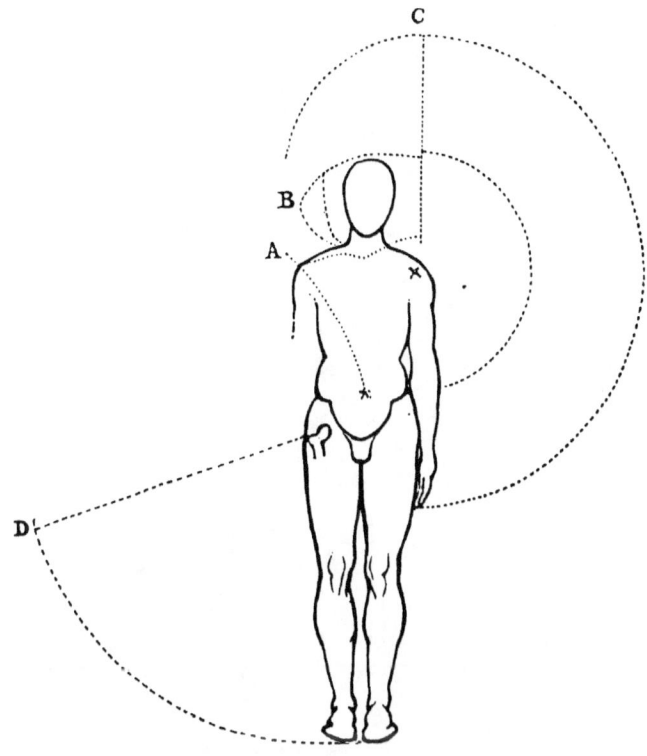

NOTE.—*The dotted line is the Line of Motion. When it is interrupted by a cross, that joint moves no farther in that direction.*

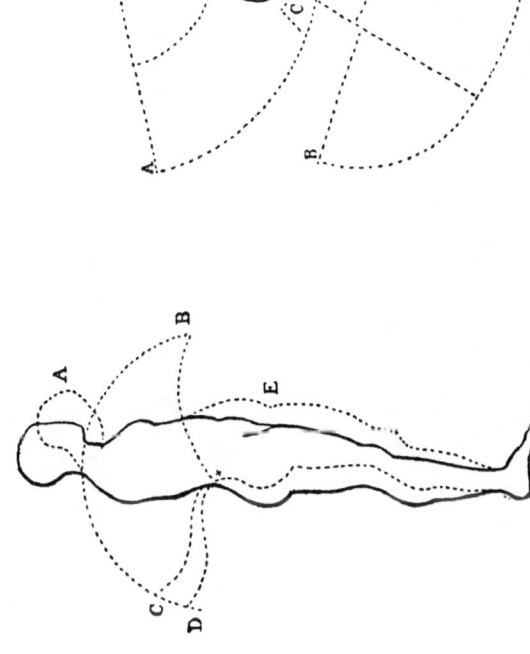

PLATE XXVIII.

EXTENT OF MOTION IN THE SKELETON.

A. Inclination of the head to the breast.
B. The extreme bend of the back over the legs without changing their position.

C. Extreme line of the back bent backwards without changing the position of the legs.
D. When the back is bent as far as D, the thighs and legs will project as at E.

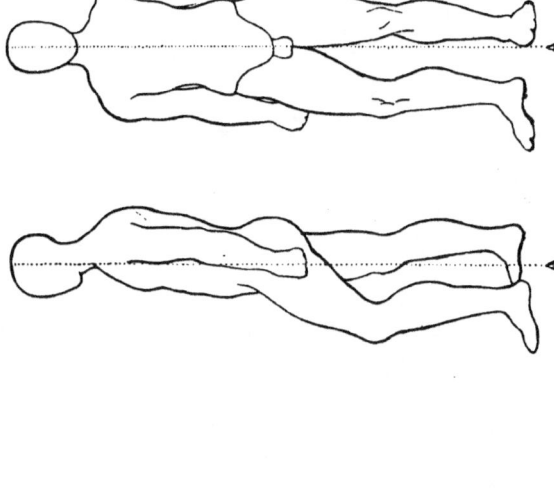

PROPORTIONS.

BALANCE.

PLATE XXIX.

Side.
Equally supported on both legs.

Front.

Side.

Front.
Supported on one leg.

Note.—A is always the centre of gravity.

PLATE XXX.

BALANCE.

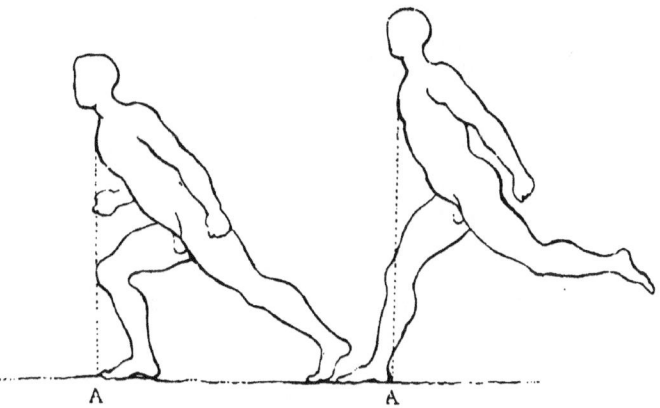

Preparing to Run.   *Running.*

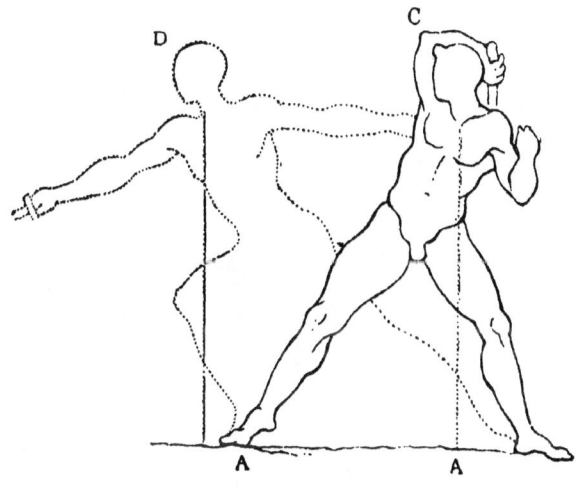

Striking.

*The force of the blow is assisted by the weight of the body conveyed
from C to D.*

PLATE XXXI.

BALANCE.

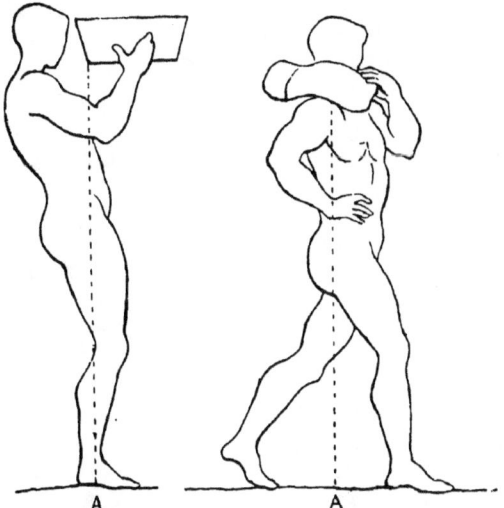

Raising a Weight.   Carrying a Weight on the Shoulders.

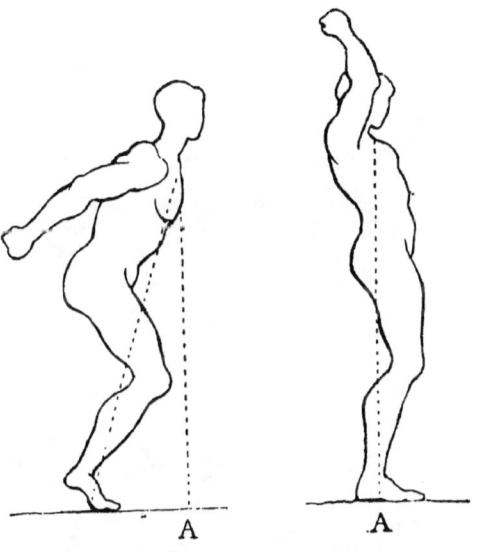

Preparing to Jump.   Alighting.

Plate XXXII.

BALANCE.

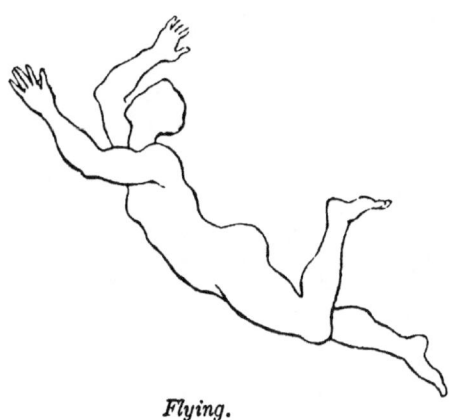

Flying.

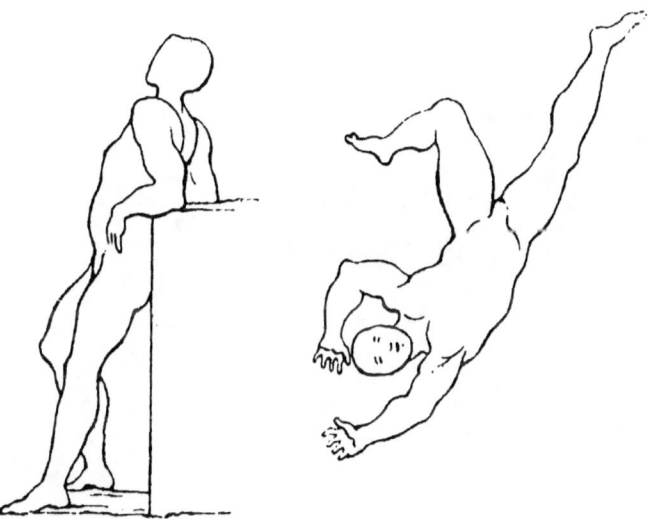

Leaning.   *Falling.*

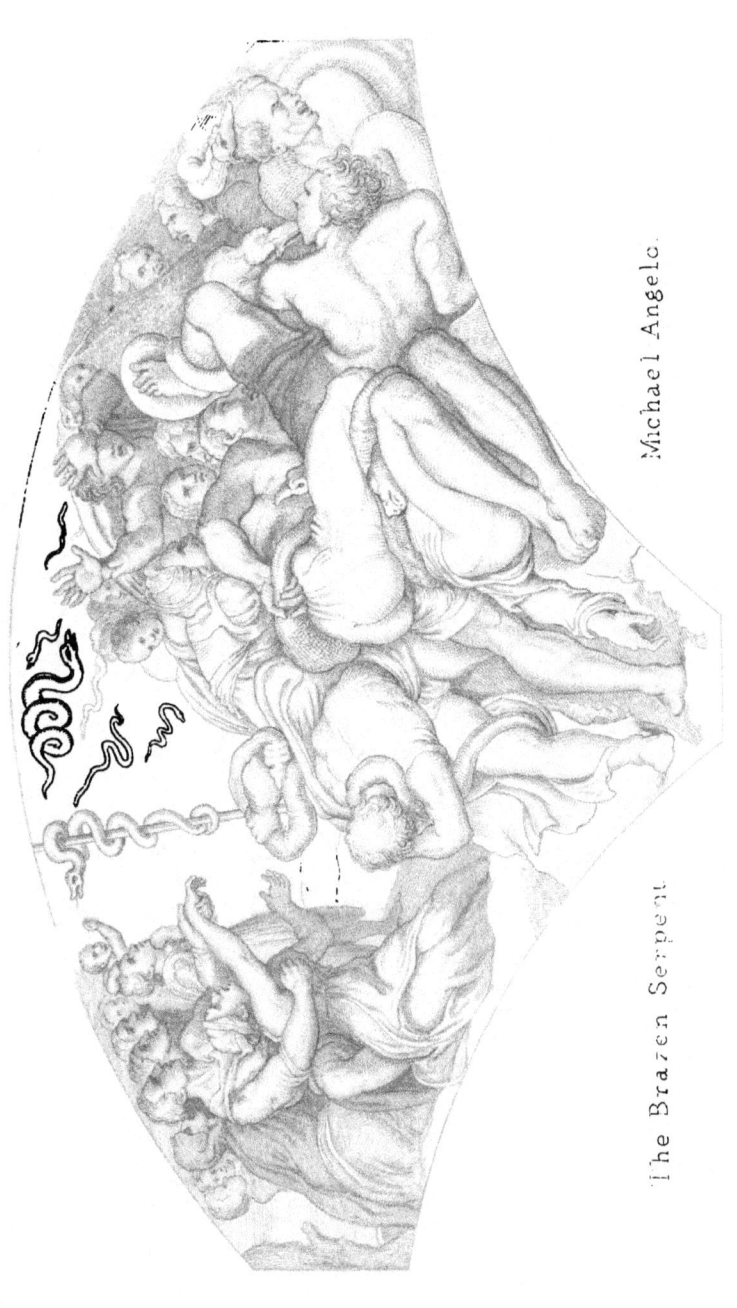

The Brazen Serpent.

Michael Angelo.

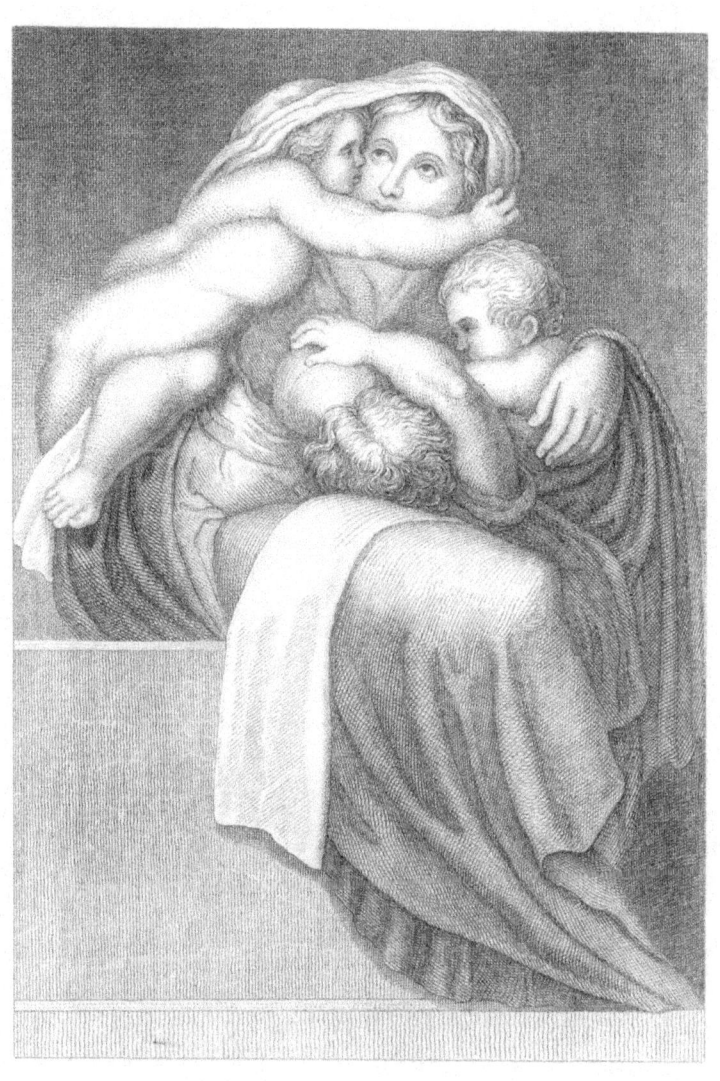

Charity ____ Mich.^l Angelo.

PLATE XXXV.

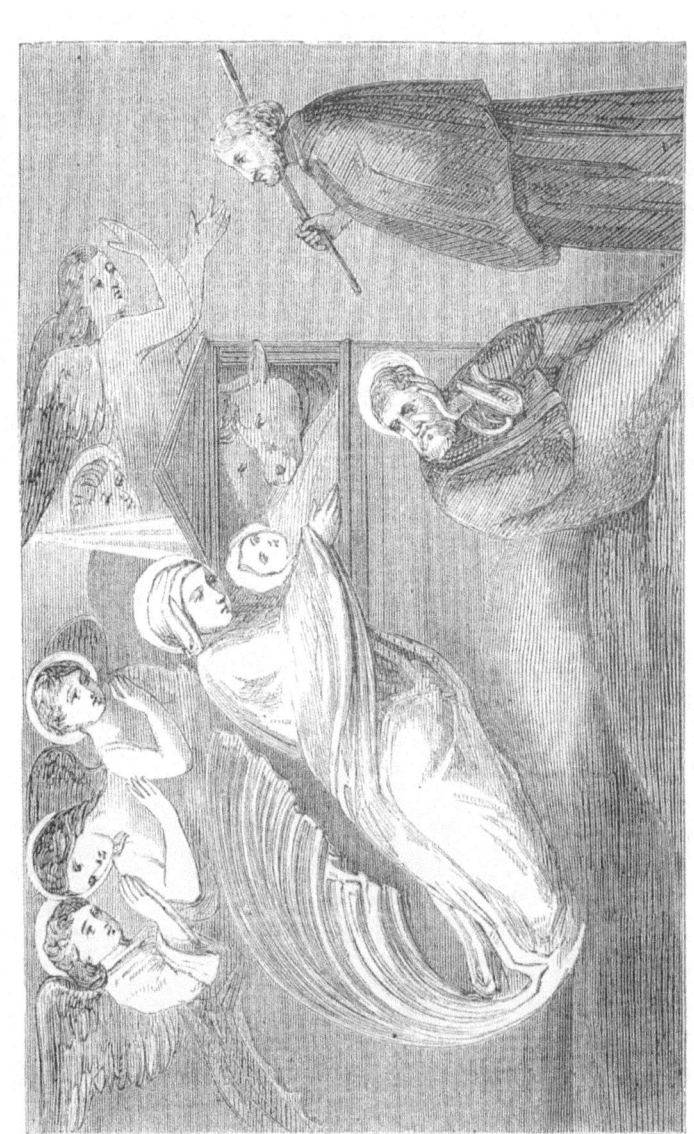

THE NATIVITY—A MOSAIC OF THE 5TH CENTURY IN SANTA MARIA MAGGIORE, ROME.

Plate XXXVI.

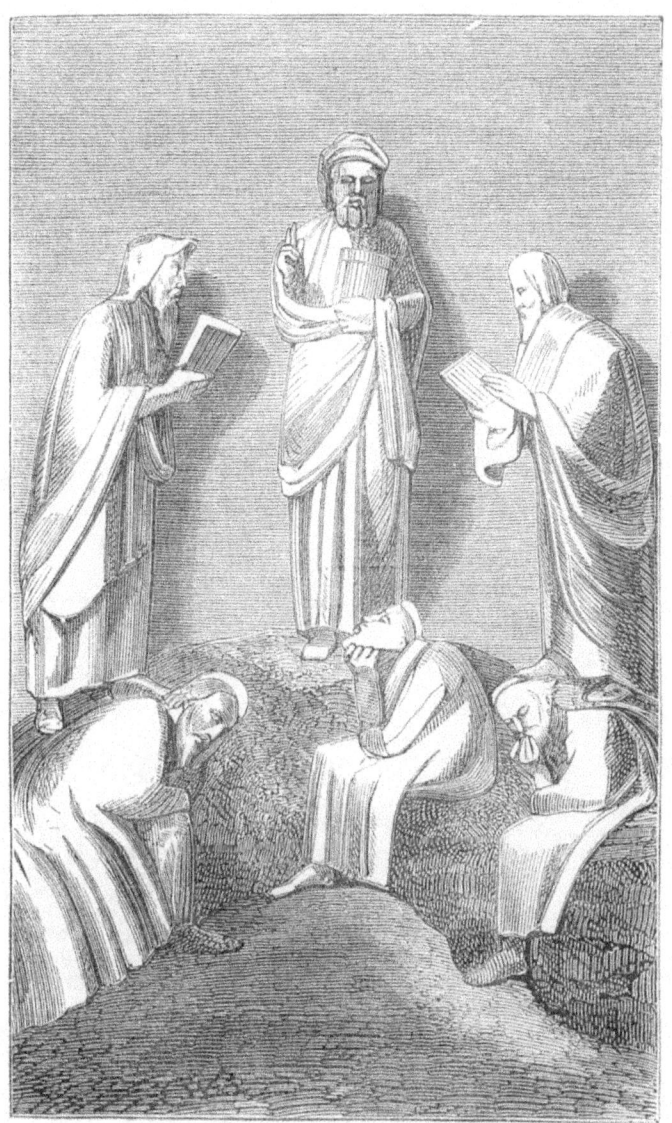

TRANSFIGURATION.

PLATE XXXVII.

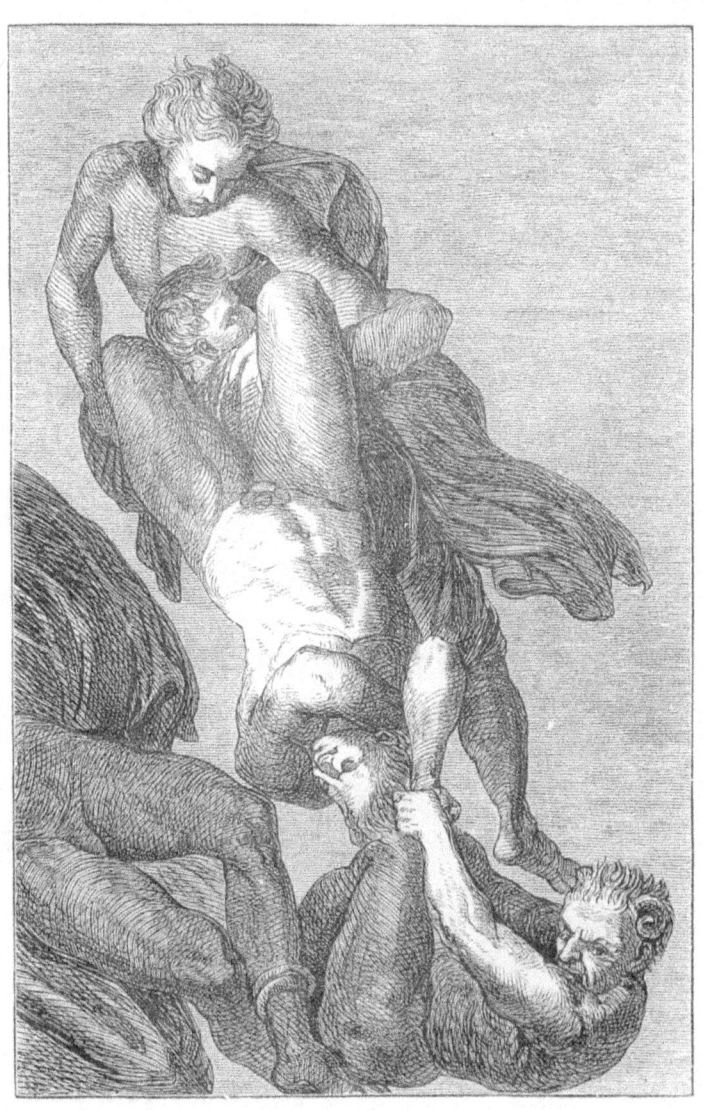

GROUP FROM THE LAST JUDGMENT—MICHAEL ANGELO.

Pl. 38.

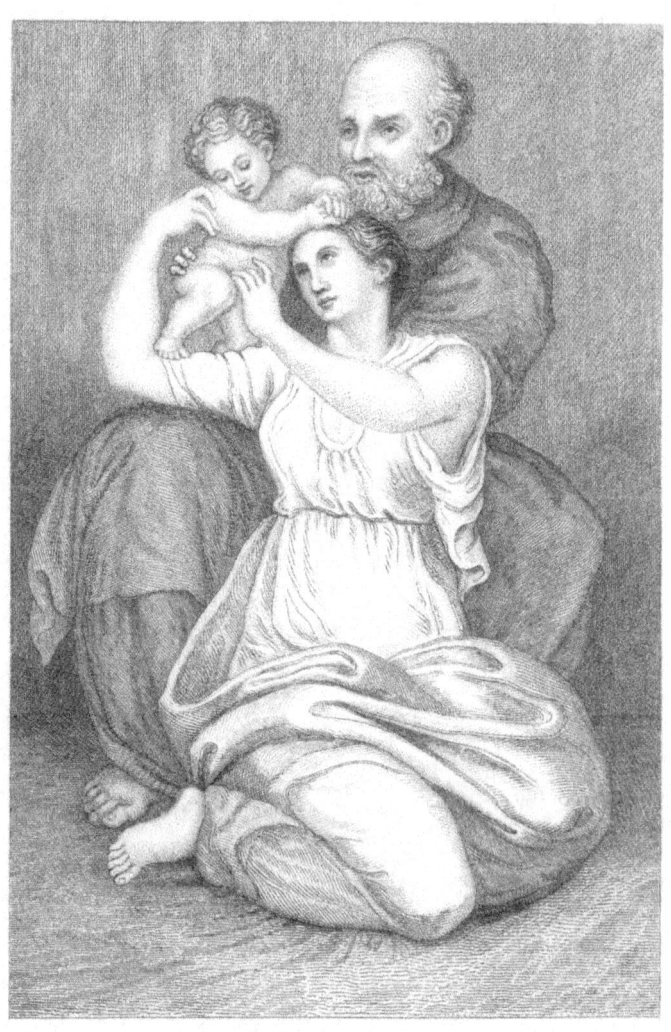

Holy Family. — Mich! Angelo.

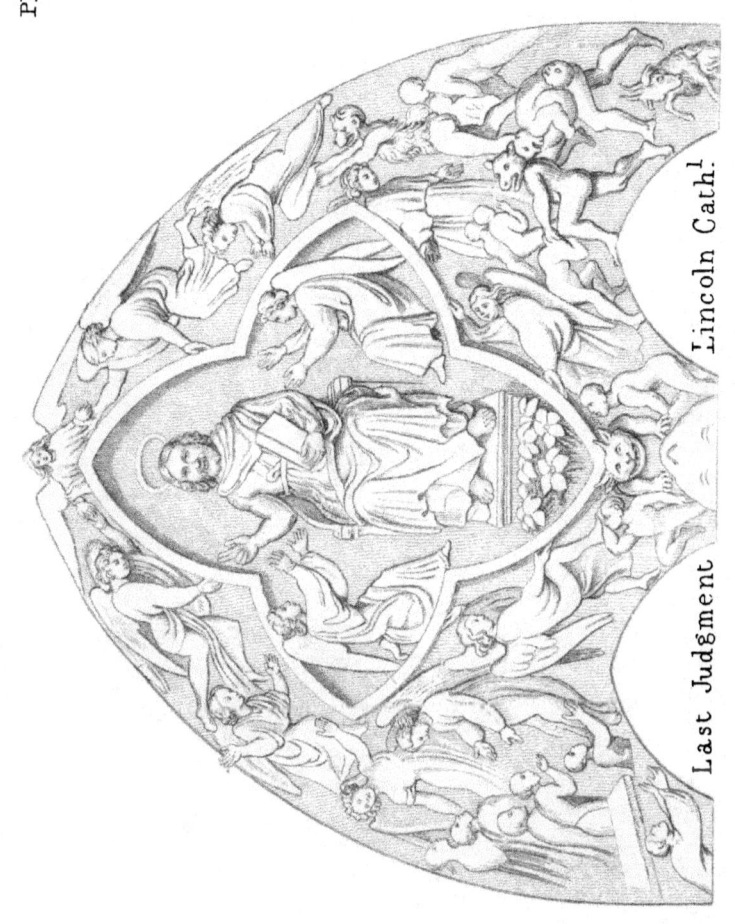

Pl. 39.

Last Judgment   Lincoln Cath.

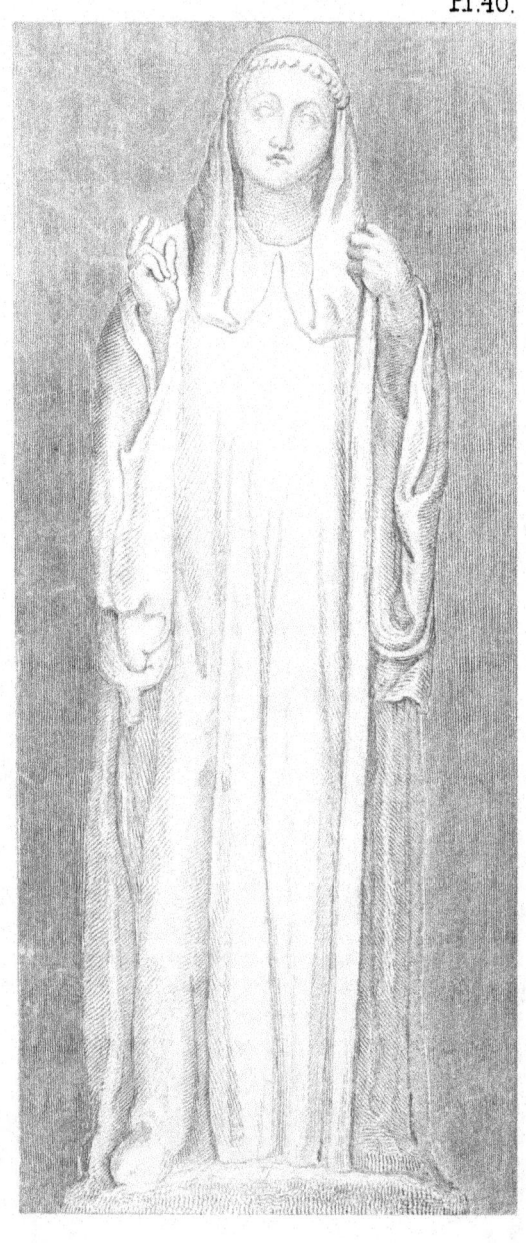

Pl.40.

Pl. 41.

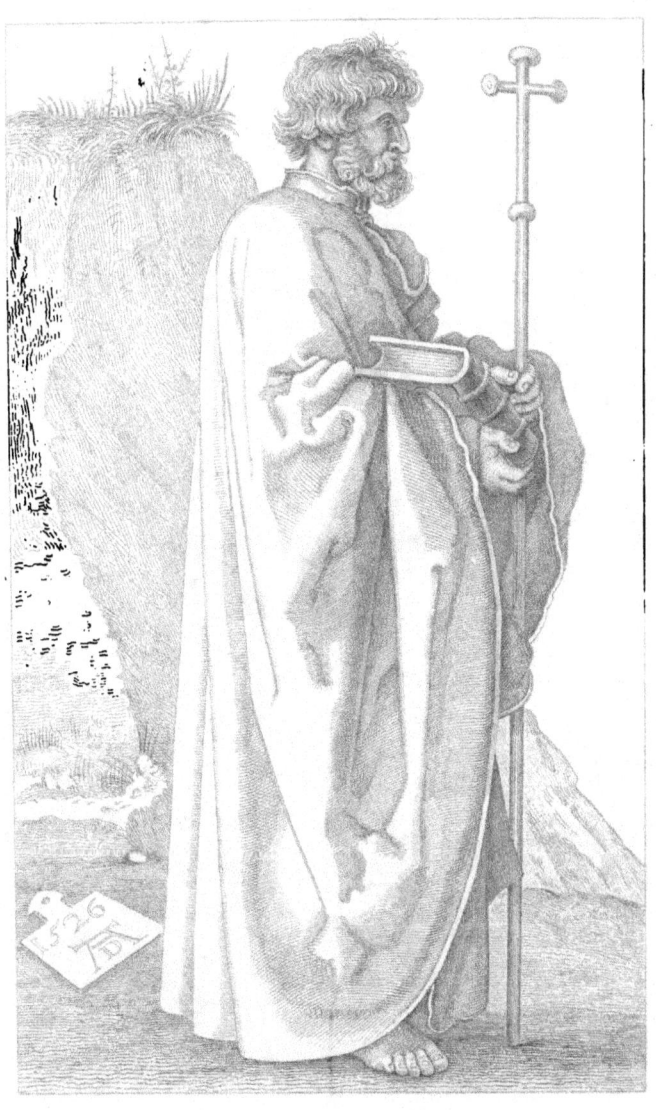

AN APOSTLE — ALBERT DURER.

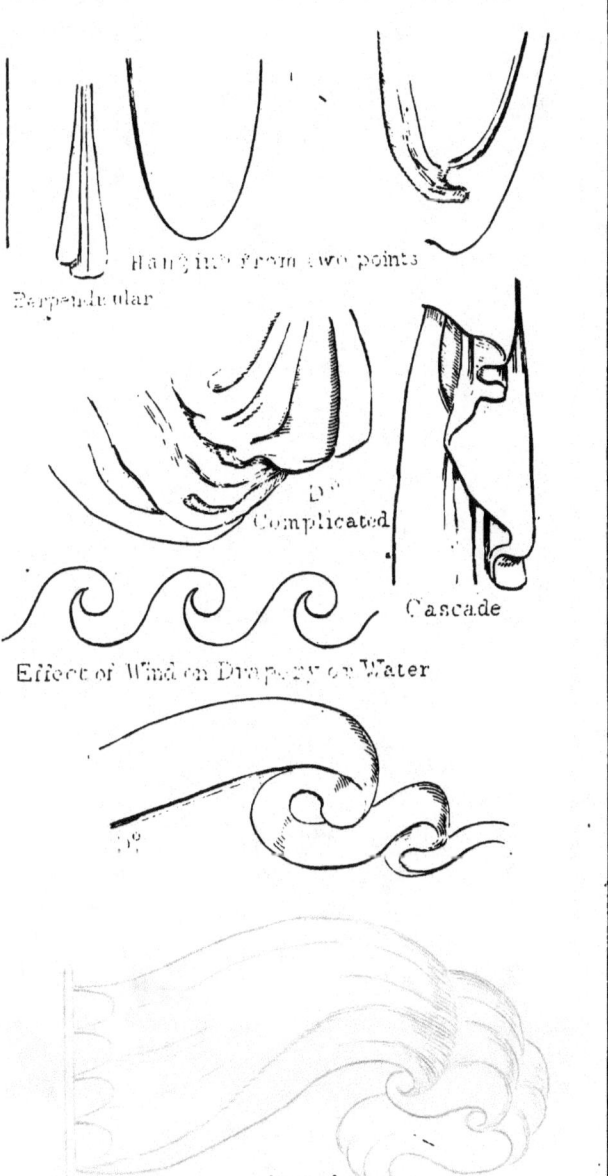

Perpendicular

Hanging from two points

Dº
Complicated

Cascade

Effect of Wind on Drapery or Water

Dº

Pl. 43

Drapery accommodated to the bosom.

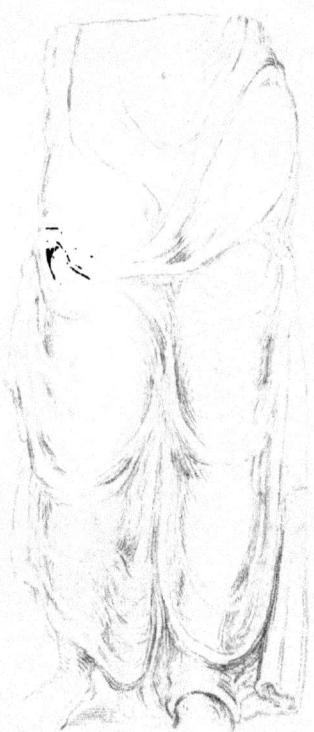

Accommodated
to the limbs

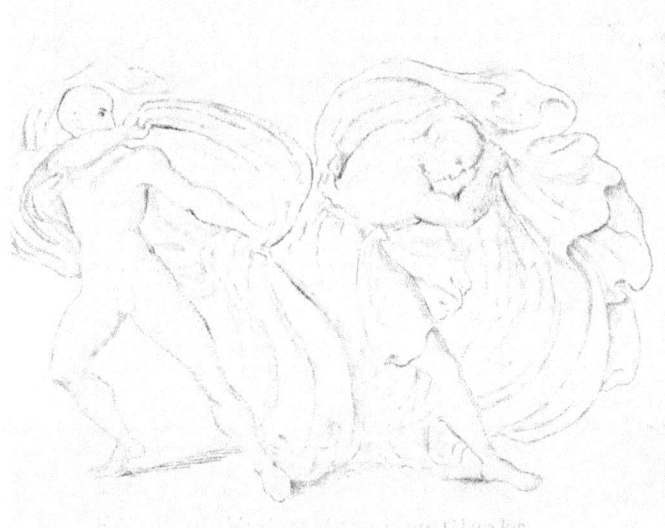

Effect of Wind on Robes or Cloaks

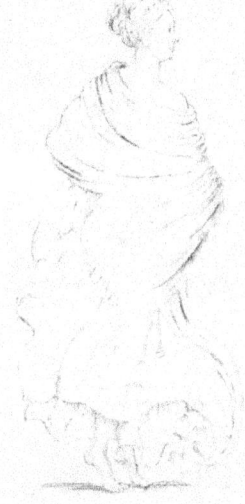

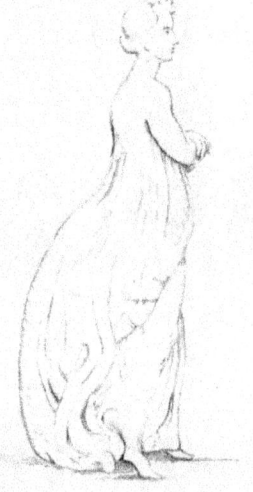

Bacchante. Drapery of the lady walking

Pl.45

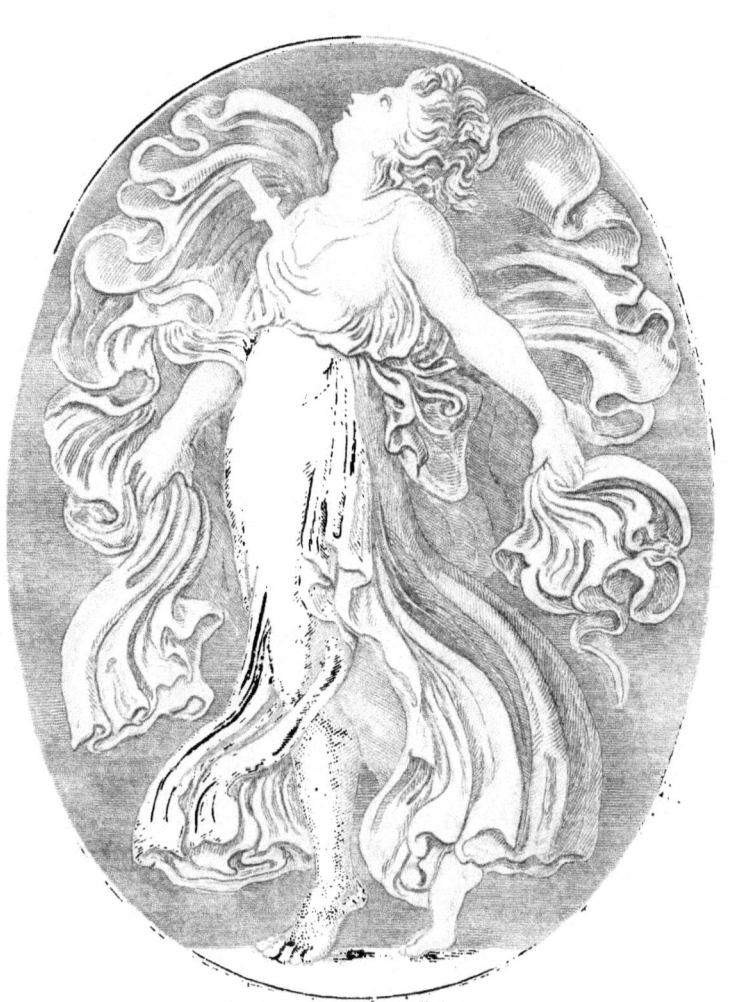

Callirhoe. from a Gem.

Pl.46.

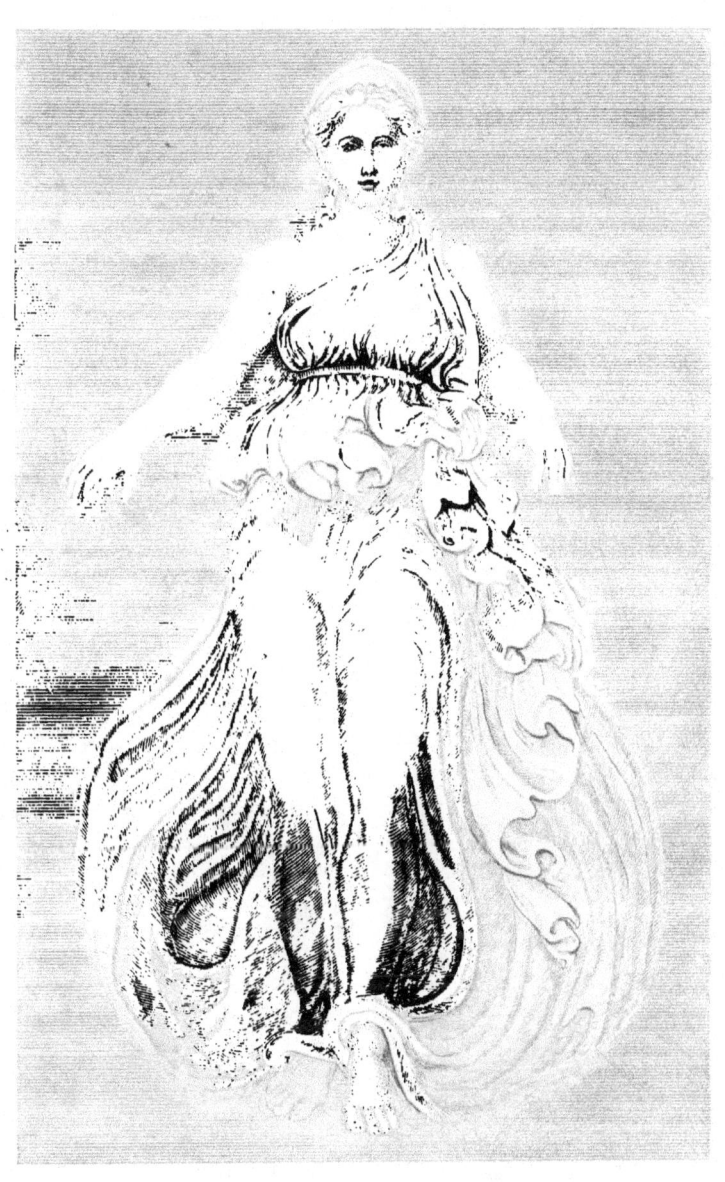

Iris descending.

Pl. 47.

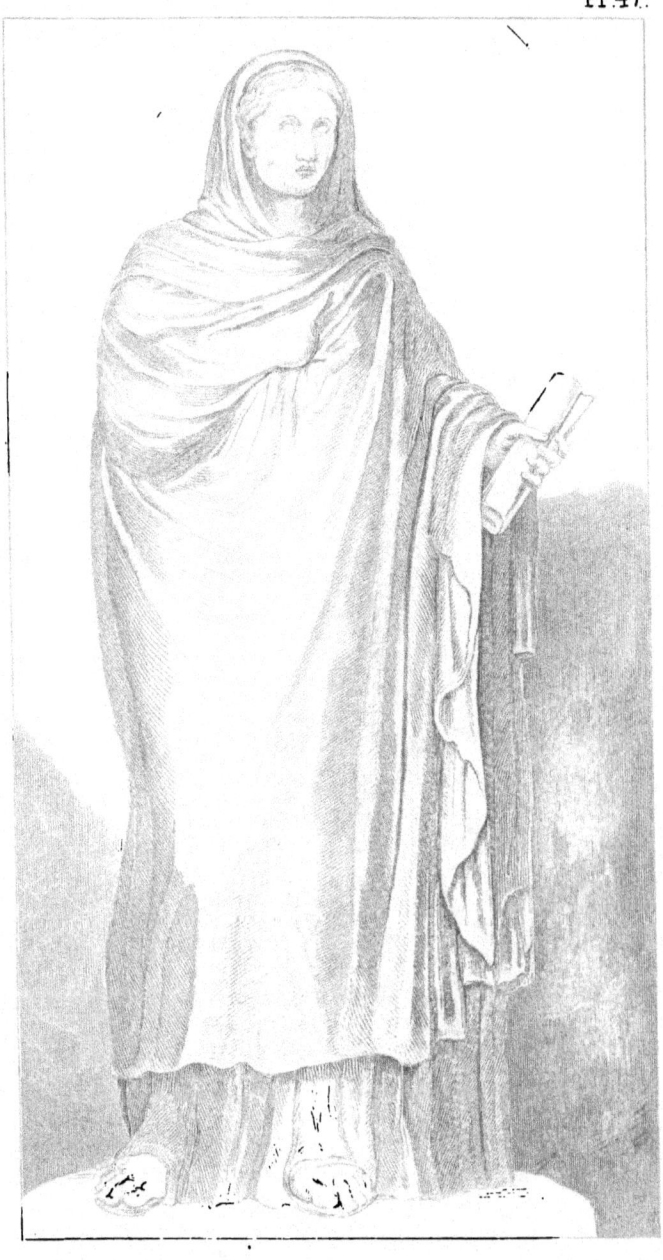

Juno Lucina.

Plate XLVIII.

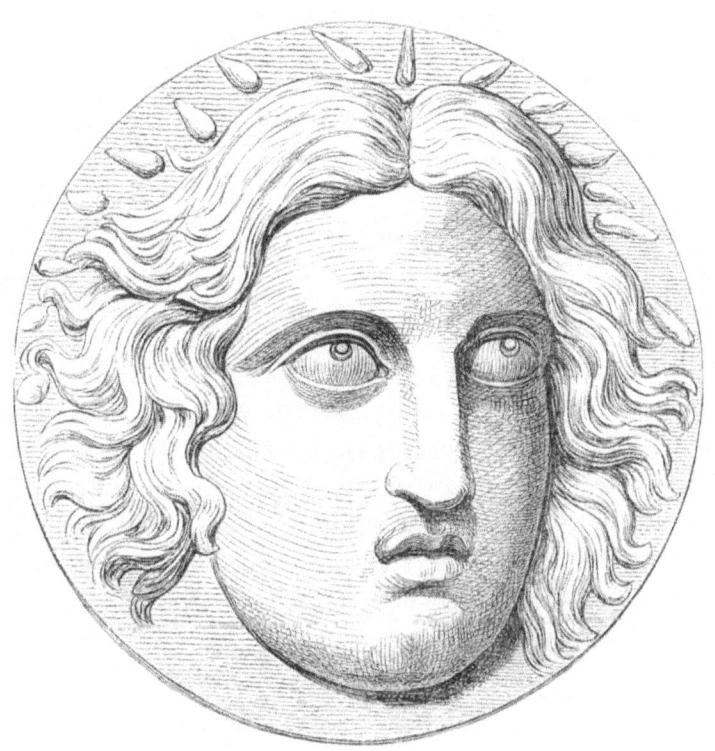

HEAD OF THE COLOSSUS OF RHODES.

Plate XLIX.

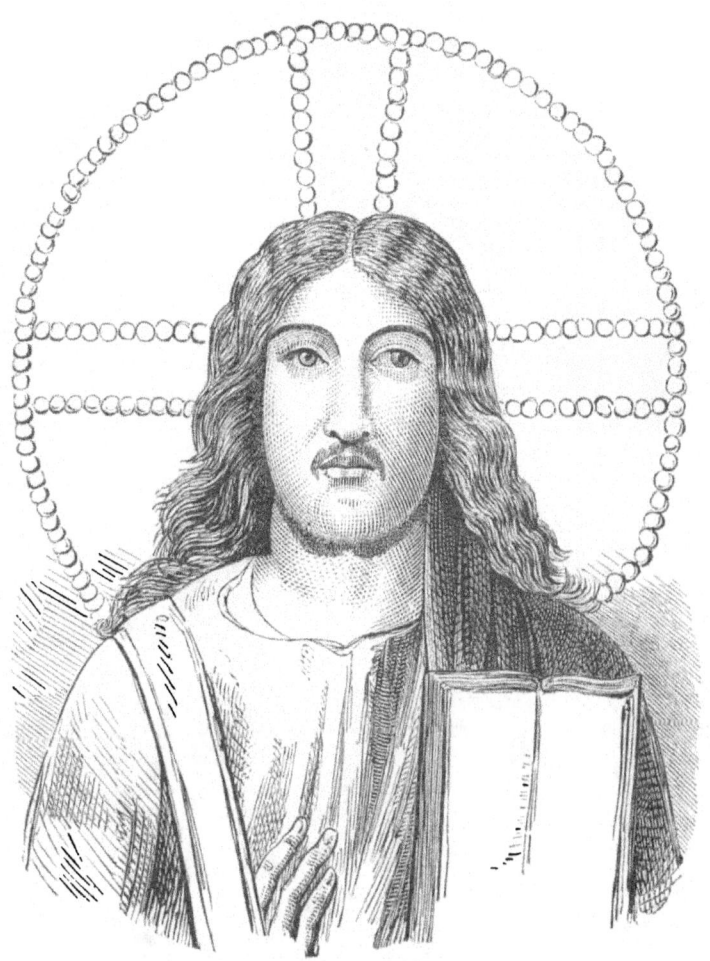

HEAD OF OUR SAVIOUR.

Pl. 50.

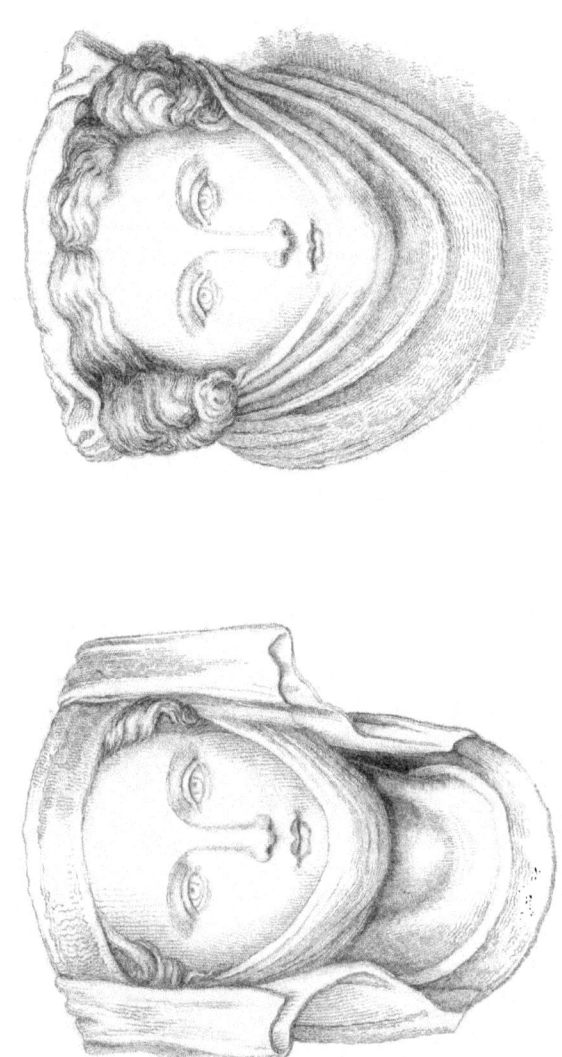

Heads from York Cathedral.

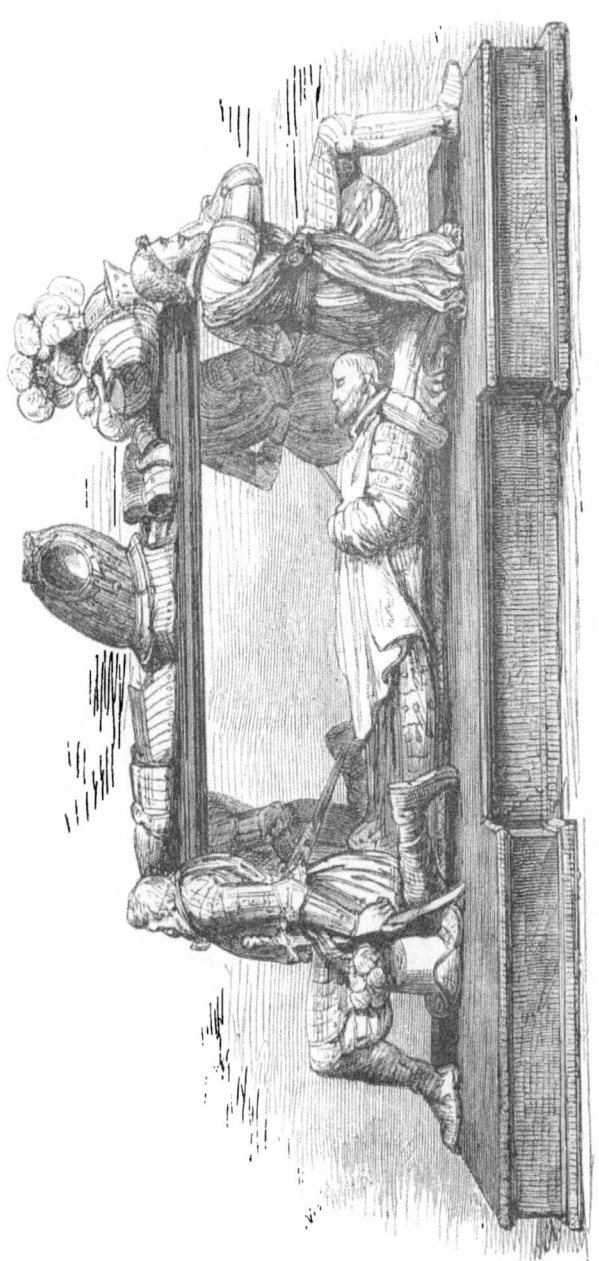

MONUMENT OF SIR FRANCIS VERE, WESTMINSTER ABBEY.

Pl. 52.

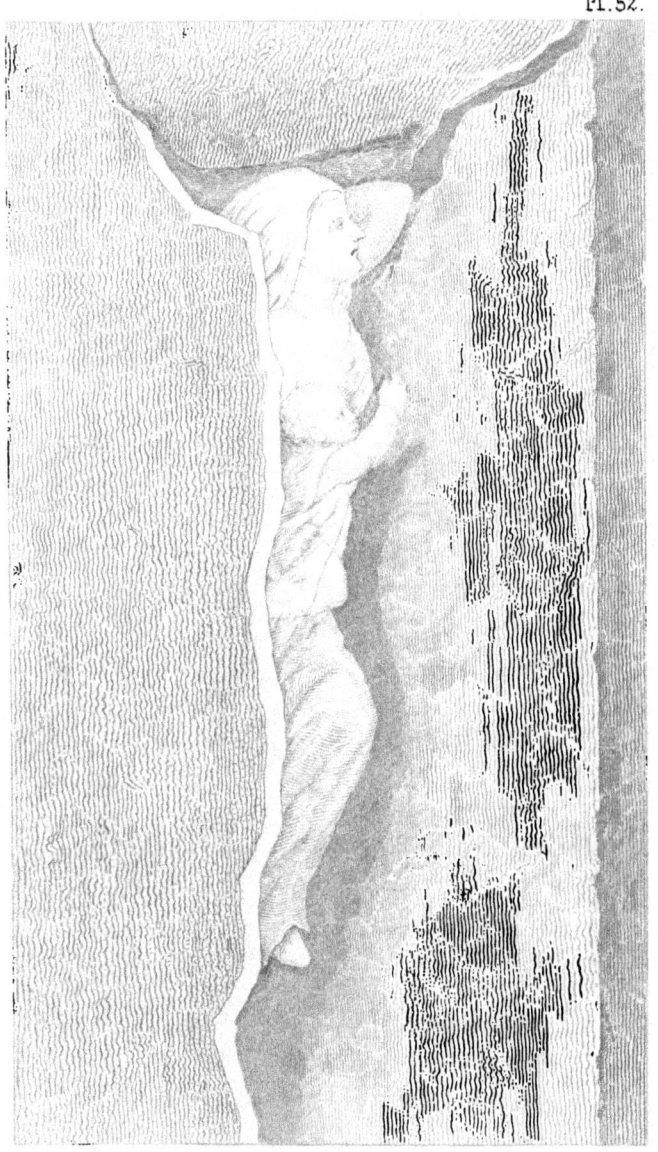

Tomb of Madame Langhahn.

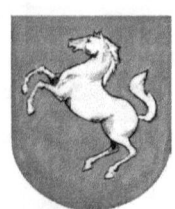

Featured Titles from Westphalia Press

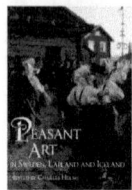

Peasant Art in Sweden, Lapland and Iceland
by Charles Holme

This particular work offers a carefully chosen selection of both the decorative and fine arts of Sweden, Iceland, and the northern most region of Finland. A comprehensive survey, it includes paintings, jewelry, textiles, metalwork, carving, furniture and pottery.

The Rise of the Book Plate: An Exemplative of the Art
by W. G. Bowdoin, Introduction by Henry Blackwel

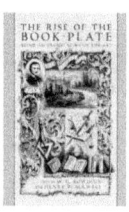

Bookplates were made to denote ownership and hopefully steer the volume back to the rightful shelf if borrowed. They often contained highly stylized writing, drawings, coat of arms, badges or other images of interest to the owner.

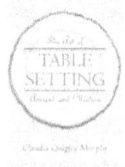

The Art of Table Setting, Ancient and Modern
by Claudia Quigley Murphy

The arrangement of a table in terms of cutlery, arrangement, serving style, and timing of courses has changed a great deal over time and now is enjoying renewed interest. The History of the Art of Tablesetting was written by a true expert in the field, Claudia Quigley Murphy.

Understanding Art: Hendrik Willem Van Loon's
How To Look At Pictures by Hendrik Willem Van
Loon, Introduction by Daniel Gutierrez-Sandoval

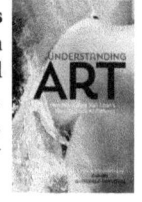

Hendrik Willem van Loon was a Dutch-American professor, journalist, prolific writer, and illustrator. His most famous work, "The Story of Mankind" earned him the prestigious John Newbery Medal.

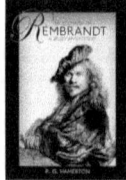

The Etchings of Rembrandt: A Study and History
by P. G. Hamerton

Philip Gilbert Hamerton (1834-1894) was an Englishman who was devoted to the arts in numerous forms. Due to the praise, Hamerton stuck with art criticism, and went on to write other works. He also wrote novels, biographies, and reflections on society.

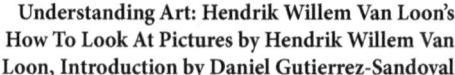

Lankes, His Woodcut Bookplates by Wilbur Macey Stone

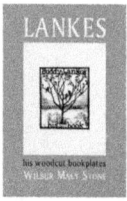

Julius John Lankes was born in Buffalo, New York in 1884, and became a prolific woodcut print artist, as well as an author and professor. As a child, he enjoyed working with the scraps of wood his father brought home from the lumber mill where he was employed. Lankes had a lifelong interest in art.

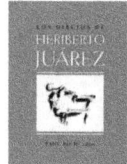

Los Dibujos de Heriberto Juarez / The Drawings of Heriberto Juarez, Edited by Paul Rich

That the drawings here are from life in México is not surprising because Juárez is constantly, and at times impishly, putting art into life and getting art from life. He doesn't think of art as some thing that is done just in a studio or for that matter kept in museums and looked at on Sundays.

The History of Photography: Carl W. Ackerman's George Eastman by Carl W. Ackerman, Introduction by Daniel Gutierrez-Sandoval

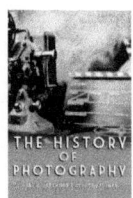

The life of George Eastman is very much a part of the history of contemporary photography. Founder of the Eastman Kodak Company, Eastman was an enthusiastic photographer himself who became instrumental in bringing photography to the mainstream.

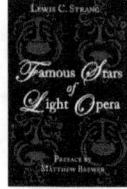

Famous Stars of Light Opera by Lewis C. Strang, Introduction by Matthew Brewer

Strang's attempts to quantify the humorous elements of each performer, as well as quotes from the performers themselves attempting to explain their own success, are an interesting exercise in attempting to explain the inexplicable.

Wood Sculpture: From Ancient Egypt to the End of the Gothic Period by Alfred Maskell F.S.A.

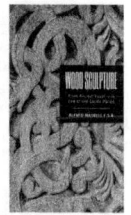

Alfred Maskell was an artist, primarily a photographer, who worked tirelessly to advance the art. Maskell, along with Robert Memachy, helped to develop the gum-bichromate printing, which is able to create a unique painterly image from negatives. This work highlights a variety of wood-based art over time.

westphaliapress.org